George M. Dutcher, Samuel S. Hall

My Escape from King Alcohol

George M. Dutcher, Samuel S. Hall

My Escape from King Alcohol

ISBN/EAN: 9783743435575

Printed in Europe, USA, Canada, Australia, Japan

Cover: Foto ©Lupo / pixelio.de

More available books at **www.hansebooks.com**

MY ESCAPE

FROM

KING ALCOHOL

WITH

TRIALS AND TRIUMPHS

ON

TEMPERANCE TRAILS.

BY
GEORGE M. DUTCHER
AND
SAMUEL S. HALL
(BUCKSKIN SAM.)

ILLUSTRATED.

"I must fight King Alcohol, or else I may yet die a drunkard."

PUBLISHED BY SUBSCRIPTION.

HARTFORD, CONN.
COLUMBIAN BOOK COMPANY.
1878.

PREFACE.

This narrative of my checkered life has been written at the suggestion of numerous friends in the United States and British Provinces. They have assured me that my sad history, if made public, would prove a blessing to many a young man who, taking warning therefrom, would firmly resolve to touch not, taste not, handle not, the intoxicating glass.

I may truly account myself as a brand plucked from the burning. Many long, miserable years did I plod on in the downward road to ruin, tossed hither and thither like a wreck on the dark, tempestuous sea of Intemperance; at times a penniless stranger in strange cities—then a homeless wanderer on the earth; suffering from cold, hunger, and insatiate thirst, and encountering many dangers while under the influence of strong drink.

My final redemption from the awful bondage which rum imposes on its victims came at last; and with it the dawn of hope and happiness. For six years past I have labored to prevent others from following the path which I once walked in.

With a spirit of devotion to the cause of Temperance and Humanity, and feeling more than thankful for my own great deliverance, I submit this book to the public, trusting that the banner of Temperance may wave between its many imperfections and unkind criticism.

G. M. D.

CONTENTS OF PART I.

CHAPTER I.

PAGE.

My Parents—Their Children—My Birth-place and Early Days—Our Log-Cabin Home by the Catskill Mountains—A Beautiful Retreat—Intemperate Habits of My Father—Turned Out by the Sheriff—A Sorrowful Time—Incidents of my Boyhood—My First Earnings, and What Became of Them—Comforted by My Mother—School-days—Ridiculed by the Boys—Taunts and Blows—A Sister's Protection—The Sorrows of a Drunkard's Son—Obliged to Leave School............................... 25

CHAPTER II.

Working on a Neighbor's Farm—New Acquaintances—How We Passed Our Evenings—Cider, Whiskey and Rum—Our Sundays In the Barn—Where Our Neighbors Hid Their Rum Jugs—How We Emptied Them—Morning Disappointments of the Owners—My Employer's Prophecy—How We Went to the Village and How We Came Back—Up Hill and Down Hill—"Clear the Track"—The Run-away Horses—"Considerably Shook Up" .. 32

CHAPTER III.

My New Employer—Our First Breakfast—Treating the Baby—How We Began Our Day's Work by Taking a Drink and a Nap—Out of Whisky—I Go for a New Supply—Portrait of "Doll"—Adventure with Village Boys—"Doll" Anchored—A Compromise—An Old Veteran—How I Gladdened Him....... 38

CHAPTER IV.

Ploughing-Bees—Carrying Around the Jug—Drunk for the First Time—How I Bridled the Horse—A Saturday Night Excursion—The Start—A Sad Story—The Hasty Blow—Flight of the Fraticide—On the Refugee's Trail—A Terrible Picture—Spearing Eels—Wet, but Dry—Winding Up of the Spree—A Ruined Home—The Jolly Landlord—Years afterwards.............. 51

CHAPTER V.

Twelve Years Old—My Father Stops Drinking for a Season—A Happy Winter at Home—Chopping Wood with Father—Our Dinners in the Woods—Pleasant Evenings by the Fireside—Engage as a Bark-peeler—A Forty Mile Walk—An Evening in a Country Tavern—New Acquaintances—A Festive Occasion—Start for the Woods—A Motley Crew—The Forest Primeval—The Bark-peeler's Camp—Building a Lodge in the Wilderness—Lackawascow Valley—Sundays in the Forest—The Old Woman's Rum Shanty—Bad Habits on the Increase—Unable to Stand the Hard Work—In a Demoralized Condition—Out of the Woods.. 58

CHAPTER VI.

Bound for Home—Sights on the Road—The Old House by the Woods—A Free Fight—End of the Battle—My Thoughtful Host—"Dash Down the Cup"—Invited to Ride—The Generous Scotchman—How to Travel Without Money—A Wonderful Transformation—Putting on Airs........................ 64

CHAPTER VII.

Home Again—Haying—A Long Illness—Encounter with a Scamp—A Critical Case—Winter—The Associations of my Youth—Wasted Hours—A Short Sermon—Self Made Men........... 70

CHAPTER VIII.

Visit to the Village—My Father's Friends—The Deacon—The Squire—The Lawyer—The Politician—The Farmer—The Horse Jockey—Loafers in General—All Willing to be Treated—Town Meeting Days—The Village Hotels—Fate of the Rumsellers—A Remarkable Circumstance................................ 74

CHAPTER IX.

Intoxicated by Cider—How I Got In at the Window—A Revival of Religion—My Old Employer in Meeting—"Go It Dolly"—The Discomfited Minister—My Mother's Example—Impressive Scenes—At the Altar—From Darkness Unto Light—A Great Blessing to the Neighborhood........................... 80

CHAPTER X.

Backsliding—An Accident and the Consequences—A Fourth of July in a Country Village—Good-Bye to Home—Experiences at Albany—Buying a Hat—Brother Jonathan Outdone—On the Cars—An Excitable Old Gentleman—Arrival at Rome—I Steal My Own Trunk—An Explanation—Treating the Crowd—A Pair of Lovers—The Stage-Ride—Arrival at My Uncle's—Attempt to Frighten Him—His Welcome—A Job Sawing Logs—Cheated and Discouraged—In Disgrace—Return Home............... 91

CHAPTER XI.

Removal—A Severe Winter—Driving Team—Spring—A Tramp into the Country—Looking for Work—On the Road—Looking for Lodgings—" We Don't Keep Beggars "—Hospitality at Last—Out of Money—I Sleep in a Barn—Arrival at Fort Brewerton—A Free Passage On Steamboat—Treated by the Engineer—Arrival at Home... 98

CHAPTER XII.

On the Wing—Adventure at Syracuse—"A Pretty Good Fellow" At Buffalo—A Prey to Hotel-Runners—At the Forest City—Make an Acquaintance—I Visit My Sister—Become a Carpenter—The Whistling Irishman—Discontented................. 105

CHAPTER XIII.

In a Country Store—My Employer—Our German Customers—I Take Lessons in Dutch—Lively Times—A Glass on the Sly—An Excursion—Dinner at the Hotel—Fun at My Expense—Attend a Ball—A Mistake Corrected—Invited to Study Medicine—A Disappointment—Adrift—A Deck Hand—At Chicago............ 113

CHAPTER XIV.

On the Pier—My Friend Dennis—In a Bar-Room—Chicago River Bummers and Dead Beats—Spoiling for a Fight—"Stranger, We'll Drink With You"—On the Lake Steamer—Working My Passage—An Eccentric Captain—A Gale on Lake Erie—An Accident—A New Acquaintance—Arrival at Buffalo—My Muscular Friend—Too much for Hacky—An Astonished Thief—At Albany—Visit My Relatives—A Long Illness—At Home Again—The Glass-Blowers...................................... 126

CHAPTER XV.

A New Start—A Wayside Tavern—The Hilarious Landlord—Phrenology—A Rough Specimen—Untitled Heroes—In the Snow-Drifts—The Canal Grocery in Winter—A Swearing Community—"Wake Up Tim"—On the Tow Path—Rest at Our Inn..... 134

CHAPTER XVI.

Among Strangers—I Peddle Essences—On the Road—At a Country Tavern—A Drink and the Consequences—A Friendly Strife—All Night in a Bar-Room—The Midnight Parley—An Indian's Victory—Dead Drunk—Return to Consciousness—My Companions of a Night—Renewal of Hostilities—I Surrender the Field 140

CHAPTER XVII.

Effects of the Spree—Sufferings from Thirst—New Enterprises—A Trip to the Lumber Regions—At the Checkered Tavern—Denizens of the Bar-Room—An Old Story—Immense Snow-Drifts—A Village in the Woods—A Blood-Thirsty Set—Return Home.. 149

CHAPTER XVIII.

Looking For Business—A Ride with an Editor—A Bargain Struck Up—I Enter His Employ—Tempted—The Fatal Demijohn—On a Spree—Sober Again—My Newspaper Enterprise at Syracuse—The Central Advertiser—Pursued By My Old Enemy—Fallen—"Where Am I?"—Rats—Striking a Light—Robbed—Locked Into a Cellar—Escape—Row in a Grog Shop—Ruined Financially—Meditate Suicide—Disgraced and Discouraged—Fate of a Companion of An Hour............................... 159

CHAPTER XIX.

Visit Philadelphia—The Scotch Baker—In New York City—Looking For Work—Disappointed Young Men—A Sad Incident—In a Bad Way—Longing for Rum—Power of Kindness—Resolves to Reform—Temptations Resisted—Work Obtained at Last—My Improved Appearance—Woman's Influence—Saved by a Song 169

CHAPTER XX.

A New Occupation—A Traveling Salesman—News from Fort Sumpter—The Rally Around the Flag—Great Excitement—Visit New York To See Major Anderson—My First Appearance As a Public Speaker—Volunteers—I Enlist a Company—Hard Drinking, and the Results—A Long Illness—Left Behind—Up the Hudson—An Old Acquaintance—Our Spree at Albany—My Five Gallon Keg, and How We Emptied It 179

CHAPTER XXI.

The Friendly Bar-Tender—Arrival at Home—Plenty of Cash and Rum—My Parents Expostulate—A Specimen of Navigation—Two Days In a Rum-Shop—Start To Walk Home—A Nap By the Wayside—On the Borders of Delirium Tremens—A Haunted Road—Attacked by a Copperhead Snake—Dreadful Sufferings—Drinking Off the Horrors—Delirium Tremens—The Reaction 187

CHAPTER XXII.

An Unexpected Caller—Arrested—Sorrow of My Parents—In Jail—My Cellmate, "Jockey Jim"—Equine Propensity—Three Weeks Amusements—Our "Poems"—Tried and Acquitted—A Man in the Snow—In New York—Experiences in a Gambling House—Fighting the Tiger—Enlisted—Discharged—Dead Beat—Brutally Assaulted at a Hotel—A Free Pass to Albany...... 194

CHAPTER XXIII.

Adventures at Peekskill—A Hatless Vagabond—Nearly Frozen—On the Frieght Train—At Poughkeepsie—The Kind Brakeman and His Wife—A Benevolent Society of Drinking Men—Making Ploughs—Pulling Hop Poles—Carpentering—A Victim of Delirium Tremens—A Drunkard's Epitaph—Adrift in Mid-winter—Hay-Mow Experiences—A Night in a Boiler Room—At Troy—Kind Policeman—Drugged and Enlisted—Camp Wool........ 203

CHAPTER XXIV.

Unfit for Service—Discharged—In Worcester—Ten Cents Left—The Hospitable Irishman—Looking for Work—A Blue Sunday My False Friend — Befriended— Generous Deed — Work Obtained—Buying Rum Instead of Shoes—A Long Carousal—Under the Cart Wheels—In the Lower Depths—True Friends—At Work Again—An Astonished Inebriate—Again Fallen....... 213

CHAPTER XXV.

At Springfield—Out Of Funds—Try to Sell My Vest—A Kind Offer of Work—Employment As a Joiner—Abstinence From Liquor—A Sunday's Ride to Suffield, and the Result—A Prolonged Spree—Turn Up in New York—Start To Walk to Springfield—"Afoot and Alone"—Fall From a Bridge—In the Ditch—A Light In the Window—A Kind Old Lady—Her Wandering Vagabond Boy—A Good Cry—A Night On the Railroad Track—On the Bridge—A Fearful Adventure—Sell My Coat, and Take Cars for Springfield.................................... 221

CHAPTER XXVI.

Carousals at Springfield—In the Saloon—Three Days a Raving Maniac—Return to Consciousness—A Fearful Ordeal—The Horrors of Delirium Tremens—Dreadful Sufferings—A Debt of Gratitude—Become a Book Agent—A Friendly Glass, and the Consequences—Delirium at Fitchburg—Wanderings Afoot—A Night in a Swamp—Tempted to Suicide—A Memorable Night—Teddy O'Neil—Befriended by a Blacksmith—Travels Resumed Reach My Father's House—My Mother's Request—My Solemn Promise... 234

CHAPTER XXVII.

Resolve to Tell My Experiences—Saturday Night at Pittstown—Interview With a Clergyman—Discouraging Advice—Interview With Rev. Mr. Creag—My First Talk at a Temperance Meeting—Speak at Stockport, Stuyvesant Falls, and Other Towns—Incidents of the Meetings—"Cold Monday"—Rev. Mr. Mead...... 239

CHAPTER XXVIII.

Go to Worcester—Assisted by Mrs. John B. Gough—Cordially Greeted by Temperance Men—Join The Sons of Temperance—Visit Old Bay State Division—Meeting at Mechanics Hall—Calls to Speak in Various Places—Visit Maine—A "Little Fellow" Among Giants—Speak Before the Legislature—At Lewiston, Bangor, &c.—At Brookline, N. H.—Rev. George Eaton........ 248

CHAPTER XXIX.

Lecture in Rhode Island—Join the Olive Branch Temple of Honor—Invited to New York City—A Tour Up the Hudson—Go to Pennsylvania—At Harrisburg—Interview with Gov. Geary—Speak before the Methodist Conference—Bishop Scott—Rev. Mr. Tasker—Hon. James Black—Reading—Lancaster—Speak in the College—At Philadelphia—Incidents—An Unfortunate Young Lady—I Am Victimized by One of the Fair Sex—" Her Level Best."... 254

CHAPTER XXX.

Visit Wendell Phillips—Franklin Whipple—The Sons of Temperance—Plymouth Rock—Tour Through New Jersey—At Siloam Church, Philadelphia—A Queer Freak—Three Days with a Hard Drinker—How He Kept His Promise—Engagement in Western New York—Col. Redington—J. A. Shaw—Incidents in Buffalo—A Conscientious Rumseller—A Visit to My Parents—My Father's Question—"That Don't Sound Well"—We All Sign the Pledge—A Joyful Time—The Praying Band—"How Wonderful Are Thy Ways, O Lord!"—Temperance Revival at Poughkeepsie—Visit Ohio—My Labors in Michigan................ 265

CHAPTER XXXI.

Invited to Barre, Mass.—Hon. George M. Buttrick—At Nyack and Other Places—In New Jersey—A Tour Through Vermont—At St. Johnsbury, St. Albans, &c.—Fairbank's Scale Manufactory—Visit New Hampshire—In Washington County—A Southern Lecturing Trip—At the Capital—In Delaware—At Trenton, N. J.—Visit to the British Provinces—At St. Johns, New Brunswick—Interesting Incidents—Tour Through Connecticut—Revisit New Brunswick—In Berkshire County—At Lee, Mass.—Recent Labors in Connecticut and Other Places—Ayre in Ruins—My Great Indebtedness to the Clergymen of America, and to Others—Summary of My Labors—Determination to Persevere—Conclusion 276

CONTENTS OF PART II.

CHAPTER I.
Old-time Reminiscences—A protracted Spree—A Night in a Graveyard—New Resolutions—Roamings in Texas and the Sioux Country—Return to Leominster—An old Acquaintance—Mrs. Dutcher and the Children—Buena Vista Cottage and its Surroundings—The Hall Homestead—"Gran'Pa Hall's" 284

CHAPTER II.
In the Susquehanna Valley—Local Option—The Rumseller's Prayer—Mollie Maguires—Among the Miners—Almost an Accident—An only Child Saved—The Ruined Professor—A Contrast—Tour through Northern New York—A Noble Sentiment... 293

CHAPTER III.
Labors in Massachusetts—Reminiscences of Hon. Henry Wilson—Edward H. Uniack—A lawful Business—A Trip out West—Travels in various Sections—A sacred Obligation—At Richmond, Va—A Tour through North Carolina—The Good Templars.. 303

CHAPTER IV.
In New Jersey and New York—A demoralized Bottle—Adventures in a Rum Shop—Pleasing Results—Centennial Reformers—Work in Ohio—A Wife's Request—" No Hope for Me "—Contrition and Thankfulness.................................. 309

CHAPTER V.
In the National Capital—Homeward Bound—A hasty Impulse —Major Wells—Wilmington and the Wilmington Revival— Pathetic Incidents—The common Enemy—A sympathetic Audience—Almost a Panic—A Temperance Gala Day 318

CHAPTER VI.

Captain Burrell—A Sea Voyage—Yarmouth—Enthusiastic Reception—A grand Picnic—Lakes George and Milo—Farewell to Nova Scotia—The Great Tent—Poetry of the Reform—"The Ranting Dutcher Fever"—Bridget's Lament........... 326

CHAPTER VII.

The Wilmington Reform Club—"Does It Pay?"—Col. Moore's Letter—A munificent Testimonial to Mr. Dutcher Contemplated—Building of the Dutcher House Begun................ 331

CHAPTER VIII.

Acadia Revisited—The Yarmouth Reformers—A Tour through the Provinces—Great Enthusiasm—Incidents by the Way—At Digby, Plymouth, Chatham, etc.—Wonderful Results—"Is not this the work of God?"—Annapolis Royal—Great Commotion in the Ancient Capital—A magnificent Turn-out—"Dutcher Came like Æolus"—A Midnight Farewell—Thirty Thousand Dutcher Reformers................................ 340

CHAPTER IX.

Removal of the "Tribe of George"—A bewildered Scout—"Buckskin Sam" in Trouble—Reception of the Dutcher Family at Wilmington—Description of the "Dutcher Home" 344

CHAPTER X.

Temperance Work in Washington—A Memorial to Congress—A Mother's Death—Retrospective—What Mr. Dutcher Advocates—Prohibitory Laws—No Compromise with Rum or Rumsellers—Work for the Future.. 351

TURNED OUT BY THE SHERIFF.

CHAPTER I.

THE beautiful village of Waterford, approximating the city of Troy in the State of New York, was the birth-place of my father. He was a descendant of one of three brothers who came from Holland and settled near New York city. My mother was born on a picturesque island thirty-five miles below Albany, around which circle the silvery waters of the noble Hudson. Her father was from England, and her mother from Scotland.

My father and mother were married about the year 1835, and first settled in Columbia County, State of New York. They, however, soon after emigrated to Greene County in the same State, and three children were the fruits of their marriage. One of them, a little brother, died when two years of age, but my sister is still living and is the mother of quite a large family.

My father was a poor man, and his little family were dependent upon his labor for their daily bread, but by the help of a kind mother might have been made comfortable, had it not been for the intemperate habits of my father, which crushed and blighted every prospect in life, as he bowed his manly form to the killing cup. Because he was thus intemperate he could not live in as comfortable a house as the more wealthy neighbors around him, but was obliged to occupy a log cabin, where, with his little family, he eked out a miserable existence from day to day; and in this humble home, situated on a small stream, under the shadow of the Catskill mountains in the town of Cairo, not many miles from the banks of the Hudson, on the twenty third day of June A. D. 1839, I first saw the light of day.

I was said to be anything but a prepossessing child, but being nourished upon a fond mother's bosom, I became in a little while what mothers term a bouncing boy. The first thing that I remember was my standing in the door, feeding a speckled hen with corn.

Shortly after this my father moved into another log house, and purchased a small piece of land about five miles from my birth-place; and, it being sparsely settled in that section, we were located some distance from any neighbors. In the winter season we were frequently blockaded by the deep snows which prevail in that section of the country, and I can well recollect the gladness with which we hailed the sight of any persons (they were usually hunters) who, perchance, wandered into that unfrequented region.

During the summer season, however, our's was a beautiful and picturesque retreat, and my mother, my sister and myself would frequently take our pails, and travel up the side of the mountain to pluck the juicy blackberries which grew by the path, or watch the little honey-bee as he sipped the sweet nectar from the rose and then hied away to his mountain home to deposit his precious burden, and lay by his winter store of sweet food.

It was in rambles like these that I first acquired my fondness for the beauties of Nature, which have taught me new truths, and led me to look with wondrous awe from Nature up to Nature's God.

The scenery around us during the summer months was charming in the extreme. The towering heads of the Catskill mountains reaching up to the clouds, covered with thick foliage and tinted with every color of the rainbow, presented a scene sublimely grand, which neither the eloquent pen of the poet, nor the skillful hand of the accomplished artist possesses the power to truthfully portray. Far below, in the valley, were seen fields of golden grain waving in the sunbeams, while here and there the neat white cottages of the inhabitants dotted the landscape, and the voice of the husbandman echoed and re-echoed up the mountain side, as he trudged behind his plough while turning over the smooth yellow clay, preparing for his next year's crop; and, mingled with the song of the milkmaid was heard the roar of the cataract, as it coursed its way to mingle with the tide of the far-famed Hudson, and with its cerulean waters roll on to the dark blue sea.

But this charming mountain home was not to be ours for any great length of time, for my father was unable to pay the price demanded for the land, or a clear title could not be obtained, and we were turned, without money, from the humble cottage which, though poor as it was, had endeared itself to our hearts; and, though then very small, I can well recollect when the sheriff came and took even the crane which hung in the old-fashioned fire-place, around which my mother had prepared for us many a simple meal.

I can remember how sad we all felt as we left that lowly spot, which was the only place we had ever yet called our own, and the tears flowed thick and fast down my mother's and sister's cheeks, as well as my own, and even father's lips quivered and his bosom heaved; for we all cherished a deep and fond affection for our indigent yet romantic mountain home. Not more sorrowful is the emigrant, leaving his native land around which all his fond affections cluster, to seek a home in the new world, where no friend greets him and no familiar face meets his gaze as he steps upon the shore, than were we, as we packed up the few little articles of household furniture which constituted all our earthly possessions, and with sad and heavy hearts wended our way along the old familiar path by the edge of the orchard—the name which we gave a few scattered trees under whose branches my sister and myself had often gathered sweet ripe fruit in autumn—to the main road, which led down to the valley below, and passed onward to seek a home in some secluded spot, we knew not where.

This was a discouraging time for my father, and to banish the thoughts of sorrow and care he began to drink deeply, and laid the foundation of years of sorrow for himself and family. Oh! if this book should fall into the hands of a father who has a little family depending upon him for support, and, to drive away the cares of a laborious life, he is resorting to the maddening bowl, expecting to gain consolation thereby, let me warn him that he is only adding fuel to the flame which in time will consume his body, and send his never-dying soul, unprepared, to stand condemned in the presence of the Living God.

And if there is a father who has just began to tamper with the wine cup when in the company of the gay and thoughtless, or who has placed it on his own table in his happy home—oh! stop and consider before you farther go; for the Word of God declares, " that wine is a mocker; that at the last it will bite like a serpent, and sting like an adder, while he who is deceived thereby is not wise."

We found a little house into which we moved, and began housekeeping in as comfortable a manner as our poor circumstances would allow. We all then began to look around us for something to do to furnish us with bread. My father resorted to chopping wood and burning coal some distance from our home, while my mother earned what she was able to by working for our neighbors, and my sister and myself would pick berries, or gather old wood in the forest near us with which to cook our humble meals, or catch fish in the brook, to give my mother a good meal when she returned from a hard day's labor.

We soon began to find that the intemperate habits of my father increased, and the money which should have contributed to furnish us with the comforts of life, found its way into the rumseller's till. He would be gone for weeks at a time, squandering his hard earnings, and leaving his family in suffering and want. I recollect his once going away on a winter's day with a dollar and a half, to purchase us something to eat, leaving nothing in the house but a small quantity of buckwheat flour and a few dried apples, promising to return that same night. But he did not return for many days, during which time we had nothing to sustain life but the flour and the dried apples; and hour after hour, and day after day, we stood looking out of the little narrow window down the unbroken path, hoping to catch a glimpse of him bringing something to make us comfortable; but he came not until ten days had passed away, and we were all in bed when he rapped at the door.

When he entered, he set down a basket filled with a few salt fish, and commanded my mother to get up and cook some; but for the want of nourishing food she had become so weak she could scarcely stand, while my sister and myself were so reduced we could hardly get from the bed to the table.

I give this incident, which was no uncommon one in our family in the days of my early boyhood, as illustrative of the sufferings we endured because my father was intemperate; and it is but a fac-simile of the condition of many thousands of families in our broad land, who, like Lacoon of old, are wound up in the coils of this terrible habit—a condition which calls in thunder tones for the statesman and politician, the moralist, the philanthropist, and the christian, to rally around the standard of Temperance and roll back the mighty tide of evil which is sweeping over our land.

The following year—having become a boy of eight or nine years of age—I began to look about me for something to do, to render my mother substantial aid and furnish myself with some necessary clothing, and, small as I was, undertook to cut down two acres of bushes for our nearest neighbor, for which, when finished, I was to receive one dollar and fifty cents.

I commenced my labor with a stout heart and willing hand, happy in the thought that I was doing something towards being useful, and I toiled hard from morning until night for three weeks. My hands were blistered, and my feet were torn by the briars and bushes; and, cold setting in my blistered hands I nearly lost the use of one of them.

But I persevered and finished the job, and after my hand had become well I called upon the man for my dollar and a half; but he almost broke my heart by telling me he had paid my father, and with tears in my eyes I returned to my mother and laid my sorrows at her feet; and I can well recollect how she placed her cool hand on my burning forehead and wiped the tears from my cheek, saying—

"Never mind, my son; you will be a man one of these days, and then no one can take your hard earnings."

Having learned to read a little from pieces of newspapers and a few dilapidated old books that were about the house, it was thought best that I should be sent to school, and my sister and myself, being clothed as well as our poverty would permit, trudged off the distance of three miles to what was then—and now is—called the old Dutcher School-house.

Nearly the first thing which greeted my ears on meeting the school-boys were these terrible words, and they sank deep down into my heart—

"*Your father is a drunkard.*"

"*You are the son of a drunkard.*"

"*You have got no shoes.*"

"*Your pants are patched.*"

"*Your hat is not as good as mine.*"

"*Your coat is ragged.*"

"*You have nothing but rye bread and no butter to eat,*" and many other taunts which I could have borne, and found consolation in the silent tear as it often, unnoticed by them, trickled down my boyish cheek. But they were not satisfied with this, and frequently resorted to blows; and I recollect at one time a large stone was thrown at me by one of the boys, which struck me on the temple, and laid me senseless on the ground. My sister, two years older than myself, would often jump between me and the club which was raised by some of the large boys to strike me, and for her sake they would sometimes desist. Whenever I went in the neighborhood, the boys took the opportunity to call me hard names, or set their dog upon me, or throw me down upon the hard ground; and these were always the sons of those who owned a few acres of land, and were members of the church; and when I told one of them that his son had abused me shamefully, in the meanness of his heart he laughed me to scorn, and, boy as I was, this almost drove me to desperation.

All this torture and misery I suffered because my father was a drunkard. When I see an intemperate man, at the present time, the question often arises in my mind, Has he a little son? and, Is he suffering as I have suffered? If so, could he but know the feelings of his boy, I know he would dash to the ground, that cup which has so long stifled his parental feelings and robbed him of the spirit of manhood; while, raising his trembling hands and streaming eyes to Heaven, he would exclaim, "O God, give me strength to resist this terrible appetite. Save, O save, my boy from being cursed by a drunken father."

It was impossible for me to attend school and endure the abuse that I then received, scorching my young spirit, as the burning volcanic lava blights the young sapling which stands in its fiery pathway along the mountain side; or as the burning winds of Sahara withers the tender plant.

So I went to my father, and disclosed to him my many sorrows, and I doubt not his heart was touched, for though intemperate he yet loved his family, and he said—

"My son, you need not go to school any more."

CHAPTER II.

SOON after this I engaged to work upon a farm for Mr. W——, who, though born in poverty and obscurity, had by hard labor become the wealthiest man in our town. My wages were very small—about eighteen cents a day—and I toiled hard from morning until night. He thought it impossible to do his labor without introducing the whisky-jug into the field, and, although I had occasionally drank cider before that time and tasted of spirits left in the bottom of the glasses, it was there that the fatal habit was formed which caused me so much misery in after life.

Here let me say by way of explanation, that Mr. W—— had acquired his wealth and property by industrious labor, and it was not until he had become in easy circumstances that he drank to any extent, or introduced spirituous liquors among his employees.

When, however, I began to work for Mr. W—— he was known throughout the community as a drunkard, and no man or boy was expected to labor on his farm without, at least, taking a drink of whisky before breakfast, one before dinner, one before supper, and one before retiring. And the reader can readily see that under such circumstances the prospects of my turning out to be a sober man were slim indeed. I soon found myself able, with the help of tansy and sugar, to take my glass with as much ease and pleasure as any man on the farm.

About this time I formed the acquaintance of a number of boys of about my own age, who at first treated me with considerable kindness owing to my having become a laborer on the farm. They would frequently call at Mr. W——'s house, and he always allowed me the privilege of giving them something to drink; and being able to drink, smoke, and chew with them, I became quite a favorite, and our evenings were spent usually in visiting the houses of neighbors who were in the habit of keeping cider and liquor in their cellars, and we were always invited to partake.

One of us generally carried a pack of cards in his pocket, and we would gather around the table and play cards and drink cider and whisky until late at night, and, on our way home, reeling under the influence of the potations in which we had indulged, we would make the night hideous with our noisy demonstrations.

Our Sabbaths were usually spent in some neighbor's barn, with a bottle of rum in each of our pockets, playing cards—the loser of the game being obliged to stand treat; we would sometimes stay until after the stars peeped out at night, having fallen asleep over empty bottles and cards.

Thus it is that boys are led on, step by step, gradually, not only in rum-drinking, but in card-playing and Sabbath-breaking, until vice so completely overmasters them that, even in boyhood, they are beginning to enter the broad road which leads down to the gates of hell.

If the reader should happen to be just entering this same path, let him stop and consider in what direction he is traveling, and, to use a military term, let him "*right about face*," and retreat on the "double quick" from such an enemy; for he will show far greater wisdom in so doing, than in facing a deadly foe, whose principal weapons are tempting and pleasurable allurements. Little threads will soon become transmitted into chains of brass which will require more than the strength of a Samson to rend asunder, and none but God can set the victim free.

After laboring for Mr. W—— for some length of time our family moved into a tenement house situated on his farm. One of the little rooms was allotted to me as my sleeping apartment; and many a time, after remaining out late at night, fearing to enter at the front door, I have crawled in at the back window in a partially intoxicated condition, got into my bed, and slept the unquiet and uninvigorating sleep of those who indulge in intoxicating drinks.

In prowling about the neighborhood at night I soon acquired valuable information—that is, valuable information for one like myself. It was no less than finding the hiding-places in which our thirsty neighbors kept their rum jugs. Mr. A—— kept his jug in a fanning-mill; Mr. B—— had his deposited in a hay-mow; Mr. C—— kept his in a manger; Mr. D—— had his behind a stone wall; Mr. E—— his in a clump of bushes near the house; Mr. F—— in the hen-coop. Wherever I would ramble, I could constantly regale myself with my favorite beverage, and being always accompanied by a number of youths about my own age, we usually enjoyed what Bacchanalians call a jolly time.

I doubt not, that many a morning when chanticleer gave his shrill warning of the break of day, many a thirsty victim, with swollen tongue, parched lips, and trembling hands, has leaped from his bed, and with eager haste, ran to the well-known hiding-place and clutched the jug to take his morning dram, who, while lifting it to his lips, has stood chained to the spot with astonishment; for—oh what a fall was there my countrymen!—behold the jug was empty; and with blasphemous ejaculations and a heavy heart he has wended his sorrowful way homeward, minus his "bitters."

My employer kept a number of horses, and I soon learned to drive them with perfect ease; and finding me handy at all kinds of work he raised my wages to twenty-five cents a day. Having no children of his own he proposed that I should have my name changed to correspond with that of his own, and remain with him as his own son; but I preferred to retain my own name, and continue to work for him as before. Often, when handing me the whisky-jug after having partaken thereof himself, he would place his rough and sunbrowned hand upon my shoulder, and, patting me gently, say—

"Bubby George, you will make a man yet."

Whether he prophesied from the activity which I displayed in my labor or the manly gusto with which I drank, my youthful mind was then unable to comprehend.

Under this manner of treatment I soon began to consider myself of no little importance, and the castles I built in the air were of the first magnitude. I have no doubt Mr. W—— intended to show me kindness, for it was then the custom in that part of the country for every one to treat, and be treated with spirituous liquors; and I feel assured that though leading me in the path of dissipation, in the kindness of his heart he wished me well.

He was in the habit of taking me along with him to the nearest village, to transact his business and get a supply of liquors, and we would generally imbibe pretty freely before starting for home. His constitution being partially broken down, he could not stand much liquor without becoming greatly under its influence; and being noisy and talkative he would attract considable attention, from the boys in particular. He was considered by sober people to be anything but a sober man.

He usually drove a span of young horses, attached to a lumber wagon without any springs; had old Dutch harnesses with rope traces, and a double chair with splint bottom placed in the wagon-box for a seat. The chair was not fastened down, and, as the reins were long, in going up hill with the horses at full spring, it would move gradually back, and on arriving at the top of the hill we would find ourselves at the very hind end of the old wagon-box. I generally held the lines and he flourished the whip. He would raise it far above his head, and with his coat-tails streaming in the wind, scream at the top of his voice—

"G'lang!"

The horses on hearing him would increase their speed until they almost raised the old wagon from the ground, and then rush down hill with the speed of the wind, the whiffletree striking their heels and they kicking at the same time. The old wagon would bound from stone to stone like a rubber foot-ball, while the rumbling noise it made could be heard the distance of a mile on a clear day.

Every team we met would give us the whole road, and the occupants, throwing their hats in the air, would scream out—

"Clear the track."

When going down hill our seat would travel towards the forward part of the wagon-box, and, as we drew a tight rein upon the horses, gathering up the lines shorter and shorter, the old chair kept moving forward, and when the horses, panting and trembling in every limb, were stopped by reining them up to the fence on the level ground below, instead of finding ourselves in the hind end of the wagon as a few moments before while going up the hill, we found we had changed our location some twelve or fifteen feet, to a position in close proximity with the horses' heels; while the whisky-jug, having reversed the general order of things and being itself thrown from the centre of gravity, was found to be hugging the front end of the old wagon-box.

Then, while the horses were resting, we pledged luck and prosperity to each other by taking a drink.—This same scene being enacted several times during our homeward ride, the panting horses would at last be reined up at his door.

In driving home one time from the village, Mr. W—struck the horses a heavy blow with his whip, and they sprang several feet at one tremendous bound, the old wagon-seat flew from under us, and, having the reins in my own hands, I saved myself from falling; but he, having nothing to support him, and being half seas over, struck heavily upon his back on the bottom of the wagon. I was unable to stop the horses, the road was rough, and at every jump the horses made, the old fellow bounced up about two feet, striking the bottom of the wagon-box every time he came down.

He went bumpity bump; bumpity bump, for nearly the distance of a mile before the horses could be stopped. He then found himself considerably "shook" up and not a little bruised, and much more sober than when he flourished the whip so gaily.

Immediately after finishing haying upon his farm that season, I left him, and engaged to work for Mr. P——, who owned a small farm some two miles distant. He occupied a portion of his time upon his farm, and the balance of the time he **burned and peddled charcoal.**

CHAPTER III.

THE first morning I went into breakfast there were three glasses placed upon the table, and they were filled about half full of whisky. One was for his wife, one for himself and one for me. His wife stepped up to the table and drank her's off as though it was nothing unusual. He drank his down a little slower, and, wishing to exhibit my proficiency in that direction I raised my glass to my lips, and throwing back my head I undertook to gulp it down at a single swallow; but it was very strong liquor, and it strangled me in the attempt, and I gasped for breath several times while it brought tears to my eyes.

Mr. P——,looking at me in perfect astonishment while his wife stood motionless, ejaculated—

"Can't you drink that?"

Then pointing to the cradle where his little babe was lying, he exclaimed—

"That little child can drink that," and, suiting the action to the word, he poured some liquor in the glass, and gave it to the child, who drank it down with as much relish as though it was warm milk from its mother's breast.

After partaking of breakfast, Mr. P——and myself repaired to the field, he taking the whisky-jug in his hand. Instead of going to work we sat down at a cold spring some thirty rods from the house and began to talk. He finally proposed that we should take another drink, which I unhesitatingly assented to, and we both drank from the jug. Sitting it down in the spring to keep it cool we again began a lively conversation, and, the liquor beginning to work upon our brains, we forgot all about our intended labor, and as our conversation became more lively we drank more frequently, until at last becoming stupefied, we stretched ourselves upon the ground and slept until sunset.

The reader may judge of our astonishment upon waking up to find the shades of night approaching. We then took one or two pulls at the jug, and, shouldering our implements of labor, with jug in hand, we went home to supper.

The following Saturday night the whisky gave out about four o'clock, and he said to me—

"George, whisky with me is victuals, drink, and lodging."

I did not then consider it "lodgings," but have since found out that it has furnished me lodgings in many places that were anything but desirable. If the reader of these pages possesses a strong appetite for drink, and is indulging day by day, he will find before long, that of the three, it will furnish lodgings first; and it will not be upon a bed of down, nor upon the flowery beds of ease, but by the side of the road, or behind some stone wall, where the cold winds will search him through and through; or within some massive walls, with iron bars, where chains clank and the ponderous lock closes him in from the sight of man, with no kind hand to soothe his throbbing temples, will his place of rest be found.

The whisky, as I said before, having been exhausted, Mr. P—— informed me that I must go to the nearest village and get a fresh supply, for it was impossible to get over the Sabbath without his usual allowance. So, his views and my own with regard to this matter coinciding, I readily consented to go. Going into the barn he brought out his horse called "Doll," which animal, upon making its appearance, caused me to stare at her in perfect astonishment, and compelled me to arrive at a hasty conclusion from the looks of the animal, that the crows had a mortgage upon her; or if not mortgaged to them they at least owned stock in her, and would soon present their claims for a dividend.

A more sorrowful looking animal I have never beheld. Her head was twice the size it should be in proportion to her body; she had lost the sight of one eye completely, and I concluded she needed a pair of glasses to see out of the other. Her neck was long and slim, while her mane stuck up like porcupine's quills. She was lame in one of her fore legs, while the hair was worn off her breast by coming in contact with the hard collar. Her back-bone was so sharp you could almost shave yourself with it, and you could count every bone in her body at ten rods distance. On one of her hind legs she had a bone spavin, and, taken gether, presented so mournfully distressing an appearance that no artist could take the animal's portrait and refrain from weeping.

Reader, laugh if you will, but this is a true and faithful picture of a drunkard's horse, and if the society for the prevention of cruelty to animals had then been in existence, an opportunity would have been furnished them to at least consider the case and prevent further cruelty to a forlorn specimen of a once noble horse.

Mr. P——placed a two-bushel bag filled with straw upon her back for a saddle and putting a jug into each end of another two-bushel bag he laid it across her back, the jugs dangling at each side, and, with bits in her mouth, he mounted me upon the paraphernalia.

With hat drawn over my eyes to prevent being recognized, for I had some little pride at that time, I rode slowly from the barn to his house, he running by my side crying, "Git up, git up." When we reached the gate, he gave me money with which to buy the whisky, and also gave me ten cents to buy some brandy for myself.

"Now," said he by way of advice, "George, brandy is six and a quarter cents a drink; but if you get one drink right after the other, you can get them both for ten cents."

With this valuable information, and the admonition to hurry back as soon as possible, I rode slowly away, presenting an appearance as ludicrous as Don Quixote astride of Rosinante.

In time the village was reached, my jugs were filled,

HOW I WENT FOR WHISKY.

and having purchased my two drinks of brandy, I mounted old Doll and prepared to leave for home. But the village boys had been watching me, and, coming through the alleys and behind the buildings, they met together in the street.

Headed by one of them as captain, they charged after me in double quick time, and before I had reached the top of the hill leading out of the village they caught up with me, and several of them, catching hold of that part of old "Doll" which goes over the bars last, held her perfectly still. Being considerably frightened I applied the whip, and she scratched gravel in her best style, but it was no go; they held her transfixed to the spot. Finally, it was agreed that if I would treat two or three of the larger boys they would let me go. So I dismounted, and taking the jug from the bag gave each of them a drink. I then took one myself, placed the jug back in the bag, and proceeded on my way.

When I had got near home I was obliged to pass a house where an old man lived who was a great veteran. Not a veteran who had distinguished himself in the service of his country, for he probably never drew a sword in her defence, but he was a great veteran at drinking whisky. I thought I would stop and rejoice his heart by giving him a drink from one of the jugs.

So reining old "Doll" up to the fence, I called out to him at the top of my voice, and as he was deaf I was obliged to repeat it several times in order to make him hear. My voice finally reached him, and he came out of the house, leaning upon his staff, his white hair falling upon his shoulders and his limbs trembling in every nerve as he tottered to where I was standing, with a smile upon his countenance, for he had espied the jug which I had taken from the bag and held in my hand, and he knew that he was going to be treated.

Placing the jug in his shaky hands, he slowly carried it to his lips, and, closing his eyes, poured the fiery liquid down his throat; and he continued to drink so long that I feared my employer would miss some of his whisky; and, as I was looking out for myself as well, I was compelled to make the old veteran desist. He seemed thirsty enough to drink the whole of it. I approached him as near as I could, crying in his ear at the top of my voice—

"Don't drink it all up."

At the same time I placed my hand upon the jug and drew it gently from him. He placed his withered hand upon his parched throat and said—

"That tastes good; I wish my neck was a mile long."

I said to myself, "Uncle, if it takes as much as that to wet your neck at its present length, I should hate to moisten it for a mile and pay for it at four dollars a month,"—the amount that I was then receiving.

On arriving home and placing the poor old horse in the barn, we went in to supper, and all took an opportunity to test the quality of the contents of the jug.

CHAPTER IV.

I WORKED for Mr. P—— for some length of time, and, between working and drinking we managed to get along as well as could be expected under the circumstances.

In those days it was the custom to have ploughing bees; or, if a man wished to get up a quantity of wood he would invite his neighbors to come with their teams; and while some chopped, others would haul the wood to his door.

The whisky-jug under those circumstances was indispensable. Many would go home at night feeling in extraordinary good spirits; while some would be considerably intoxicated.

Being sent one afternoon to one of these gatherings I was delighted to carry around the jug, and, drinking as often as any of them, for the first time in my life I lost entire control of myself, and became so much intoxicated that my reason left me. Reeling beneath the load I fell prostrate upon the ground, and remained in a state of stupefaction for some time.

How I got back to my employer's house has, up to

this day, remained to me a mystery. Suffice it to say, when coming back to consciousness I found myself there, and getting upon my feet I found I was able to walk about, though considerably stimulated.

There were several men sitting upon the grass in the front yard, among them my own father. The jug was being passed around, and they invited me to drink. I accepted the invitation, and felt somewhat relieved after drinking.

My father said that as it was Saturday night, they were going down to the Catskill Creek to spear eels, and they had arranged for me to accompany them to carry the whisky-jug, while some held the torches, and others used their spears.

It was agreed that Mr. P——'s teams should be used upon that occasion, and I was sent with bridle in hand to bring the horses from the field. As I was considerably stimulated I could not see straight, and instead of getting the bits in the horse's mouth I got the head piece where the bits should have been, and the bits on top of one of the horse's head.

When I came to the men sitting upon the grass, leading the horses, they saw the blunder at once, and bursting out into roars of laughter, they said—

"George, you must be drunk."

I concluded myself that they were about right.

After considerable delay we got ready to start, and about fifteen men were piled promiscuously in the long wagon-box, while I was seated in front to drive. Taking one drink all around, they placed their hats upon the ends of their spears and held them above their heads, while I brandished the long whip triumphantly in my hand.

Then they shouted, "All on board," and we moved off at a pretty good speed. The whole of the party, having drank rather freely, felt as though they owned a consideration of the surrounding country, and one of them remarked as he took another swig at the jug—

"What is the use of being poor, when a shilling expended in whisky will make you rich?"

Between singing and hallooing, laughing and joking, we attracted much attention as we rode along; and feeling well myself for a boy of my years I made as much noise as any of them.

Having said something which displeased my father, who was seated in the wagon, he reached over the shoulders of those in front of him, and with his spear handle struck me a heavy blow upon the top of the head, which nearly knocked me from off the wagon. Upon this some of them caught him by the coat collar, and, flourishing their spear handles above his head, cried—

"Don't you do that again, for no man can abuse George while he is with us."

One of them then pulled the stoppel from the jug and poured some of its contents upon my head, rubbed gently with his hand the bump raised by the spear handle, and said to me—

"Don't be frightened; you shall not be hurt any more."

After the external application with the help of another drink I felt quite well again, and we proceeded gaily on. My father, being a good deal intoxicated, struck me, probably, a heavier blow than he intended; and though a good, kind father when sober, even in his intemperate moments he loved his only boy, and, on second consideration, he acknowledged himself sorry for having struck the hasty blow.

Oh! how many fathers, at the present time, in their sober moments love their children with all the fondness of their parental affection, and would face even death itself to save them from surrounding danger, who, when reason is dethroned and their fond affection blighted by the fell destroyer, have often struck the fatal blow which has laid their darling child low in the icy arms of death.

Here let me draw a picture of but one case out of many thousands that constantly occur in our land Mr. C—— was known in the neighborhood in which he lived as a kind man when sober; and he toiled hard every day to give his wife and children the necessaries of life. But when reeling under the influence of the maddening bowl, it would seem as though the very demon of the damned had taken possession of his soul, and he was ever ready at such times to wreak his vengeance upon his helpless family.

Coming home one night, staggering under the potations that he had taken during the day, upon entering the house he demanded of his wife to tell him if his little son aged ten years, had done the work he told him to do when he left home in the morning. She answered him, that shortly after he left the boy was taken quite ill and had been unable to finish his task.

On hearing this he stamped upon the floor, and clenching his fists he said—

"D—— him, I will learn him, sick or well, not to disobey me."

Then rushing out of the door he soon re-entered with a club in his hand, clambered up the stairs, entered the little room, and called out to his son—

"You young rascal! why didn't you do that work?"

The little boy turned over in bed, with feverish cheek, tears starting in his little eyes, and trembling at the sight of his enraged father said—

"Oh! father, I was sick. Oh! don't whip me for I feel very weak, and if I had been well I would have done the work."

But the father's heart was turned to steel and he was impervious to the moanings and entreaties of his little boy, and uttering a terrible oath he approached the bed, and raising the club that he held in his grasp said—

"I'll teach you better conduct than to disobey me."

At the same time he struck the boy a blow on the temple with such terrible force that the blood gushed from his nostrils and from the wound, soaking the pillow on which his little head rested.

Seeing at a glance that he had struck a heavier blow than he intended, he hurried down the stairs. The sight of what he had done had nearly sobered him, and taking his hat in his hand with his cheek pale and bloodless, he told his wife he believed that he had killed his boy, and, darting out of the open door, he ran at the top of his speed to the nearest physician and told him what he had done, requesting him at the same time to go to his house as soon as possible, and ascertain if the little fellow was really dead.

Then he started for the nearest piece of woods, where he could conceal himself and at the same time could get a good view from beneath the underbrush of his own house. He saw the physician come and go away; then he saw others come, remain a short time, and go away; and for three days he watched from his hiding place without eating a mouthful of food or drinking a drop of water. On the third day at ten o'clock, he saw teams coming from every direction loaded with people, and stopping in front of his house. He then knew his little boy was dead.

He remained in his hiding-place until night, when he silently stole away on foot, over fields, through swamps and forests, with his face towards Canada. The north star was his only guide through the long hours of night as he pushed on, fleeing from the hand of Justice, goaded with the terrible thought, his bosom heaving with emotion, knowing that he was the murderer of his own child, and that rum had maddened him to commit the monstrous crime.

He traveled as far as he could at night, and in the day time he concealed himself, sustaining life as best he could by sometimes emerging from his hiding-place and venturing to the nearest farm house in the edge of the evening, where he would beg something to eat.

Then he would follow his starry guide through the long hours of night. He finally reached the outer boundaries of the United States, and concealed himself on board of a vessel which was to sail in a few hours for Canada.

But the eye of an avenging God had followed him through his solitary journey, and he was never destined to see the Queen's Dominions; for the officers of Justice were upon his track, and one of them reached the vessel in which he was hidden just twenty minutes before she was ready to sail.

The officer had nothing by which to identify him except a large scar which was upon one of his hands. He searched the vessel without at first finding him, and went on shore, telling the captain he was satisfied the man he was in pursuit of was not on board; but to make sure he went back and searched once more. He became thoroughly convinced that his efforts to find him would be fruitless, and was just about to leave the vessel when, lo! crouching close down behind and nearly entirely hidden by some timber, he saw a man with a slouched hat drawn over his face and a pair of cotton gloves on his hands.

The officer approaching him said—

"Is your name Mr. C——, and do you live in —— County in the State of New York?"

He replied that was not his name and that he lived in the State of Pennsylvania. The officer said—

"Just take off your gloves and show me your hands."

He pulled off one of them and held up his hand when the officer said—

"Pull off your other glove and let me see the other hand."

On its being done the scar was discovered, and the officer knew then he had found his man; placing his hand upon his shoulder, he said—

"Sir, you are my prisoner. I arrest you as the murderer of your own son."

The heavy irons were fastened upon him, and he was soon on his way back to the scene of the terrible tragedy.

He was tried for murder; but through the influence of powerful friends he was acquitted of the crime of murder, found guilty of manslaughter, and punished accordingly.

After a number of years a pardon was granted him, but still the image of his little murdered son was ever before his eyes, and he hid from the sight of man suffering ten thousand deaths, and was ever shunned by his fellow men. He died a few years afterwards unpitied and unknown.

Ah! rum, cruel, cruel rum, the demon of the damned, how many untold sorrows hast thou produced, how many fond hearts hast thou broken, how many hast thou sent down in sorrow to the grave? Ah! the terrible picture never can be painted. Paint a picture black as hell—paint starvation, crime and death—paint ruined houses and broken hearts—paint starving children and a mother's shame—paint skeletons of dead men and women suspended from the high dome of Heaven, with rolling thunder o'er their heads and forked lightning flashing beneath their feet—paint all these in one conglomerated mass and then you would have but the faint outline of the dark picture of every day life, could it be arrayed before us in all its horrors caused by rum.

Come forth, ye victims of intemperance and testify to this. Come forth ye bleeding hearts. Starvation, step in the ranks that we may behold thee in all thy horror. Crystal tears, come to our relief, that thy testimony may be taken. Murderer, come forth reeking with the blood of thy victim. Graves, burst open and let the victim of intemperance stalk forth with his bony fingers and frenzied glare. Hell's dark surging waves, roll back, that we may gather ten thousand legions from the dark domain of endless woe, to substantiate the horrid deeds that rum has done.

The reader will please pardon this digression from my own personal experience, for the great object in writing this book is, if possible, to lead some poor drunkard back to the paths of temperance, happiness, and virtue, and to God; and restore him reconstructed and redeemed to the arms of his own dear family, as the prodigal son returned to his father's house.

To continue the narrative begun previously to the sad incident just related, our party reached the creek about dark, unhitched the horses from the wagon and tied them to a tree, throwing before them a bundle of hay.

We then began to arrange for our night's adventure in eel catching, by filling the "lighter" with pine faggots and lighting them, in order that we might see the eels under water. We put on old suits of clothing brought for the purpose, took a drink all around to give a steady hand to hold the spear, and with a torch light raised above our heads, we marched boldly down into the stream and commenced operations.

As soon as an eel was struck it was placed in a bag brought for the purpose, and few of those that came in our way escaped that night. As we had a large supply of whisky on hand, it was unanimously voted, that whenever a successful strike was made we should all drink around, and as numbers were added to the supply in the bag we had occasion to drink quite often. As I drank as often as the men I began to feel the effects of the potations, so much so that I became unable to carry the jug any longer without reeling through the water and making a considerable noise, which frightened away the fish.

My father then directed me to wade to the shore and lie down upon the grass until I felt better, and then bring the jug out again.

This met with my approval, and without hesitation I started, and on reaching the shore I sat down the jug, threw myself upon the ground, and fell asleep.

How long I slept I do not know, but it was probably less than an hour. I was aroused from my slumbers by hearing them calling—

"George, bring out the jug; we are dry."

Feeling much better I picked up the jug and soon reached them in the middle of the stream. Before starting I had taken the precaution to fill it from the supply we had on shore, and, having had no opportunity to drink for some time, they took a deeper draught than usual, and when the last one had finished I found it nearly empty.

This course of procedure between drinking and spearing was kept up until morning, and going on shore to divide the spoils we found the night's work had been fruitful, and that each one had a bountiful supply of eels.

On the way down the night before we stopped at a hotel where the principal business done was selling whisky, and the proprietor being always ready for sport of that kind, accompanied us. After the horses were attached to the wagon and we were ready to start for home, a consultation was held, when, by invitation from the jolly landlord to accompany him to his house to wind up the spree, we all jumped into the wagon, and the horses were soon reined up at the door.

On entering his house the sport began. It being then Sunday morning they decided to remain until noon. Each one of the company was to stand treat commencing with the landlord. Without hesitation he stepped behind the bar, sat down the bottle, and placing the tumblers in a row on the counter, said—

"Come on, boys; let's drink."

From drinking they commenced wrestling; and between drinking, wrestling and singing we desecrated God's Holy Day.

The horses having been placed in my charge I declined drinking as often as the rest of them, feeling some responsibility because I knew if they all got so much intoxicated as to be unable to sit up in the wagon, it would be necessary for me to keep sober to drive them safely home. On getting ready to start, I found that my conjectures were not without foundation, for such scrambling, staggering and reeling to get into the wagon I have never seen before nor since; and though partially intoxicated myself I felt ashamed of my company.

Tumbling into the wagon, they stretched themselves out at full length, and, throwing the horse blankets over them to hide them from the sight of the people returning from church, I placed myself upon the wagon-seat, gathered the lines in my hands, cracked the whip around the horses' heads, and drove off at a rapid rate, leaving the landlord reeling in the door-way.

In that condition we reached home, feeling not a little the worse for the preceding night's adventure.

Remaining with Mr. P—— for some length of time, and learning more of his circumstances and family relations, I found out that his wife as well as himself was on the broad road to destruction, for she imbibed almost as freely as he did himself. I have known her to be so much under the influence of strong drink, in the morning before breakfast, that she would be obliged to clutch a chair to keep from falling, or place her hand upon the wall to steady herself while preparing our morning meal. Under such circumstances it would not be supposed that my employer would prosper. In a short time after I left him he was obliged to dispose of his little farm, and, gathering up a few articles of but little value that had remained in his possession, he sadly left the spot which from childhood he had called his home.

Soon after this his wife, who still retained her drinking habits, sickened and died. The little babe also died about the same time, and the mother and child were laid side by side in one grave. I leave the reader of these pages to decide what killed them, and why they came to a premature death.

The last I heard concerning Mr. P—— was that he still adhered to his old habit of intemperance, and was gaining a living by working for day's wages.

The jolly landlord who accompanied us upon our expedition, and at whose house we imbibed so freely on that beautiful Sabbath morning, was sometime afterwards laid upon a sick bed with that terrible disease, delirium tremens, and he only recovered to be stricken down again with the same malady about two years later. The last time I saw him he had just recovered, as I was informed by almost a miracle from the third attack of the same death-dealing disease.

While I looked at him, moving around the room like a spectre, his cheek bloodless and his glassy eyes sunk deep in their sockets, with stooped shoulders and tottering limbs, I scarcely recognized the once strong, healthy, and hearty-looking man, and as I took his fleshless, bony hand within my own, he looked up into my face, and with a sepulchral voice said—

"George, I am glad to see you. I am not what I once was."

I indeed felt that he was but a wreck of his former self; and it is a sad warning for others engaged in the terrible traffic of rum-selling; for surely an avenging God will not hold *him* guiltless who putteth the bottle to his neighbor's lips, and maketh him drunken.

CHAPTER V.

AS stated in the previous chapter I had left the employ of Mr. P——, and being then about twelve years of age, I considered myself competent to earn more wages than I had been receiving, and returned home to my father's house to remain until an opportunity offered. It being winter then and the snow deep there was not much to do in the neighborhood, and my father having a job of cutting wood about two miles and a half from our house, it was proposed that I should remain at home and assist him in the woods.

Many a cold morning we have shouldered our axes and wallowed through the deep snow, and finally reached our place of labor, where, toiling all day, we accomplished our task, and then, facing the cold wind and driving snow all that long distance, returned to our humble habitation, tired and weary from our hard day's labor, where, with a keen appetite, we sat down at the table to partake of the simple food which my dear mother had prepared for us. We would then retire early to bed, to enjoy that refreshing sleep which none but those who work hard can fully enjoy.

During that long and dreary winter this was our usual routine of life, and I can well recollect how sweet the coarse brown bread and cold meat tasted when we sat down to dinner on a log in the woods.

Though laboring hard to gain a subsistence amid the cold storms and chilling winds, I can truly say, that that winter is a bright spot in my life's history to which I can look back with unfeigned pleasure; for during that period of time we did not visit the village, and my father remained sober and affectionate.

Some of the evenings during the week the neighbors would gather at our house, sing songs, play games, crack butternuts by the fireside and enjoy themselves, while my father, being a good story-teller, would add to the pleasures of the evening.

In turn I would occasionally visit the neighbors, and, altogether, we spent our winter evenings during that season in a pleasant and congenial manner.

The following spring I began to look about for something to do, and, finally, a young man somewhat older than myself proposed that we should go off some forty miles from home and engage ourselves to peel bark, as they were paying high wages at that business. So we started upon foot and walked the whole distance. When we arrived at our destination we found immediate employment at twenty-six dollars a month and board, which was very high wages for those times, and we considered ourselves fortunate.

We stopped at a hotel the night of our arrival, and laborers were coming in from every direction. They comprised Irish, Dutch, native born Americans, and the dark-skinned sons of Africa were also represented.

As they were to start the next morning for their habitation in the forest twelve miles from where we then were, and as we were to accompany them, an acquaintance was soon formed, while in order to enliven the evening a violin was brought in. It was in rather a dilapidated condition and had but three strings; still, notwithstanding these disadvantageous circumstances, one of the party, an American, succeeded in grinding out some lively strains, and a dance was commenced in which the sable sons of Africa were the principal participants, displaying remarkable skill and agility.

While the music and the dance proceeded the whisky flowed freely, and the perspiration ran down the dancers' faces in streams, while their eyes glistened with evident satisfaction as they quaffed the flowing goblet and tripped the light fantastic toe.

It was not until the short hand of the clock pointed at one, and the long hand at twelve that the festive bacchanalian orgies of the evening came to a close. Then the whole of the party, taking a final drink in which they pledged long life, happiness and fortune to each other, all lay down on the benches and floor in the bar-room, and placing their bundles under their heads were soon soundly asleep.

After imbibing several potations in the morning, the breakfast bell rang, and, without respect to nationality or color we marched into the dining-room in full force, and made a desperate attack upon the eatables which disappeared in double quick time, while the penurious landlord looked on in perfect astonishment.

After breakfast we took up our line of march for the woods, and a more motley crowd it would be difficult to find together even in Water Street, New York. Some of them had their pants thrust into their boots, while others had their shoes tied together by leather strings; others had crownless hats, and some wore garments tattered and torn. Others had matted hair and bushy beards.

Taking it altogether, our uncouth-looking party presented an appearance quite equal to that of Sir John Falstaff's ragged regiment as it marched through Coventry.

We reached the woods in a few hours, and began to build a cook house and shanty for our accommodation. We did not commence by laying a foundation fifteen feet below the surface of the ground, as they do when erecting a palace on Brooklyn Heights or a palatial residence on Fifth Avenue, but began building by driving into the ground two poles some fifteen feet in length, while a stick of timber was laid on the top reaching from one pole to the other, and fastened with spikes; small saplings were then cut and placed in a vertical position, one end penetrating the ground and the other resting against the ridge-pole. They were laid a short distance apart and covered with bark.

A sleeping apartment was formed above by stretching poles across from one part of the shanty to the other about eight feet from the ground, fastening them at each end with heavy spikes, and placing loose board upon them.

Having supplied ourselves with straw beds our lodging room was completed. One portion of the apartment was assigned to the colored men, and we occupied the balance. A rough ladder was built, and a stove was brought into requisition below with the pipe thrust through a hole at the back end of the tent; and having built a rough table on which to take our meals our habitation was considered complete. If placed by the side of one of our aristocratic buildings it would be taken for a dog-kennel or a large-sized hen-coop; but it answered our purpose very well and sheltered us from the storms.

Being supplied with sharp axes and well-ground spuds we commenced operations. We were separated into gangs of four men each; two to fell the trees, one to ring and slit, and the other to use the spud. As the bark was in a position to peel well we made considerable progress; and the sound of fifty or more axes reverberating through the forest and along the mountain side caused the wild animals to leave their hiding-places and seek a refuge in the more remote wilds, farther back in the dense forest which covered the deep valley of Lackawascow.

We would have enjoyed our labor and humble fare had it not been for the millions of gnats which swarmed about us, settling down upon our hands and faces, biting us most unmercifully.

The use of rum was strictly prohibited by our employer, who instructed his foreman that none should be allowed to any of us while in the woods. However, an old woman and her two daughters came up, and built a shanty near the line of the large tract of land where we were working, and having stocked it with a large supply of liquors for our especial accommodation soon drove a thriving business.

Sunday being with us an idle day, many of us resorted to her habitation to enjoy ourselves and drink to our heart's content, and, alas! I am sorry to say that many a hard-earned dollar found its way into the old hag's well-filled purse.

We had established the principle of equal rights to all in the matter of drinking, and he who could stand the greatest quantity of liquor without becoming drunk, whether white or black, commanded the most respect. Many a holy Sabbath evening, we have returned to our humble habitation in the woods—to use an expression not uncommon—thoroughly soaked with rum. After remaining there some length of time I found myself unable to stand the hard work. My appetite left me, and I subsisted for many a day on nothing but bread and molasses. I wore on my feet an old pair of cowhide boots, and the deep creases formed in the thick boot-leg chafed my ankles, causing me much pain, while I soon dwindled down into a mere skeleton.

My face was scorched and browned by the burning sun, and my hands were blistered; my clothing was torn in shreds, and a collar and wrist-bands were about all that remained of a garment which most men find to be an indispensable article of clothing, so that I presented a picture at once ludicrous and sorrowful.

Could I have been supplied with the wings of an eagle, and suddenly alighted on fashionable Broadway, the charming, well-rigged damsel, with paste diamonds and pinch-beck watch and chain, with hair imported from the catacombs of Egypt and garments resplendent with all the colors of the rainbow, when she saw me would have lifted up her hands in astonishment and exclaimed—"Ah! how horrible;" at the same time preparing to faint, but watching the opportunity to fall into the arms of some highly-perfumed young swell, and be borne in his tender embrace to the nearest physician.

When Saturday night came I informed the foreman I could not remain any longer. He gave me an order on my employer for the money due me, and I began to make preparations for leaving that same night, but some of them urged me to stay over Sunday and we would have a jolly time before I left.

We were up bright and early on Sunday morning, and having taken a bite of something to eat started for our usual place of resort, heedless of the injunctions contained in the fourth commandment. When we arrived there I immediately treated all hands. Many times during the day we drank the poison down, until our reason reeled and our incoherent utterances plainly demonstrated the fact that we were anything but sober, and that night we all slept the sleep of the drunkard.

CHAPTER VI.

ON the following day I called upon my employer for my money. He at first refused to pay me, giving as his reason that I was one of the best hands he had in the woods, and that he would rather lose almost any other one.

He finally said he would pay me if I promised to return upon my restoration to health, to which I agreed; so, with this understanding, he gave me a draft on the nearest bank, thirty miles distant. Thanking him, I shouldered my little bundle and trudged along on foot towards the town where the bank was located.

After traveling about one mile and a half, as I came in sight of a house near the edge of a small piece of woods, my ears were greeted with a terrible mixture of sounds, composing swearing, screeching and screaming in several different tongues. On approaching the spot from whence the melody proceeded I saw over the door the simple sign "lager beer," and while I stood transfixed to the spot, gazing and wondering, the door was suddenly burst open, and through it several queer-looking specimens of humanity made a hasty exit, and commenced a free fight which resulted in one of the most terrible and bloody rough and tumble encounters that I ever saw.

They continued coming out of the old house until they numbered about twenty individuals, in which several different nationalities were represented. Some were supplied with clubs, others had axe handles, some had knives, while pots, kettles, bottles, tumblers, brickbats and stones flew in every direction. I noticed in the crowd one old woman with her gray hair streaming in the wind, holding above her head a large frying-pan with which she dealt many a hard and well-aimed blow.

The battle waxed hotter and hotter, while the blood flowed more and more freely, and many a poor wretch bit the dust stunned by heavy blows, only to renew the contest upon recovery.

In the meanwhile, through fear, I ensconced myself behind a fence where I became an unobserved and astonished spectator of the wonderful scene which had thus unexpectedly presented itself before me. And I inwardly thought as I looked upon this drunken battle, that if Satan and all his imps had come up from Pandemonium, to hold their infernal conclave over the wailings of their victims, a more devilish panorama could not be presented to the observation of the beholder.

What the *causa belli* arose from I could not determine. They were all "very drunk," and they struck each other promiscuously without seeming to have any other purpose than to keep the battle raging.

After fighting for a long time, with bruised faces and blackened eyes they threw down their arms as by mutual consent, and all re-entered the house. When the last man passed in the door, and it was closed, I emerged from my hiding-place and went on my way, hurrying past the house as quickly as possible. Though poor and unhappy, as I then was, I surely did not envy the condition of its occupants.

The shades of night found me some distance on my road, and coming about that time to a hotel I concluded to stay over night. After taking two or three drinks the bell rang for supper, and going in with the rest of them, feeling tired and hungry, I did justice to the food placed before me. The good-natured landlord happened to be an acquaintance of mine, having once lived in our neighborhood. So we spent the evening pleasantly, cracking jokes and occasionally taking a drink (of poison) until the clock warned us that it was bedtime, when, after imbibing a parting drink, the landlord filled a tumbler full of whisky for me to take to my sleeping apartment, in order that I might have my early morning bitters. I then retired, and soon forgot my troubles in quiet sleep.

On awaking early next morning, feeling very thirsty I reached out and grasped the tumbler containing the whisky, and sitting up in bed drank down its fiery contents. Oh, how many a poor drunkard after a night's debauch has woke up in the morning and, reaching out his shaky hand from under the blankets, grasped the goblet to pour down his throat the death-dealing poison, which would give him artificial strength while it sapped his very life's blood.

What a sad thought it is to realize, that man, born in the image of the God who made him, endowed with faculties but a little lower than the angels, will destroy the beauty of that image and eternally damn that immortal spirit, robbing Heaven of a sparkling jewel.

"Dash down the cup; a poison sleeps
　In every drop thy lips would drain,
To make thy life's blood seethe and leap
　A fiery flood through every vein.

A fiery flood that will efface
　By slow degrees, thy God-like mind,
Till mid its ashes not a trace
　Of reason shall be left behind.

Dash down the cup; a serpent darts
　Beneath the flowers that crown its brim,
Whose deadly fangs will strike thy heart,
　And make thy flashing eyes grow dim.

Before whose hot and maddening breath,
　More fatal than the Simoon's blasts,
Thy manhood, in unhonored death,
　Will sink a worthless wreck at last.

Dash down the cup; and on thy brow,
　Though darkened o'er with many a stain,
Thy manhood's light, so feeble now,
　Shall bright and steady burn again.

Thy soul shall, like the fabled dove,
　From its own ashes upward spring;
Till fountains in thy breast be stirred,
　Whose living waters joy shall bring."

After breakfast I engaged to ride with a farmer who had a few years previously emigrâted from Scotland. After treating him to a drink we got on board of the wagon, and started for the village of K—— where my draft was to be cashed.

Having but little money in my pocket after paying my hotel bill I informed him of the fact, when he ejaculated—

"Never mind; I'll teach ye how to travel without mooney."

It being a plank road, much traveled, hotels had sprung up only a few miles apart, and as they sold rum they were all well supported. On coming to the first inn he reined up his horses, and leaping from the wagon, with a knowing wink, said—

"Coom young mon, will ye have a dram o' whisky?"

To his invitation I readily assented; so going into the house, we took a drink together. This operation was repeated several times before we reached the village.

Arriving there at last I thanked him for my ride, and was about to bid him good-day, when he said—

"Hold, young mon; ye are a fine laddie; hae ye not traveled weil without mooney?"

I acknowledged his generosity, and, pulling off my old hat, bowed respectfully to him and went on my way.

Presenting my draft and letter at the bank, the cashier peered through his glasses over his desk, eyeing me from head to feet, and I thought I discovered a smile playing upon his features; for my personal appearance would cause even the reader to smile could he have seen me. I wore the same old boots and ragged garments that I had on when in the woods; but the letter disarming all suspicion, he counted me out the money. I thanked him and left the bank, and as quickly as possible found a ready-made clothing establishment which I entered, and, after a long parley, struck up a bargain for a suit of black clothes. Having replaced the wristband and collar with a nice new shirt, I threw off my old garments and donned my new suit, feeling that with a few other necessary articles I would present quite a respectable appearance.

The next place I visited was a boot and shoe store, where I procured a pair of new calfskin boots. Then going to a hat store I obtained a new hat, and, last but not least, my steps led me towards the barber's shop, where I got my hair nicely trimmed. Then flattering myself that, with the requisite graces, I might be taken for a young clergyman just emerged from college, I stepped exultingly down the street. Could the old, good-natured Scotchman have then met me he would not have believed that I was the "laddie" of a few hours before.

Feeling quite dignified I would not stoop so low as to enter a common groggery to procure a drink, but went to the first hotel in town, where, stepping up to the bar with head elevated and shoulders thrown back, I called for a glass of the best brandy, and drank it with as much importance as though I was a member of Congress. I then took my bundle in my hand, and walked down to the river with as much pomp as though I was going to attend the marriage of a king.

CHAPTER VII.

STEPPING on board of a steamer that lay at the wharf, I was soon on my way up the river for home, where I arrived about dark. My mother was glad to see me, and my sister ran to meet me at the door.

After getting considerably recruited, it being then about haying time, Mr. W—— came to see if I would not help him in haying, and I agreed to do so, for my mother did not wish me to go back to the woods again. Mr. W—— being a hard-working man, thought a youngster of my age ought to mow as much as a strong man; and, trying to do as much work as any other hand in his employ at mowing, I injured myself, and was in consequence laid upon a bed of sickness from which I did not recover for many long and weary weeks.

When able to get around again I was obliged to go to the village with a basket on my arm to get some fish, for my father was off some distance in the woods burning coal. When about half way to the village I was met by a young man somewhat older than myself who, knowing that I had a drunken father, took the liberty to abuse me, and threw me heavily upon the ground. After lying there some time, feeling weak, I finally managed to regain my feet and proceeded on to the village, purchased my fish, and with much effort, as the distance was long, carried them home.

The injury I had received from being thrown down by this notorious scamp soon became apparent, and I was again confined to my bed. My mother thought my fall had injured me internally, and a physician was summoned, who thought my case critical, and applied blisters to different parts of my body. My father was sent for, and without hesitation he came quickly to my bedside.

Learning what was the cause of my sickness, he started immediately for Mr. W——'s house and told him what his son had done, and further, that if I did not recover he should hold him responsible. Mr. M—— said he was sorry that his son had done so, and that he would punish him severely, which I presume he did, for he never troubled me again.

Having a kind mother to minister to my wants I in time got better. The autumn had then set in, and as winter was not far distant I concluded to remain at home. There was a great deal of snow upon the ground that winter, and horses, cattle, sleds and shovels were brought into frequent requisition to keep the roads open, and as so much snow had fallen but little work could be done in the woods. My father had laid in quite a stock of provisions, and, with a large wood pile in front of the door, and a good large fire-place in the old house, though bleak and cold as it was, we considered ourselves fortunate in being so comfortably provided for.

My time was principally spent in visiting the neighbors' houses with the other youths of my age, and drinking cider, playing games, and smoking pipes. Could I have then seen things as I now see them, instead of spending the precious moments of life in drinking, smoking and card-playing, I would have laid by a store of knowledge, which, at the present time, would cause me to look backward to those days with pleasure instead of pain. But my associations were of such a character that, being continually in the company of the intemperate and uneducated, I was not privileged to drink of the pure fountain of wisdom which many other lads were then enjoying.

And now, in my sober moments, when I see young men frequenting billiard saloons, smoking and drinking in grog shops, and standing on the corners of streets idly wasting precious time, that which can never be regained, I feel as though I would like to point them to the end of the course they are pursuing. If they could realize that only those who plant in spring-time reap the golden harvest and garner up health and happiness for the winter of age, how soon would they leave their course of idleness and seek a life of industry and usefulness.

Think of this, young man, now in the days of your strength and youthful vigor; ponder well the fact that precious time was given us for useful labor, and that every moment we allow to pass without doing something to mark its progress is lost forever. Lost wealth may be restored by industry; the wreck of health regained by temperance; alienated friendship smoothed into forgetfulness; even forfeited reputation itself won by penitence and virtue; but who ever again looked upon his vanished hours, recalled his slighted years, stamped them with wisdom, or effaced from Heaven's record the fearful blot of wasted time?

In the present age, supplied as it is with literature and free libraries, young men can acquire a practical education and fit themselves for the various walks of life. And with free education, liberty of speech and freedom of the press, a young man, though born in obscurity and cradled in the lap of poverty, can, in America I am proud to say, prepare himself, by perseverance and integrity, to hold the highest office in our nation's gift.

From our institutions of learning have emanated many bright stars in our nation's galaxy who did not throw away their opportunities for acquiring knowledge through vicious habits of intemperance, or waste their precious time in billiard halls or company of the gay and thoughtless as, sad to relate, many young men, at the present day, who are blessed with the same educational advantages are in the habit of doing.

We have also seen those in our land occupying enviable positions, who have never entered the doors of the Yale, the Harvard, the Dartmouth, the Williams, or the Brown University, but who have arisen from the humblest condition of life, and, having fought their way upwards with indomitable courage and perseverance, improving every moment of time while laboring under many difficulties, have gone down to the grave leaving honored names upon the pages of our country's history. The race is not always to the swift nor the battle to the strong; so, reader, no matter what your condition in life may be, do not give up in despair but improve the golden opportunities that God has given you, and let this be your motto, "*I will by the help of God do my best.*"

If you are a drunkard, reform at once. You can do it. If you are indolent, remember that drowsiness will clothe a man with rags. If you are poor in this world's goods, take courage, for from these conditions have arisen many of our celebrated public men. Rely upon the promise of God and persevere in well-doing.

The peace of mind only found in the path of rectitude, and the approving smile of God are of more value than wealth or fame. You may have sorrows that are hard to bear, but this is the common lot of all; let them not cause you to repine or despond, but use them as stimulants to hopeful, earnest exertion. Many can truly say, "It is good for me that I have been afflicted; it has inspired me with higher aims and nobler ambition to suffer, dare and do."

> "Lives of great men all remind us
> We can make our own sublime,
> And departing leave behind us
> Foot-prints in the sands of time.
>
> Foot-prints which perhaps some other,
> Sailing o'er Life's stormy main,
> Some forlorn and ship-wrecked brother
> Seeing may take heart again."

History tells us that Homer the prince of poets was once a beggar; Christopher Columbus was a weaver; Sir Francis Drake was a shepherd boy; Æsop, the immortal author of the fables which bear his name, was once a slave; Lord Tenterdon, one of England's greatest judges, was the son of a hair-dresser, and when a boy he helped his father in his humble trade; Cardinal Wolsey was a butcher's boy; Rawlins, one of the greatest historians of the nineteenth century, was a common day laborer; Curran, the Demosthenes of Ireland, was the son of a poor man in the county of Cork; Horace Greeley was a poor printer of Poultney; J. Gordon Bennett was said to have found his first sixpence in the streets of New York; N. P. Banks was a bobbin boy; Henry Wilson was a shoemaker; General Grant was a poor tanner; Abraham Lincoln was born in a log cabin and split rails for a living; Andrew Johnson boasts that he was a tailor, and that no better tailor could be found in all Tennessee.

On one occasion, when Mr. Lincoln was urged to furnish wine to distinguished guests, he replied in the noble spirit of his manhood—

"Gentlemen, I never drink wine and I cannot furnish it now; but if you wish to drink my health we will drink it in a glass of pure cold water."

Had Johnson had the same moral courage he would not at his inauguration have caused our nation to blush with shame.

CHAPTER VIII.

DURING the whole of the winter last spoken of I remained at home, and my father and myself occasionally rode to the village with Mr. W—— and others of our neighbors. My father had good credit at all the places where rum was sold in the village, and could always get plenty to drink whether he had the money or not. When he entered the town the rummies would all flock around him, expecting him as a matter of course to treat; and such an uncouth-looking set of men as followed at his heels it would be hard to imagine.

Among the crowd was to be found the long-faced sanctimonious-looking deacon, whose tombstone countenance gave the impression that he had lived for years in the necropolis of the clouds. Also the jolly-faced squire, ever ready to take a drink when invited, or crack a joke in order to get one. Next came the village lawyer, with his witty sayings and rum-blossomed nose, tossing off his glass with the air of a man of importance. Then the wire-pulling politician talking knowingly of his inalienable rights as an American citizen, and criticising the administration with a knowing wink.

With this bacchanalian crowd would be seen the hard-working farmer in his homespun suit of brown, telling of the large amount of corn he had raised, and the fat hogs he had killed; being too stingy to buy rum himself he would wait patiently for some one to treat. Conspicuous among all was the smooth-tongued horse jockey, with his eye peeled, ready to strike up a trade with the farmers and cheat them if he could.

Then last, but not least, came the large body of loafers who are always to be found frequenting bar-rooms, their little children at home crying for bread, while in tatters and rags they proved a curse to themselves and a disgrace to the community in which they lived. In this crowd I received those instructions which paved in a great measure my course in life.

Upon town meeting days such characters came in from all directions to cast their votes, and many a poor drunkard on such occasions sold his vote for a glass of rum—rum being freely used to bribe voters. Before night drunken people were very plenty, and the day was usually wound up with a grand fight, which was considered indispensable to the close of any great occasion in the village.

There were then four hotels in that village, besides the low groggeries, dispensing rum freely; and it may not be uninteresting to the reader to know what became of some of these rumsellers.

The oldest one had a very promising son, but he

drank deeply, and his reason became dethroned. One of the other rumsellers, in a fit of desperation, cut his throat from ear to ear. The family of another became broken up and scattered through his intemperate habits; and the proprietor of the largest hotel hung himself one cold night to the post of his bedstead, where he was found in the morning.

I happened to be in the hotel the morning he was carried down from his room a lifeless corpse, and the scene made a great impression on my mind at the time. Could some one who is now dispensing the poison to his fellowmen have looked upon that lifeless lump of clay and considered his untimely end, would he not pause in his murderous career? Verily, as the Scriptures tell us, the way of transgressors is hard.

Although the rumseller may prosper for a time in his nefarious business, and his eyes stick out with fatness, yet, as true as there is a God in Heaven, that God will bring down vengeance upon his head, and he will find at last that it is a fearful thing to fall into the hands of the living God.

If the rumseller could, by some chicanery, crowd his way through the gates of Heaven and behold there the purity around him, and then be permitted to look back again to earth and view the terrible work he had done, while contrasting his own wretched life with those around him, he would find Heaven to be more intolerable than the deepest pit in hell.

Another man who kept a hotel on the mountain came to a very sad end. He was opposed to Mr. Lincoln's administration, and when he heard that the president was shot remarked that he was d—— glad of it. Then leaping into his wagon he started down the mountain on his way to our county seat, but was never permitted to see the end of his journey.

His horse became frightened, and, wheeling around with the quickness of thought, threw him over a steep cliff. He struck his head against a sharp stone at the very spot where the ball entered the president's brain, and was instantly killed. This may seem incredible, but is nevertheless strictly true. The sudden manner of his death caused considerable excitement in the circle in which he moved.

Should any young man embarking on the sea of life choose for his business that of rumselling, let him ponder well the fate of these men, and then judge whether in the end his business will pay or not.

The height of my ambition was at that time to become a bar-tender; for when I saw other young men of my own age standing behind the bar dealing out rum to their customers, with their hair nicely combed and their sleeves rolled up, I envied their position, and would have been willing to sacrifice anything that I might engage in the same calling.

The following summer the opportunity was offered me for one day only. One of the hotels having changed hands, the new proprietor engaged me for the Fourth of July to help tend bar.

In the morning, when I took my station behind the counter, no young man living could have felt more proud of his position, and I would not have exchanged it for the presidency of the United States.

CHAPTER IX.

THE winter season referred to in my last chapter, was not barren in interesting incidents in my life. Some were painful; others of a pleasant nature. I occasionally visited the village with my father, as I said in the foregoing pages, which tended to relieve the monotony of an idle life. Upon such occasions I invariably drank freely.

When no opportunity offered for me to ride to the village, I would often, in company with several of my youthful acquaintances, resort to some places in the neighborhood where cider was plenty. We were generally furnished with all we could drink, and, it being possessed of a good deal of strength, we generally felt its effects. Many times we were quite boisterous after drinking freely.

One night in particular, I remember going into a cellar with another young man, and drinking a large amount of cider. We then started through the woods to visit a house some two miles distant, where we drank cider again, and then started for home. It seemed to have a powerful effect upon us, and, with few exceptions, I have never been more intoxicated in my life.

How we got home that night I can scarcely tell; I have a faint recollection that the door was fastened, and, for fear of disturbing my father and mother I undertook to get in at a back window. As near as I can calculate, I pulled off my boots in the deep snow, losing my hat at the same time; then, working myself through the window, I got into bed, where I found myself next morning.

On rising, I found to my utter astonishment that I had no hat or boots to put on. They were afterwards found in the snow; and I came to the conclusion that if the attempt was ever again made to get into the window, it should be done with my hat and boots on.

My head ached all that day and the next, and, feeling miserable, I solemnly vowed in my own mind never to drink so much cider again.

Soon after this I went some six miles to visit a family. Mr. E—— had once held quite a high position; his intelligence, which was above mediocrity, made his conversation very interesting. But while connected with his office he had contracted the habit of drinking to excess. He was a noble-hearted man, and no needy person ever went empty from his door.

His wife was of a generous disposition, and had a warm heart; an idea of being penurious had never, probably, entered her mind. As a wife and mother she was a model woman. One of her sons subsequently married my sister.

The afternoon after my arrival the old gentleman proposed that we should go down to the nearest hotel, which we accordingly did; and, as a matter of course, we drank together for some time, until we both began to feel rich. The first thing I knew he began to pull large quantities of silver from his pocket and throw it around the bar-room, as you would scatter grain. I gathered up the coin and put it in my own pocket, and, upon going to his house that night, gave it all to his wife.

About this time a revival broke out in the little Methodist Church in our neighborhood, and people began to flock from all directions to attend. Some would come for a good purpose, and some to make sport; in the evening there would be a mixture of all classes.

Sometimes, on the way home from the village, not a few would stop to attend the meeting, and among that number was Mr. W——, my former employer. He was not in a condition, usually, to attend such a place, and most always intoxicated; and he would sometimes disturb the meeting by conversing in a loud tone during the service.

One time, in particular, I remember he sat down by the side of Mr. B——, and in a loud tone began to talk about pulling stumps.

"Why," said he, "I jest went into the field with old Doll, and, hitching her to the stump, I would jest raise up my hand, and holler, 'Go it, Dolly,' and out would come the old stump. That's so, Jake," continued he, at the same time bringing his fist down on the bench.

His friend at his side would move farther from him, in order to avoid his incoherent conversation; but this only made matters worse, for he would then speak out much louder. Finally the minister stopped short in his address, and said—

"When that gentleman gets through his conversation we will be prepared to go on with the meeting."

"Oh," said he, "never mind; go ahead, Colonel Crockett;" much to the discomfiture of the worthy minister, who had no other desire than to save souls.

Finally Mr. S——, a member of the church, and a man much respected by every one, laid his hand gently upon his shoulder, and persuaded him to leave the meeting.

The servants of God were not discouraged, but continued the meetings, and were soon rewarded by seeing a few come to the altar, while others, profiting by their example, followed also. Among that number was my own mother, and a tear gathered in my eye when I saw her start; for though bad at heart as I was, yet I loved my mother, and thought more of her welfare than of my own.

The next night I went again as usual, and just as meeting had commenced the minister came down the aisle, shouting, "Glory to God," and singing the beautiful hymn—

> "Come, ye sinners poor and needy,
> Weak and wounded, sick and sore;
> Jesus ready stands to save you,
> Full of pity, love, and power."

As he reached the place where I stood he held out his hand towards me, and I involuntarily laid mine in his; pressing my hand tenderly, looking at me earnestly in the face, with his rich, sweet voice he finished up the hymn, singing—

"He is able, he is willing,
He is able, doubt no more."

This made a powerful impression on my mind. My heart came to my throat, and the cold perspiration stood upon my brow, while the tears rolled down my cheek, dropping upon our clasped hands as he asked—

"Do you love Jesus?"

He then said—

"I love you, and Jesus loves you too. He is waiting to receive you. Will you come and drink of the water of life freely?"

He returned to his desk, offered up a fervent prayer, and gave an invitation for those who wished to serve God and get to Heaven to come forward to the altar, and commenced singing the beautiful hymn—

"There is a fountain filled with blood
Drawn from Emanuel's veins;
And sinners plunged beneath that flood
Lose all their guilty stains."

It seemed as if the power of God had settled down upon me, and that moment I felt the need of a Saviour, and, without one moment's hesitation, was the first one to leave my seat to go up to the altar. When the Christian people saw me going, they shouted, "Glory to God,"—"Blessed be His holy name,"—"Hallelujah,"—"Amen,"—and then began to sing—

"The dying thief rejoiced to see
That fountain in his day;
And there may I, though vile as he,
Wash all my sins away."

Kneeling at the altar, I covered my face with my hands, and the scalding tears trickled between my fingers; but they were tears of penitence, and gushed up from the deep fountain of my heart. It seemed to make a deep impression upon the other young men present, and one by one they began to come to the altar, until it was crowded to overflowing.

When mothers saw their sons going, it touched their hearts, and with trembling hands they, too, knelt by the side of their children to seek the Saviour.

The fathers held out as long as they could, until, groaning in spirit, while their tears flowed thick and fast, God sent the arrow of conviction to their hearts, and, nerving themselves for the conflict, they rushed to the altar to seek forgiveness for their sins.

There must have been rejoicing in Heaven to see father and son, mother and daughter, kneeling together around the same altar, pleading for mercy. Earnest prayers were offered, and that very night light began to break through the murky darkness, and Jesus spoke to the troubled soul in that still, small voice, saying, "Peace be still. Thy sins which are many are all forgiven thee;" some, rising from their knees, sang hymns of praise.

I have reason to believe, that during that revival many souls were converted, and it proved a great blessing to our neighborhood. For my own part, I felt that I had been changed from darkness unto light, and from the power of Satan unto God, and I endeavored to walk in the fear of God.

CHAPTER X.

WHEN spring came I engaged to work for Mr. E——, who was a pious man. My work consisted of burning brush, and plowing a new piece of land with a yoke of cattle. It proved very hard work for me, for the ground was rough and stony, while the plough, striking against a root, would nearly throw me off of my feet. The cattle were not very well broken in, and my patience was exceedingly tried.

Under such circumstances I forgot my profession of religion, and began to swear at the cattle like a pirate. My heart became hardened, and I soon found myself as wicked as before. Some of my companions who started at the same time in the good way had also backslidden. Oh! the deceitfulness of sin. Satan is ever ready to pounce upon his victim, and when once the young convert yields to his seductive influence nothing but the powerful hand of the Almighty can turn the poor sinner from his grasp.

Young man, how stands this matter with you? Have you entered the path of rectitude? Do you feel that you are blessed with God's approving smile? If so, resist the adversary of your soul, falter not in your good resolution, but with a steady step and your eye upon the Cross, press on like a true and faithful soldier, remembering that Jesus is your Captain.

After working a short time for Mr. E——, I left him, and engaged to work upon a farm for Mr. M——. Nothing of much importance transpired excepting that I returned to my old habit, and drank whisky when the opportunity offered as freely as ever.

I worked for him a while, until one day while ploughing in the field in company with Mr. M—— we drove the horses upon a slippery rock, when one of them lost his foothold, fell heavily upon his side, and broke his leg.

Though it was not through my carelessness the accident happened, yet I felt grieved about it, and immediately told Mr. M——that if my life must be spent toiling upon a farm, I should seek some section where rocks were not so plenty.

Finding me determined not to remain he paid me my wages, and, bidding him good-bye, I went immediately to my father's house. Mr. M—— was a good Christian man, and seemed inclined to be anxious for my welfare. The last thing he said to me was—

"George, whenever you want work come to me."

I was never permitted to look upon his face again, for shortly afterwards I learned of his death.

Shortly after I left him the fourth of July spoken of in the last chapter came, when, as stated, the opportunity was given me to tend bar for that day. The position I thought to be a great honor, and with evident pride I waited upon the thirsty customers as they crowded around the bar. Many a sixpence I took from the trembling drunkard, giving him in exchange the poison which was fast eating up his vitals.

The town was filled with pleasure seekers. Whole families came, some in lumber wagons drawn by a yoke of cattle, others in more stylish equipments, while many a pedestrian wended his way to town. Amid the explosion of fire-crackers, the thundering of the cannon, the music of the fife and drum, speech-making, eating, drinking and fighting, the day was spent.

When the shades of night came on, with empty pockets and battered heads, drunk and noisy, the revelers turned their faces towards home. Some not being satisfied remained in the bar-rooms and drinking-places until long after midnight, and then went noisily through the streets like a pack of wolves, howling, cursing and swearing.

What a great contrast between these men celebrating the fourth day of July, and that sedate body who, struggling for American liberty, met in the old Court House in Philadelphia, and, invoking the Divine favor of God upon their proceedings, boldly placed their names upon that precious document—The Declaration of Independence.

Having made up my mind to leave that part of the country I gathered together about fourteen dollars, and, bidding my friends good-bye, left with a heavy heart, to battle alone against a depraved appetite and a cold, unfeeling world.

Going down to the village of C——, with a small trunk which contained all my earthly possessions, I swallowed down a large glass of brandy to nerve me for my journey. Stepping on board of a steamer we were soon ploughing through the waters of the Hudson on our way to Albany.

We arrived there in the afternoon about three o'clock. My trunk was placed on shore, and, stepping from the boat, I went through the usual ordeal of being attacked by a number of hackmen; but not wishing to engage any of them, and having heard of Dr. Franklin when he began business in Philadelphia wheeling home his own paper, which gave the people confidence in him, I proposed to carry my own trunk.

With this resolution I shouldered it, and went up town to a small hotel. Leaving it in charge of the proprietor, I sauntered out to take a view of the city. Then for the first time I began to ponder upon my situation, realizing the sad fact that I was indeed a stranger in a strange city. As I passed hundreds of people I looked eagerly into each face, to see if I could not recognize the countenance of some one whom I had seen before; but not one familiar face met my gaze, and I felt lonely and desolate; for though surrounded by thousands, yet not one could I call my friend.

To drive care from my mind and make me forget my lonely condition, I stepped into a saloon and obtained a drink. This seemed to invigorate me, and after drinking three or four times more I felt quite at home.

I then formed the resolution to visit my uncle living

in the northern part of New York State, and, repairing to the railway ticket office, secured a passage through to Rome. My next move was to carry my trunk to the depot, where I presented my ticket and received my check.

Having a few moments to spare before the train started I walked out into Broadway, and in passing Frothingham's hat store my eye caught the sight of a tall, white fur hat in the window, and I walked in and purchased it for the sum of two dollars. It was second-handed. Placing it upon my head I stepped up to the large mirror, and, upon viewing myself, came to the conclusion, from a picture I had once seen, that Brother Jonathan stood before me.

My clothes were not of the most stylish pattern. I had on a blue swallow-tail coat with brass buttons; a red checkered vest with velvet collar; my pants were light-colored and striped, and about six inches too short, leaving the whole length of my boot-leg exposed. They complimented me very much on my personal appearance in the store, and said the hat was a great improvement.

This gave me quite a high opinion of myself, and, pulling my hat down so it rested upon my ears to keep it from blowing off, I made my way proudly along to the depot, stepped on board the cars, and was soon out of the city.

An old gentleman occupied a seat at my side, and he informed me that he had never been on a train of cars before in his life. Every time the train stopped he supposed it was at his station. It was amusing to watch the doubts and fears that constantly perplexed the old gentleman in this his first experience in railway travel. Whenever the whistle blew for the train to stop at a station, he would rise quickly from his seat, and scream out—

"What place is this? Is this Little Falls?"

On being informed by a gentleman in front of us, that it was not, he would settle back in his seat and wait for the whistle to blow again, only to ask the same question and receive the same answer. This he continued to do until, arriving at his station, he got out of the car.

This left me alone in the seat, and for the first time since leaving Albany I thought of my trunk, and showed my check to a gentleman in front of me, who quieted any apprehension I might have had in regard to its safety by telling me it was probably on board of the same train, and that on my arrival at Rome I would find it all safe.

After that I felt easy about my trunk, but, like the old gentleman, I now began to fear that they would carry me past my stopping place. When the conductor came in I ventured to ask him in regard to it; he told me that the brakeman would give me notice, and that the train would stop there some length of time.

We reached Rome about midnight, and my first thoughts were concerning my trunk. I made my way with haste to the baggage car, where, after watching the removal of trunks for some length of time, I at last discovered my own.

Pressing my way in front of the baggage-master I seized my trunk and started off with it as fast as I could go, when, hearing quick steps behind me, I looked around. At the same moment a heavy hand was laid upon my shoulder, and a man said in a gruff voice—

"Stop! Where are you going with that trunk?"

It frightened me very much, and I explained to him that it was my trunk; but he said—

"You can't come that on me."

Taking me by the coat-collar, he jerked me unceremoniously back to the baggage car. He then wanted to know if I had a check. I told him I had, at the same time producing it. He took it from my hands and compared it with the one on the trunk and found they corresponded. Then laughing heartily, he turned to me and said—

"Young man, you must be crazy."

I told him it was my first attempt at traveling, and apologized for the mistake. He seemed to take quite an interest in me then, and in the morning assisted me in getting tickets, and checking my trunk on the other road. After having done so we stepped into a saloon near by and took a drink. I then went on board the cars, bade my newly-made friend adieu, and was off.

On arriving at the station of M——, where I was to take the stage, I found it was not to leave until evening; so I went to the hotel near at hand, proceeded up to the bar, and called for something to drink, at the same time extending an invitation for all in the room to partake with me, which they readily consented to do. This opened an acquaintance, and we chatted and drank until dinner time. After dinner the conversation and drinks were resumed, and the more we drank the more interested we became in each other, and we continued enjoying ourselves until the stage-driver's horn warned me that it was time to leave.

The stage was drawn by four horses which stood pawing the earth, when I went out of the door, anxious to be off. There were two or three ladies who had engaged seats, and one old lady I noticed had three or four band-boxes in her hands. One lady had a small child in her arms screaming at the top of its voice, and last but not least came two lovers gaily dressed. She was leaning on his arm and looking up with a silly smile into his unmeaning face, as much as to say—

"Won't we make the country people stare?"

The odor arising from their clothing gave the impression that they had been muskrat-hunting. When she beheld the uncouth stage she said–

"Why Chawley; how hawible!"

To this the dandified specimen of humanity replied—

"Y-a-a-s ; but then we are in the country now."

She didn't faint however, but catching up her little poodle in her arms gathered up sufficient courage to take a seat in the repulsive-looking vehicle. The rest of us got in without ceremony, and after the trunks were safely stowed away the driver took a seat on the box; crack went the whip, and round didn't go the wheels, for a bright idea seemed to strike him, and he yelled out—

"Whoa!"

Then leaping from the box, he entered the bar-room, swallowed down a hasty drink, and soon made his re-appearance on the box with a short, black clay pipe in his mouth, shouted to the horses, and the coach rolled away at a rapid rate.

This was my first experience in stage riding, and the motion of the coach had the same effect upon me that Jonah had upon the whale, for it made me sick. I held out till we came to the first stopping-place, and feeling very unpleasant, I went into the bar-room and called for a glass of brandy with a few drops of peppermint in it.

This seemed to relieve me somewhat, and when the stage started I took my position on top of the box. Stretching myself out at full length, with a carpet-bag under my head, I rode in that way the whole distance.

The coach arrived at my destination about midnight; going to my uncle's door, I gave several raps without receiving any answer. However, I soon discovered a light through the window, and my uncle called out—

"Who's there?"

I answered by saying—

"I am an officer, and have a warrant for your arrest."

He immediately came and unbolted the door, saying—

"All right; come in."

Looking into his face, I said—

"Sir, do you know me?"

Scanning my features closely, he ejaculated—

"I think I have never seen you before."

After some further delay I informed him who I was, when, grasping me by the hand he said—

"George, you are welcome."

Next morning we strolled out to view the town. It was located upon the shores of a beautiful lake, while in the distance I saw several vessels plying upon its silvery surface. Many lumber men were at the dock loading their vessels, and the busy saw was cutting out lumber in the mill close by. The lumbering business and the manufacture of glass seemed to be the principal employment of the inhabitants. The land around the village had been recently cleared, and here and there tall, black stumps could be seen, and the sound of the wood-chopper's axe rang out clearly in the distance.

Remaining idle for a few days, time began to hang heavily upon my hands, and I looked about for something to do.

My efforts were soon rewarded, for I engaged to saw quite a large quantity of logs of different lengths preparatory to their being hauled to the mills.

This was new business for me, and as I needed assistance, I employed a colored man and my uncle's eldest boy to help me. We commenced in earnest, and on the evening of the first day we scaled up the amount we had cut, and found, to my great satisfaction, that after paying all expenses I had made about four dollars. This encouraged me very much, and, finding I was likely to make money at the business, I worked hard every day with a right good will.

When the job was finished and I called upon my employer for payment, he managed to figure me out of quite a share of my hard earnings. This had a tendency to discourage me somewhat, and I went to a village some three miles distant and got drunk, spending a good deal of money.

On becoming sober I made up my mind to return home where I arrived about the middle of autumn. My father was anxious to leave that section of country, and formed the resolution to move out to my uncle's. So we packed our scanty furniture in boxes, and prepared to leave our place of abode.

CHAPTER XI.

ON arriving at our destination we hired a small house and began house-keeping. My brother-in-law soon found a job of work, and my father and myself engaged to chop cord wood. We continued at this business until the beginning of winter, when I left home and contracted to work for my cousin, Mr. Blanchard, and I remained working for him the space of one month; after which Mr. H—— offered me ten dollars per month and board to drive team for him, hauling wood some six miles to a glass factory, and I accepted the offer.

That winter was very severe, the snow covering the ground to the depth of four feet in some places. We were obliged to dig the wood from under the deep snow, load it on the sled, and drive to the glass factory, the excessive cold penetrating my body and almost freezing the blood in my veins. This work I continued until nearly spring, when I left Mr. H——, and engaged to saw logs in the woods for Mr. B——.

I continued to work for him until the snow had left the ground and the red-breast robin began to carol his sweet song in the spreading branches, while the warm rays of the sun had melted the ice from the surface of the lake, and all Nature seemed to rejoice at the return of Spring.

No opportunity being offered me to work after leaving Mr. B——, I put a change or two of linen in a small valise, and started off on foot to seek my fortune, or, at least, to find something to do. My purse was slender, containing but a few shillings, and with a heavy heart I trudged along the dusty road.

When night came I found that I had traveled twenty-five miles, and, footsore and weary, I stopped at a small inn by the way-side.

Not having eaten anything since morning I felt terribly hungry, and told the landlord to prepare me some supper. Then stepping up to the bar I called for something to drink, and as I drank it down in eager haste it aroused the slumbering demon in my bosom; without leaving the bar I poured out another glass brimming full, and gulped it down almost with a single swallow. Having taken nothing for so long a time it seemed to have a powerful effect upon me, for it coursed its way, almost in a moment's time, through every nerve and sinew of my body—even causing my finger-ends to tingle.

Although it was artificial stimulus, yet I must acknowledge that it eased present pain. When I sat down to supper I had already forgotten my hard day's journey, and with a well-filled table before me felt quite happy.

The following morning my knees were so stiff I

could hardly get down stairs, but knowing what the remedy was from the previous evening's experience, I made my way immediately to the bar and drank three or four times before breakfast. This produced the desired effect for the time; but after traveling a few miles on my way, I found that I felt much worse than on my arrival the night before.

I am satisfied, from this fact, that alcohol does not give strength to the body, but only excites the brain; and when exempt for a short time from this artificial stimulant the body relaxes into a state of torpor and disease.

All that long day I traveled on, not knowing whither I was going, stopping ever and anon at the little streams crossing the road, to bathe my face and take a drink of pure cold water, and at the different farm-houses along the road to enquire for work. At every place I stopped I was unsuccessful, and as the shades of night gathered thick and fast around me I felt almost like giving up in despair.

But taking fresh courage I still pressed on. It soon became so dark that I could not see to walk very well, and I began to realize that I must be looking about to find some place to spend the night.

After traveling about a mile further I came to a large farm-house, and in looking through the window I saw the table spread, and the family sitting around taking their supper. On going to the door I tapped gently, when some one said in a rough, harsh voice—

"Come in."

I walked in and said, "Good evening;" when a man said in the same gruff voice—

"Good evening, sir;" at the same time looking me over in a scrutinizing manner, while the old lady peered through her glasses, seemingly as much surprised as she would be if some horrible hobgoblin had broken in upon them, for my personal appearance was anything but prepossessing. My pants were thrust into my boot-legs; I had an old satchel strapped upon my back, and my whole exterior was covered with dust.

They might have taken me for a thief or robber; but I quieted their fears if any they had by telling them that I had started out to procure work and wanted some place to stop over night; but he immediately said in that same gruff voice—

"We don't keep beggars here."

I at once told him that he was laboring under a mistake; I was no beggar, although very poor. He continued eating for a few moment's longer, when he looked up and said—

"We cannot keep you."

Then putting on my hat I said to him—

"Sir, the day will yet come when I shall have a home of my own, and no man, however poor he may be, if he comes to my door and asks for a night's lodging, shall be denied."

Then bidding him good-night, I left, impressed with the consciousness that though he had the form of a man, yet a soul he did not possess. I felt as a gentleman did who, when telling about a small-souled person said—

"I believe his soul is so small that you could blow it through the quill of a humming-bird into a mosquitoe's eye, and not make him wink."

This comparison was surpassed by an old lady, who said some souls were so small that you could put ten thousand of them in a mustard seed and, by shaking it, hear them rattle. And now, when looking over my past life I am constrained to say, that if this man's soul was not as small as one of these it approximated closely to it.

After passing about a mile further, groping my way as best I could, my eyes caught the glimpse of a light in the distance, and I made my way towards it as fast as possible. It led me to a small house by the roadside, and I saw at a glance that they were living in much more humble circumstances than at the house I had just left.

Without hesitation I knocked at the door, and it was opened by a plainly dressed woman, holding a small child in her arms, who, peering at me through the darkness, asked me to walk in. When I entered I saw that they were quite poor, for their scanty furniture evinced the fact. At the table sat the husband reading a book; raising his eyes from the pages, he said in a pleasant voice—

"Take a seat."

I did so; and then told him what my object was in calling. He said—

"Certainly you can stay over night if you will take up with our humble fare."

Engaging in conversation with him, I soon felt quite at home. His wife spread a clean table-cloth, and prepared me some supper which I ate with a sharpened appetite. I found in the course of conversation that he had seen better days, but owing to misfortune he had become reduced in circumstances.

The next morning, having a shilling or two left, I offered it to him for my entertainment; but he refused to take a cent; so, thanking him for his hospitality, I left his humble habitation feeling that though poor he had a noble heart.

All that long, weary day I plodded on in a south-easterly direction towards Fort Brewerton. At nearly every house I called at to enquire for work I received the same discouraging answer, to the effect that they had help enough; and I began to wish myself home again.

When noon came I stopped at a large farm-house, and asked them for some dinner. After eating it, I asked the lady how much it would be. She said I might give her what I thought it was worth; taking the last twenty-five cent piece from my pocket I laid it in her hand, and left the house, penniless, and among strangers.

When night came, having no money, I crawled into a barn, and slept until morning. Getting up very early I started on my weary way, and traveled on at a rapid pace until I came to Fort Brewerton at four o'clock in the afternoon, or thereabouts. The little steamer that plied on the lake was about ready to leave for the village of B——, in which my father lived. Captain R——, who owned the vessel was a perfect stranger to me, but I told him how I was situated, when he put his hand in his pocket and placed a passage ticket and fifty cents in my hand. He said the boat would not leave for a few minutes, and told me to get something to eat and drink.

Following his advice I went to the nearest hotel and got two drinks of whisky and a cold lunch. I then went on board the steamer, and we were soon under way up the lake.

During the passage I made the acquaintance of the engineer who, going to a little closet, brought out a decanter of brandy, and invited me to drink with him. This was repeated several times on the voyage.

I arrived at home fully impressed with the idea that "Be it ever so humble, there is no place like home."

Nothing occurred of any importance until haying time, when I engaged to work for a man in the neighborhood through haying. When finished I once more packed up my few effects in a valise, and prepared to leave on a journey to the state of Ohio to battle again with the stern realities of life.

CHAPTER XII.

BIDDING my dear mother good-bye, and pressing my father's hand, I left them with a heavy heart, not knowing when I should see them again; stepping on board of the little steamer, I was soon on a second expedition, in order if possible to better my condition.

I arrived in due time at Fort Brewerton, and from there took stage to the city of Syracuse. On arriving at the depot I found it literally crowded with the people, and there was a great deal of confusion. Elbowing my way to the ticket office, I purchased a ticket for Buffalo.

As the train was not to leave for an hour and a half, I occupied my time by strolling about the city. While walking down one of the streets near the cànal, just as I came opposite to a rum saloon, the door was hastily thrown open, and a man ejected with terrible violence into the street, striking flat upon his face on the hard curb-stone. The blood flowed from his nostrils, and he lay as if dead.

Having been in many rough places I felt an inclination to step in to see what was the trouble. On doing so, the state of affairs in the saloon indicated that a severe fight had been going on, while a more miserable drunken set of vagabonds could rarely be seen. Among the number were three or four drunken women, cursing and swearing fully as bad as the men.

From past experience I concluded it wise to beat a hasty retreat, and was about doing so when one of the women placed herself against the door, saying—

"No; you don't go out of this door until you treat."

"That's so," exclaimed three or four others; and gathering around me, they rudely pushed me to the bar, and, considering discretion the best part of valor, I told the bar-tender to set on the glasses. They accordingly arrayed themselves in front of the bar, and drank at my expense. After which one of them approached me, and slapped me on the shoulder, saying with an oath—

"You seem to be a pretty good fellow;" and with this, they allowed me to depart without further molestation.

Then going to the depot I stepped on board the express train, and we were soon flying over the iron track, towards Buffalo. We reached that place sometime in the early part of the evening, and being a perfect stranger in the city I scarcely knew what to do or which way to go.

The hackmen seeing my dilemma pounced upon me like a pack of hungry wolves, and I was really afraid I should be torn into pieces. A runner from one of the low hotels actually seized me by the collar, and said—

"Come along with me young man; I will show you where you want to go."

I permitted myself to be dragged along like a sheep to the slaughter. Entering a small hotel, he took my satchel from my hand, and gave it to the man behind the bar, at the same time informing him that I would remain over night. Then turning to me again he said—

"Can't you afford to treat?"

I agreed to do so, and we took a drink together. My mind was made up to go to Cleveland, Ohio, and I asked him if there was a steamer that left for Cleveland that night. He informed me that there was not.

Not liking the looks of the man I doubted his word, and, stepping out into the street, I enquired of a nice-looking gentleman passing by, who told me that the steamer would leave in one hour, from —— wharf.

With this information I marched indignantly into the hotel, and said to the man behind the bar—

"Sir, I want my baggage."

With seeming astonishment he replied—

"What do you want your baggage for?"

"Because," said I, "you have deceived me; the boat leaves to-night for Cleveland, and I am going. You thought to get my money, but you will find yourself mistaken this time."

So he gave me my baggage, charging me twenty-five cents for his trouble, and I departed, impressed with the idea that I had at least learned one lesson.

On arriving at the wharf I found the steamer nearly

ready to start; so I went on board and purchased my ticket for Cleveland. The wind blew heavily during the passage, and the lake was rough, and some of the passengers were seasick. I didn't sleep much that night owing to the motion of the vessel; but the kind hand of Providence safely guided us over the waves, and toward morning the wind died away. So that when we entered the harbor of Cleveland scarcely a ripple could be seen upon the clear waters of Lake Erie.

It was a beautiful morning, and the city presented a fine appearance. I thought, as I beheld the stately trees that lined the sidewalks and heard the sweet birds singing in their branches, that it justly deserved the title of the Forest City of the West. No noisy hackmen pounced upon us as in the city of Buffalo, for they were not allowed to go beyond a certain limit to solicit passengers; and a stranger under these circumstances could not be otherwise than favorably impressed.

My next thought was to satisfy the cravings of a hungry appetite, and, having fallen in with a gentleman upon board of the steamer who was acquainted in the city, he told me he knew where we could get a good breakfast for twenty-five cents a piece. We went immediately to the place in question, and after taking two drinks made a hearty breakfast.

Then we strolled about the city in different directions, and, finally entered the old Court House, to get a more extensive view of the surroundings. Looking out of the window we saw the light-house standing upon a rocky eminence overlooking the fine harbor, while in every direction could be seen vessels sailing to and fro. The sea-birds were skimming over the crested waves, and ever and anon their silvery wings would flash in the morning light, as they rose to plunge beneath the surface in search of their finny repast.

I could not help thinking as I looked on that wave-beaten light-house, how many vessels, at the midnight hour, battling with the shocks of the tempest, have been saved from becoming wrecked upon the adjacent rocky reefs; and, now, even to-day, in our many Amercan pulpits, clergymen and God-fearing men are standing up with extended arms, warning the old, the middle-aged and the young to beware of the rocks of sin and dissipation, in order that at last they may find a safe mooring in the haven of peace.

In the afternoon I made my way to the depot and took the cars for the village of H——. After arriving there and partaking of something to eat, I started off on foot to visit my half-sister who lived in a neighboring town; she was my mother's daughter by her first husband—my mother being a widow at the time of my father's marriage with her. She had at that time, three sons and one daughter.

The contents of my purse began to get slim, and, sitting down by the side of the road, I counted over my money and found that I had one dollar and seventy-five cents left all in silver. Then shouldering my valise, I trudged on the dusty road and arrived at the village of R——, where my sister, lived late in the afternoon.

Reparing to a hotel, I arranged my toilet, brushed the dust from my clothing, and walked up to her house. My relatives, having never seen me before, were overjoyed on learning who I was. They prepared me an excellent supper, and treated me with great kindness.

After resting a few days, I engaged to work for Mr. H——, my sister's husband, planing boards in his carpenter shop. Although I had worked at that business a very little, I soon found it needed considerable experience to plane the board smoothly; for in that part of the country instead of using pine, they use whitewood, which is harder to work. However, by dint of perseverance, I soon learned to work it quite well, and entered into a contract to remain an indefinite length of time, and if I liked the work to stop until I had learned the trade. Our first job of any importance was upon a brick school-house in the village; while there I made the acquaintance of quite a large number of the leading citizens who were interested in education.

There was one peculiar character in that village whom I well recollect. He had emigrated from the Emerald Isle previously, and was a good-natured, intelligent, hard-working man. In whatever position he might be placed, he was noted for his even temper. Any morning you might hear his hearty laugh, as he trudged along on his way to work, with shovel or pickaxe on his back. He was the finest whistler I ever heard; he could imitate the fife or clarionet, or warble like the birds; on account of his good-nature and intelligence he was quite a favorite in the village.

They engaged him to do the digging around the school-house; and every morning he made his regular appearance with his implements of labor, whistling as merrily as a lark. Being so far away from home I became many times very lonely, and at such times would ask him to whistle for me, to cheer me up. He would then say, as he looked up into my face—

"An sure, its mesilf too that's often ben lonely, begarra, since I came til Ameriky; for isn't it Biddy and the childer that I lift behind, beyant the say in Tipperary—God bless it! But, thank the Holy Vargint and the blissed St. Patrick, wasn't it my own hands that earned the money to bring them over to this counthry where they are living with me now, sure! It's mesilf, Garge, that knows how yeez feel, and, bejabers, I'll whistle for yeez."

He would then throw down his tools, and strike up some lively Irish jig, which would soon cause me to forget my sorrow.

After completing the school-house and finishing a small job for Mr. D——, we commenced work upon a large building some three miles from the centre of the village. We would walk to our work and return at night after laboring hard all day.

After working there sometime I began to feel quite unwell, and one morning, feeling very bad I left the building, and went into the woods some distance off, where I lay down at the root of a tree and lay some hours contemplating my condition in life. It was nearly evening when I reached home where I remained two or three days when I began to feel better.

CHAPTER XIII.

ON going down to the post-office one morning I met Mr. B——, the leading merchant in the village. He told me his clerk was about to leave and he would like to engage me to fill his place. This proposition was very acceptable to me, and without hesitation I told him I would be glad to come.

Early next morning I went to the store where I was to receive my first instruction in mercantile life. I entered upon my duties with a firm determination to do my best.

The first day I found out that there was a great deal to do, as the customers were very numerous. A regular country trade was carried on, the most of our customers being Germans, who would bring in butter, eggs, dried-apples, cheese, lard, wheat etc., and exchange them for goods. The work was more laborious than I expected, and the first night upon my returning home from the store I was so tired I could hardly eat my supper.

My employer was a native of Connecticut, who,

years before, when a boy, left his home on foot to seek a residence somewhere in the West. He took a little trunk filled with Yankee notions to pay his expenses on the way. When he arrived about at the spot where the city of Rochester now stands, his stock in trade gave out, and he could travel no further. He began to look about for something to do, and finally engaged to chop wood for about thirty cents a cord. He worked faithfully until about the middle of winter, when one day on cutting down a tree, it fell in the wrong direction from what he intended, struck a valuable cow and killed her instantly.

"That," said he, " was a trying time, and I never felt more like running away than I did then."

But instead of leaving he formed the resolution to chop wood until the cow was paid for, which he accordingly did. Then leaving, he worked his way through until he arrived in Ohio, where he learned the cabinet-makers business, married, and finally began in a small way to sell goods.

He had thus worked himself up from obscurity to a position of standing in the community. He had enlarged his store several times, and when I engaged with him he had been twenty-five years upon the same spot. His motto was "Honesty is the best policy;" his customers had unbounded confidence in him. He said to me on first entering his employ—

"Give good weight and measure."

It was a one-price store and all customers were served alike. Sometimes a new settler, coming in that vicinity from Germany, would call at our store to purchase some article, and after examining the goods would offer a few cents less than the price, when we would immediately lay the goods upon the shelf, informing him at the same time that we sold only at one price; when he would say in broken English—

"Dat's ves vrights; yous ve honest; I takes 'em."

These Germans were generally a hard-working people. The women would toil all day long in the fields, and do nearly as much work as a man; after which they would take their baskets, filled with butter or eggs, and come on foot to trade at our store in the evenings.

I soon became convinced that it would be necessary for me to learn something of their language, and whenever opportunity offered I would question them in regard to the names of the goods we sold them. In a short time I could understand them so well that I could show them any article they called for.

One day, however, an old Dutch lady came in who had not yet learned to speak a word of English. Coming up to me she tried to imitate our language by asking for a "*touch kalenar.*" This put me to test, and I stood for a moment to consider what she wanted; but I was completely nonplussed. The old woman came up close to me and took hold of my coat-sleeve, while she kept saying—"*touch kalenar, touch kalenar.*"

I motioned to her to look about the store to see if she could find what she wanted. She seemed to understand what I meant, and immediately commenced a thorough search. It was some time before she was successful, when, finally going behind the desk where we kept our stationery, she soon returned to the place where I stood, holding in her hand a Dutch calendar. She laughed heartily, and clapped me upon the shoulder, as much as to say, "You will learn yet."

Our customers were not all of this kind; we had many of the best families in the neighborhood to trade at our store, and, as we kept silks and embroideries as well as groceries, crockery and hardware, oils etc., the business kept me constantly on the go from one part of the building to another. Sometimes up stairs, and sometimes down in the cellar.

Frequently I would come up out of the cellar with a jug of oil in my hands, when a young lady would say to me—

"I would like to look at some silk."

On going to the water tank to remove the oil from my hands, another customer would say—

"Can you draw me a jug of molasses?"

On the way back, some lady would say—

"Can you show me some embroidery?"

Another again would cry out—

"Let us have some coffee!" or, "Cut off this piece of cloth as I am in a great hurry."

So with butter to weigh and eggs to count out, I found but few spare moments. In the middle of the day when our customers were not so plenty, I would find time to pack eggs or butter for market. I was generally the last one to leave the store at night, and the first one to open it in the morning. I would generally rise about three A. M., and have the store all swept and dusted by daylight, when the German customers would begin to come to do their trading in order to get time to do a day's work.

We kept liquors in the cellar, to sell for medicinal purposes to our customers. Occasionally I would go down in the evening, after all had left the store, and draw a tumbler about half full of some kind of spirits, and after sweetening it I would drink it and imagine that it did me good. It was far better liquor than they have at the present day and did not have the same effect. I doubt not that many a young man has formed the appetite for strong drink by taking an occasional glass, being deluded with the idea that it would do him good. My appetite at that time was strong for drink, and I should have imbibed more freely had it not been for a desire to do justice to my employers. They soon gained confidence in me, and I was intrusted with the key of the safe, and nearly all the money taken in passed through my hands.

We had accumulated some sixteen hundred dollars in silver and gold in our safe, when it was proposed that I should go to the nearest bank, some twelve miles distant, and procure a draft on New York. Mr. B—— harnessed up his horse and carriage; and, having taken in a young lady, I started off in high spirits.

On arriving at the bank I procured the draft. We then went to the largest hotel in the town and ordered dinner. On sitting down at the table I found myself face to face with those whom I supposed to be merchants, and gaily-dressed ladies. I felt very much embarrassed, and made awkward work at waiting upon the lady who accompanied me.

The first thing I did was to upset the coffee, and at the same time I accidentally dropped my knife upon the floor. There was a general tittering around the table at my unfortunate mishap, which embarrassed me still more, and started the perspiration which ran streaming down my face. How I got through that meal is more than I am able to tell; but I made up my mind that in future, whether merchants or princes should happen to be at the table, I would try to keep from being excited.

We started for home, and there came up one of the heaviest thunder showers I ever experienced. The roads began to get muddy, and when we arrived home we presented a far different appearance from what we did when we left in the morning.

I remained in the store all the next winter without losing but one or two days. We had but little snow and the roads were generally very muddy indeed. Whenever we had a short run of sleighing, the young folks improved it by going off to balls or parties in the evening. I was generally invited to accompany them, but invariably refused with one exception.

There was to be a ball some twelve miles from where I lived, and they sent a special invitation for me to come. Two ladies were to accompany me. We started off in a snow storm, and on arriving at our destination we found the clerk who was my predecessor in the store.

As I never danced I thought it best not to learn, and therefore, giving the ladies in charge to my friend, I felt at liberty to do as I pleased, so long as I did not get intoxicated. So going down to the bar-room I took a drink. When supper time came, I sat down at the table beside the same young lady, with considerable less embarrassment than on a former occasion.

It was piercing cold the next morning; and after having taken a parting drink with my friends, we got into the sleigh, covered ourselves up with the robes and rode home.

This was in the year 1857. Many of my readers will remember that there was great financial embarrassment during that year all over the country; and especially did they feel it in the West. No money passed current at that time in that state, excepting the State Bank bills of Ohio, and, of course, gold and silver. There might have been a few banks whose bills passed current, but they were very few.

One day a German physician came into the store and purchased a few small articles, giving me in payment a ten-dollar bill on one of the banks in Sandusky City—we both supposing it to be good. When my employer came in he told me at once that it was worthless, and I said—

"Sir, I will get good money for it before night."

I immediately went to the stable, harnessed the horse, hitched him before the carriage, and started in pursuit of the doctor. I drove up to the door just as he entered the house, presenting him the bill, telling him that it was not good; he immediately counted out good money in exchange for it, and, wheeling round my horse, I drove back to the store in time to wait upon my evening customers.

I remained in the store until about the middle of spring, and was then nearly nineteen years old, when Dr. W—— proposed to me to enter his office for the purpose of studying medicine. As there was some difference of opinion between myself and my employer, I accepted the proposal and left the store; but owing to circumstances I did not enter his office. He was shortly afterwards taken ill and died. Thus my hopes of ever becoming a physician were nipped in the bud, and I then made up my mind to return home, and started with the full determination of doing so.

On arriving at Cleveland I fell in with a gentleman whom I had previously met, and we spent an hour or two together. I then took the cars for Buffalo. On reaching there, I changed my mind in regard to returning home, and when the steamer left for Cleveland the next day I returned again, hoping that I might find employment there; not meeting with success I became discouraged. Having a few dollars in my pocket, to drown trouble I began to drink, thus rendering my condition more and more miserable.

After remaining there for a day or two, suffering in a manner I will not now relate, I fell in with a man who had shipped on board a lake steamer which was going to Chicago. He procured me a situation as deck hand; I held the position until the steamer arrived in Chicago, when, being fully satisfied with my experience on the water as a deck hand, I left her.

After wandering around the sunken streets of Chicago for a day or two, I once more turned my face towards home.

CHAPTER XIV.

AT this time my worldly goods were very limited. My funds, in the aggregate, amounted to about twelve dollars. I had on a fair suit of clothes, and my carpet-sack contained a change of linen besides several other necessary articles.

While trying to find the steamboat pier, I met a representative from the Emerald Isle. I asked him politely if he could tell me at what time a steamer would leave for Cleveland; said he—

"Is it the capt'in yez take me for? By the holy St. Patrick, it's the capt'in I'm after wishing I was, and we'd soon have a wee dhrop together, and then to Cleveland you should go, free of expense, as sure as me name is Dennis O'Rafferty."

The good-natured language and appearance of this wanderer from the bogs, warmed my feelings towards him to such an extent that I asked him to take a drop of cordial with me in an adjoining groggery. Scratching his head, with the greatest satisfaction depicted on his sun-burned visage, he assented readily, heaving a sigh of relief, as though he had been wishing for that invitation all the morning. We walked toward the groggery, the old fellow remarking as we went, that he should have invited me to drink with him, but he had not had a red in his pocket since the wake of Tom Nolan.

As we entered the bar-room, which was in a basement below the sidewalk, the man behind the bar—the professional poison dispenser—looked as though he had also attended at the wake of the late Nolan, and seen the whole thing through; one of his eyes was dressed in mourning, and his nose looked like a boiled beet; The bar was situated in one corner of the cellar,—for it was nothing else—and scattered around the room, in various stages of sobriety were a number of Chicago River bummers. If there is a worse looking set of men in the civilized world, I would rather not see them.

I have rambled about the world somewhat; and no place can produce worse men than those frequenting the low haunts of crime about Chicago. The Five Points of New York is respectable to some portions of Chicago; but, thanks to Long John Wentworth, some of these haunts are destroyed. I have no desire now to investigate very deeply into the mysteries and miseries of the aforesaid city; but my recollections are not very flattering to that certain class that I became connected with that morning while taking a quiet drink with Dennis O'Rafferty.

As soon as we entered and called for our drinks two

rough-looking beats came up, and one of them said—

"Stranger, we'll drink with you, as you are a fair looking chap. Where are yer traveling?"

I paid for our drinks; I knew they were spoiling for a fight, and, rather than have any difficulty then and there, I paid for theirs also, and beckoned Dennis to come on, which he seemed very willing to do, having taken a very stiff horn. I observed that he had waited until the bar-keeper's attention was attracted, and very quickly filled his glass to the brim, covering it with his enormous fist.

Entering the street again, Dennis, wiping his mouth with his rusty sleeve, said—

"Be jabbers, if me mother gave me that quality of milk, I'd not be waned till yet."

We felt somewhat better from our slight indulgence. I speak for both, as I could judge my companion by the sparkle of his eye and confident air.

When we arrived at the dock my friend of the morning pointed out to me the Cleveland steamer, saying—

"Now me man, there is the boat that will just take yez where yez want to go, and it's a safe voige I'm wishing ye'll have, and long life to yez. You'll be after gething yer ticket at the winder, when the capt'in comes aboard."

I bade good-bye to Dennis, and with thanks for his information and good wishes for his future, I went on board the boat and sauntered into the cabin, to wait for the time of sailing. Waiting on a boat or in a depot is very dreary, as people are aware who have trav-

CHICAGO RIVER GROCERY.

eled, especially in a strange place. As I sat in that cabin, far away from friends and home, a strong feeling of melancholy came over me, and, as all know who have ever been addicted to strong drink, my only resort, feeling as I did, was to indulge again; but I gave the river groceries a wide berth, and extended my walk to a more respectable bar,—if anything in that line can be called respectable—and while there purchased a bottle of brandy, thinking it would come handy on the lake.

On my arrival again at the boat I deposited the brandy in my carpet-sack, and did not have long to wait before the captain made his appearance. I lost no time in introducing myself and stating my case to him, as I had made up my mind to work my passage through if possible. I informed him I was not very well supplied with cash, and wanted to make my way home to the East; that if there was a chance I would work my passage on this boat.

He asked me what I could do. I told him I would do anything he thought fit. He told me to take pencil and paper, and foot up the freight bills. I commenced, and in about half an hour I had them ready for his inspection. After looking them over he told me to foot them up again, which I did, and then asked him what I should do next. He said, foot them up again. I complied again with his request the third time, and had the order repeated the fourth time. I now began to think that he was testing me; and I made up my mind to keep on casting up his accounts over and over until he was satisfied. I presume that he had heard or read of the poor man's story in connection with Stephen Girard, and as it may not be out of place, and some of my readers perhaps have not heard it I will relate the circumstances.

One day, as Mr. Girard was standing on his wharf in Philadelphia, a man accosted him with a request for work, stating that he was in absolute want.

"Very well," replied the millionaire, "I will give you employment. There is a quantity of lumber in the loft of my storehouse which you may bring down and place here on the pier."

The man divested himself of his coat, and went to work with a right good will. He brought the lumber all down as ordered; then went and asked, what next, and was told to take the same back again to the loft, which he did; and, the same orders being repeated, he brought down and took up the lumber several times in succession. Then he went to Mr. Girard, and said—

"I do not see the necessity of this."

"Well, well, my man, that is all the work I have for you to do, and if you do not want to do it I will pay you off. But if you wish to work I will give you two dollars per day as long as you are satisfied."

The man concluded to continue on, and when his week was up he went to the office and drew his pay. This he continued to do for a long time, thus earning a good living for himself and family.

When I had presented the accounts to the captain the sixth time, he said—

"That will do, my boy," at the same time slapping me on the shoulder, and then exclaiming—

"God bless you! you shall have a free passage, and as good fare as the boat affords. I like your perseverance. I was a poor boy myself, and by that quality, coupled with honesty, I have made myself what you now see me."

I felt overjoyed at the kindness manifested towards me by the captain, and came to the conclusion that he was one of nature's noblest men. As he requested, I made myself at home on the boat, and should doubtless have enjoyed myself during the voyage had we not encountered one of those storms, unknown any where but on the American Lakes.

That night of storm, confusion and horror will never be effaced from my memory; and as I sit at my table writing, I seem to live over again in imagination the scenes of that dismal night. The roaring waters, crashing thunder, howling wind and creaking timbers, mingled with the screams of women and children, prayers and curses of men,—these together made me think the last day had surely come.

Sailors tell of storms in the Gulf of Mexico, and in the China Seas; but I have talked with those who have sailed the globe over, who say they have never encountered worse storms anywhere than on our Western Lakes. Storms arise very suddenly, and the short swells, and absence of sea room to ride out a long gale make our lake navigation very dangerous.

I had retired to my berth, and the first indication I had of the gale was that I was thrown violently from the berth to the cabin floor. While lying there, bracing myself in the best way I could, a man came staggering across the floor, grasping any thing he could, to hold himself up. As he came towards me he lost his balance, and fell, striking his head against one of the cabin posts or pillars that support the deck, knocking him senseless, and badly cutting his head.

My first impulse was to crawl to see if I could not render some assistance. It was impossible for me to walk. I found him, to all appearances, lifeless. My God! thought I, the man is dead. Then the thought struck me—if they find me with him they will think I killed him.

I dragged myself along to my berth, and found my bottle of brandy, which, fortunately, was nearly full, as I had only taken two drinks since we had left Chicago. I went back to the man, and found him still senseless. I moistened his lips with brandy, at the same time bathing his face and hands. He soon began to show signs of returning consciousness. Hope revived, and I kept on bathing him. Finally he opened his eyes, and in the dim lamp-light they looked glassy. I put my head down close to his lips, and he asked faintly for more brandy, which I gave him. His first words after fully recovering were, "How came I here? What did they do it for?"

This convinced me that his mind was wandering; so, binding up his head with my pocket handkerchief, and giving my blankets and pillow to make him comfortable, I returned to my bunk and clung like a barnacle for dear life. The storm still raged in fierce fury, and I thought we would all soon be in Davy Jones's locker.

About twelve o'clock the next day the fury of the storm abated, and with the exception of a slight swell we were sailing through a comparatively smooth sea. I noticed my wounded friend of the previous night walking the forward deck, looking as well as could be expected under the circumstances; but I must confess that his appearance must have looked to a person not acquainted with the events of the gale, rather pugilistic.

In due time we reached Cleveland, and I joyfully shook the spray of Lake Erie from my feet and was not sorry to plant them once more on *terra firma*. Wending my way to an adjoining restaurant, I indulged in a stiff horn of brandy and ordered breakfast. After satisfying the inner man I strolled about the streets of the Forest City.

During my perambulations it was my good fortune to fall in with a gentleman who was traveling east, and we dropped into several drinking saloons during our stay, adding to our bar-room experiences. When the time came for our departure we purchased tickets for Buffalo, by rail via Lake Shore Line, where we arrived safely at night.

The hackmen met us as only Buffalo and Niagara Falls hackmen can. They were determined we should have a hack at any rate. We judged that every hotel, one-horse eating house, and rum shop in the city was represented. We were surrounded and at their mercy.

If a Camanche warrior had stood in that crowd and heard their wild yells, he would doubtless have thrown up the sponge in their favor, and have gone back to his tribe on the plains with an exalted opinion of the yelling capacities of Buffalo runners.

One fellow more bold than the rest followed us until my traveling friend thought it was about time to show his colors; so squaring himself, *a la* Heenan, he gave him a tip in the mug, which brought the claret, and also the man to the ground, if I may be permitted to use the slang of the ring.

"Now," said my friend, "if you don't travel, and let peaceable strangers alone, I'll *hack* you finer than sausage meat, and you will have to charter a hack to take you to your place of residence."

By this time Hacky came to the sensible conclusion that he had struck the wrong crowd, and that it was about time to beat a retreat, which he did in bad marching order, with his colors trailing in Buffalo mud; and we saw him no more.

After our experiences with these city denizens, we came to the conclusion to take our immediate departure. My money had been slowly diminishing; but my friend told me that if I would extend my travels to New York City he would pay my expenses. There was existing at this time a rivalry between the New York Central and Erie railroad.

While we stood at the ticket office making inquiries, I observed a gentlemanly-looking person coming across the room towards us, and he soon stood at my side. I supposed he wished to purchase a ticket; but when my attention was attracted in an opposite direction, he deliberately took up my carpet-sack, which lay near me on the floor, and made for the door.

I saw that there was no time to lose. Springing towards him with all the energy I possessed, I grasped him by the collar just as he reached the door. In another moment he would have escaped me; but I had him fast. Said I—

"That is my satchel, sir, and I shall have to trouble you for it."

He seemed to be very much surprised, and made many apologies, remarking that he must have made a mistake; but as he had none of his own in view I could not see the point.

By this time my friend was at my side, saying—

"Just pass that chap over to me; I'll settle his hash in double quick time."

I have no doubt he would have done it, judging from what I had witnessed on our arrival, but I begged him not to harm the man as he would never have a chance to steal anything from us again.

"That makes no difference; he will steal from some one," said my friend.

But I finally prevailed on him to let the would-be thief off without any great harm. He could not however resist taking him by the ear and leading him out on the street, assisting him somewhat on the way by a slight application of boot-leather.

After these events we continued on our journey, and on our arrival at Albany, with many thanks to my comrade of a day for his great kindness in inviting me to accompany him to New York, I declined, for on nearing my friends, I naturally wished to visit them. We had several parting drinks together, and took an affectionate farewell. I have never met him since, but still remember his genial, off-hand good fellowship, and entertain a respect for his muscular developments.

Not far from Albany I found relatives, who cordially welcomed me and I had some very pleasant times in their society; many sails on the noble Hudson were not the least of the enjoyments I had during those halcyon days.

But my pleasures were arrested by a violent illness that prostrated me and confined me to my bed for three long months, reducing me to a shadow. The kindness shown me by my relatives forced on me a debt of gratitude which I can never repay; especially to my cousin John Anderson and his noble-hearted wife, at whose house I was kindly entertained during my protracted illness. My half-brother I must not forget. His frequent visits and sympathy will cause me to remember William Fuller with exceeding gratitude; also his subsequent aid in one of the darkest hours of my life.

After I had sufficiently recovered I took the boat for New York, and from thence went to New Jersey; and there I staid until I recruited my strength sufficiently, and then I made my way to Oswego County, New York, where my parents resided. They were very happy to see me after my long absence from home. Here I was again taken sick, and did not leave the house for three weeks.

During my convalescence, I used to amuse myself by watching the interesting processes in the manufacture of window glass,—a large glass factory being near at hand. As many of my readers may not have had an opportunity of witnessing the different stages in the manufacture of this indispensable article, I will describe, as minutely and intelligibly as I can, what I saw of this valuable product of American industry.

The men engaged in glass-blowing are not the most temperate men in the world. Many of them drink to excess, and not a few drink up nearly all their earnings.

In the factory at that time were several glass-blowers from England, who made larger cylinders than any other workmen there, some being nearly ten feet in length.

These cylinders were twice the thickness of ordinary glass, and required much skill in handling. They would whirl them over their heads with great velocity. The whole building would be as light as day, while the heat emanating from the furnaces and molten glass made it quite comfortable for those working in other portions of the factory, even in the coldest season.

The heat, however, was very oppressive for those engaged near the furnaces: it was so intense that men could only endure it for a moment at a time. They would run up to the pots containing the melted glass, thrust in their blow-pipes, and roll them around for an instant to gather a sufficient quantity. They would then step quickly back, at the same time blowing through the tubes, which were carried far above their heads, and whirled back and forth with great dexterity.

Finally, with blowing, swinging, and balancing, the cylinder is blown to the proper size, and is then laid away to cool. After that a red-hot iron rod is run through it, which separates it on one side. It is then taken to the flattening room, and from thence to another department where it is cut with diamonds into window-panes.

Glass is manufactured from sand and other ingredients. It is said that it was first discovered by a party of soldiers who were encamped on the sandy shores of the Mediterranean Sea. They saw, when they were about to resume their march in the morning, that the sand on which they had built their fire was in a melted state, and that it was transparent.

CHAPTER XV.

HAVING recovered my health in a measure, and not believing in waiting for something to turn up, I determined to start out immediately to see what Dame Fortune had in store for me. The snow at this time was nearly three feet deep; as I could not travel as a pedestrian I contracted with a gentleman to take me in his sleigh some thirty miles to the village of O——. The snow being so deep, our journey was necessarily slow.

The first hotel we came to my friend reined in his horses, and we entered the house. Here we met a man about half-seas over, who addressed us on sight with—

"Hill-hill-hillo stran—hic—gers. Where—hic—the d-d-devil did yer—hic—come from? Le'ss—hic—take some —hic—pen to drink—hic—I'm on—hic—fun and—hic —lousy with money," at the same time pulling a handful of silver from his pocket, several pieces of which dropped on the floor.

I picked them up and handed them to him. Said he—

"You seem—hic—to be—hic—a honest chap—hic; —but being—hic—a phrenol—hic—ogist I know you —hic—are by your—hic—bumps. Keep the—hic— change, lad, there's—hic—more where—hic—that came—hic—from."

I finally prevailed on him to take the money, after which we accepted his invitation to drink.

He certainly was the roughest specimen of humanity it had been my fortune to meet for a long time. Swearing seemed his forte. Oaths rolled over his lips like rain-drops off the back of a goose. His nose was an exaggerated Roman; and I thought at the time that he would be very proficient in the business of cherry picking and might earn good wages by the job, as he could hang on a limb with his nose, and use both hands to gather the fruit. His eye (he had but one) looked like a fried egg floating in sweet oil.

He informed us that he had a great mouth for rum, and we were fully convinced of it before we parted with him, for his regular time between drinks was just five minutes. His face was completely covered with toddy blossoms, and, take him altogether, he was a living temperance lecture—a perfect wreck of manhood, and a warning to all those who join in the social glass.

He probably started in life with as fair prospects as the average of young men have; what a loathsome sight had he now become! A few short years before he was a free-hearted, happy boy, the pride of his mother and the joy of his father. In an unguarded moment he, probably, took his first glass, which launched him on the raging sea of intemperance, where many a staunch craft has foundered, and sunk beneath the red waves.

While writing of this man my thoughts wander back to the dangerous position I was then in, fully embarked on the same traitorous tide. How thankful I am that I was enabled by God's goodness to about ship, and return to the port of temperance, to anchor at last in that harbor of security, where I hope ever to remain, safe from the storms that howl around me. What greater victory can man achieve than to conquer himself?

When a poor victim of intemperance comes trembling up to sign the pledge, I feel that he has shown himself to be a hero. We may talk of heroes of the past. We point to Alexander, the conqueror of the world; Hannibal, surmounting the snowy peaks of the Alps; Wellington, at Waterloo; Cæsar, crossing the Rubicon; Napolean, at the bridge of Lodi; Nelson, who at one fell blow destroyed the combined maratime powers of France and Spain off Cape Trafalgar; our immortal Washington, leading his thin-clad soldiers o'er the blood-stained snows of seven winters; but none of these momentous conquests, decided though they were, can be compared to the glorious victory which a poor, deluded drunkard obtains, when he defeats the serried hosts of King Alcohol, and, horse, foot, and artillery, sends them cowering to the wall.

"Let others write of battles, fought on bloody, gory fields,
 Where honor greets the man who wins, and death the man who yields;
 But I will write of him who fights and conquereth his sins;

Who struggles on through weary years against himself, and wins:
He may not wear a hero's crown, nor fill a hero's grave,
But Truth will place his name among the bravest of the brave!"

We remained at the way-side inn until our horses were rested, and during that time imbibed rather freely; the consequence was we were feeling rather jolly. Taking a parting drink with the good-natured landlord, we tumbled into our sleigh and started off to complete the journey. The road was almost impassable for most of the way, and we were tossed about like a ship in a gale of wind.

Finally, we reached a place in the road where the snow lay piled in immense drifts. While the horses were plunging, and exerting themselves to get through, the sleigh suddenly capsized, precipitating us into the snow. I found myself completely buried, but managed to clamber out, and after some difficulty gained a secure footing.

After shaking the snow from my garments, my next thought was for my companion. He was nowhere to be seen; but a pair of number nine cowhides, projecting from an adjoining drift, were rather convincing proof that he was still in the immediate vicinity.

I had not sufficiently recovered to go to the assistance of the aforesaid boots, but saw they contained life, for they were soon mimicing all the fancy steps of a French dancing-master in the air; and I had the satisfaction of seeing legs, body, and then the head and shoulders of my friend appear in a well-frosted condition.

Winking, blinking, and shaking himself, he let off a

volley of oaths that would have gained great favor with a Kidd, or any other piratical marauder.

As good luck would have it the horses were pretty well anchored in the snow, and did not seem very much inclined to proceed farther. We soon secured them, righted the sleigh, resumed our seats, and started on as well as the difficulties of the road would permit.

The next place we reined up at was what they term in that section a canal grocery. These rum shops are open during the summer months for the accommodation, or destruction, of boatmen on the canal. They usually keep a small stock of groceries, but their principal income is derived from selling bad whisky. Some say it will kill as far as a Sharpe's rifle; others that it is as effective as Jersey lightning; consequently the customers are always required to pay in advance.

Some few of these places are kept open through the winter season; and there the lowest of humanity congregate, to drink, swear, play cards, quarrel, and fight.

We were rather downcast after our snow bath, and feeling thirsty, concluded to venture in. We found the room to be about fifteen feet square, the bar occupying one entire side of the den. Overhead were several baskets, hanging from rusty nails, that looked as though they had waited a long time for purchasers. The principal stock in trade consisted of several barrels, mounted on skids, which contained more or less of O. B. Joyful, as the denizens of that locality termed it. But I should say that O. B. Sorrowful, or O. B. Damned, would be much more appropriate.

The last name reminds me of a story that was related

to me while traveling in the West. The incident happened in California some years since. While a gentleman was making his way across country on his mule, he came to Yuba River; on the opposite side was a village called Yuba Dam; but he was ignorant of the above facts. As he rode down the bank to ford the stream, he saw on the other side two red-shirted men engaged in a rough-and-tumble fight, and postponed his movements to witness the result.

In a few minutes one of the men crawled off, badly beaten, into the bush, and the other coolly sat down on a stump and began to fill his pipe. The traveler, seeing that all was over, swam his mule across, and, riding up to the participant in the late unpleasantness, said—

"Will you be kind enough to tell me, sir, what is the name of this town?"

"You-be-dam," was the surly answer, which had the effect to end further questions of the traveler. He started up his mule hastily, thinking that, judging by appearances, it would not take much to get up another fight, and that he would stand a chance to take a hand.

Riding on through the town, which consisted of three log houses, a blacksmith's shop, and a couple of groceries, he saw a woman at a door, and, being still anxious to know in what locality he was, politely asked—

"Madam, will you please to inform me what town this is?"

Her answer, in that shrill voice only heard from a woman of the frontier, was, "You-be-dam."

Our traveler put spurs to his mule, thinking that the people were not very choice in their language, nor courteous to strangers.

On reaching the outskirts of the village, seeing a little girl making mud pies, he determined to make one more effort to learn the name of this interesting hamlet, and accosted her with—

"My pretty little girl, what is the name of this village ?"

She tossed back her hair, inserted one finger in her mouth, and lisped, " You-be-dam."

This was enough for our traveler. He drove the rowels deep into the flanks of his mule, determined to put as many miles as possible between himself and a town where even the women and children cursed so frightfully.

But to return to the grocery. There was a rough bench on one side of the room, on which was seated a half-dozen of the regular customers, I should judge by there appearance. They were in all stages of intoxication, and a sorry sight to behold. One fellow had drank himself into a stupor, sleeping that sleep which only a drunkard can : his snoring capacity was extensive. His next comrade on the bench punched him repeatedly saying—

"Wake up Tim ; it's your treat."

We made up our minds to try the O. B. Joyful, and not wishing to be thought mean we invited the crowd ; it was very surprising how quick Tim awoke at that time ; he staggered up to take his allowance, rubbing his bleared eyes, and gazing wistfully at the liquor.

Our drinks brought the tears to our eyes; the liquor must have been manufactured from Prussic acid, old boots, and pig-tail tobacco.

Our stay after this experience was short, and we were soon gliding along the tow-path in good style. It was after dark when we arrived at our destination. Going directly to a public house, after stabling the horses we ordered tea; but before supper was ready I said to the landlord—

"Have you any good brandy?"

"Yes sir," remarked he, "the real old quill; try this," and he produced a black bottle from a nook under the bar.

The poison we had imbibed at our last stopping place was, I should judge, made to produce instead of alay thirst, and consequently we concluded, as we had the landlord's word the article before us was prime, that a good stiff horn would not hurt us any, as the last portion of our ride had been quite cold.

After our drink and a quiet chat by the old-fashioned fire place, we seated ourselves at a well-set table, and enjoyed the meal as only hungry travelers can. After supper we had another pull at the brandy bottle, took a smoke by the fire, and talked over our day's trip; then retired.

In the morning I settled with my friend, and, bidding me farewell, pledging me good luck in a **parting glass**, he started on his return to his home.

CHAPTER XVI.

I STOOD stood once more among strangers with the world before me. What should I do? Where should I go? I must decide both questions. I sat down to deliberate but could not conclude on anything definite, and, disliking inaction, I took a stroll through the town.

Judging by appearances business was flourishing, and there seemed to be improvements in progress at various portions of the village.

While passing a store my attention was attracted by seeing a number of bottles labeled peppermint, checkerberry, etc., etc. In an instant the thought occurred to me that these essences might be peddled through the country with considerable success. I thought I would step in and inquire the retail price per bottle; the proprietor told me they sold for fifteen and twenty-five cents according to the size of the bottles. This convinced me that the profit must be one hundred per cent, and that I might do well at that business.

No sooner had this idea of speculation occurred to

me than I resolved to carry it into effect. I went immediately to a drug store to ascertain the price of alcohol and essential oils. After ascertaining, and making my calculations, I found my surmise was correct; so I determined to commence at once as a manufacturer and peddler of essences.

It was not many days before I had quite a large stock in trade, and was ready for the road. Packing them in a hand trunk I started through the country, selling them at the farm houses along the roads. My first success was so flattering, that I thought certainly that I had by mere chance entered the road to wealth.

The third day I called at a tavern at some distance out in the country; and feeling rather tired and wayworn, I took a good stiff horn of whisky. Not having drank any for a few day's preceding, it went to my brain, and before ten minutes had elapsed the fact that I was an essence peddler had departed from my mind. There was the usual crowd of country tavern oafers seated around on the benches in the bar. I asked them to drink with me a couple of times, and was soon hale fellow well met with them.

Finally, we concluded to see which could drink the most liquor without giving in, and all that afternoon and evening we continued pouring down the fire-water, as an Oneida Indian who was one of the party was pleased to call it.

Well might he call it fire-water—the curse of his nation and his tribe. It had caused many a council-fire to become extinguished, and his once powerful

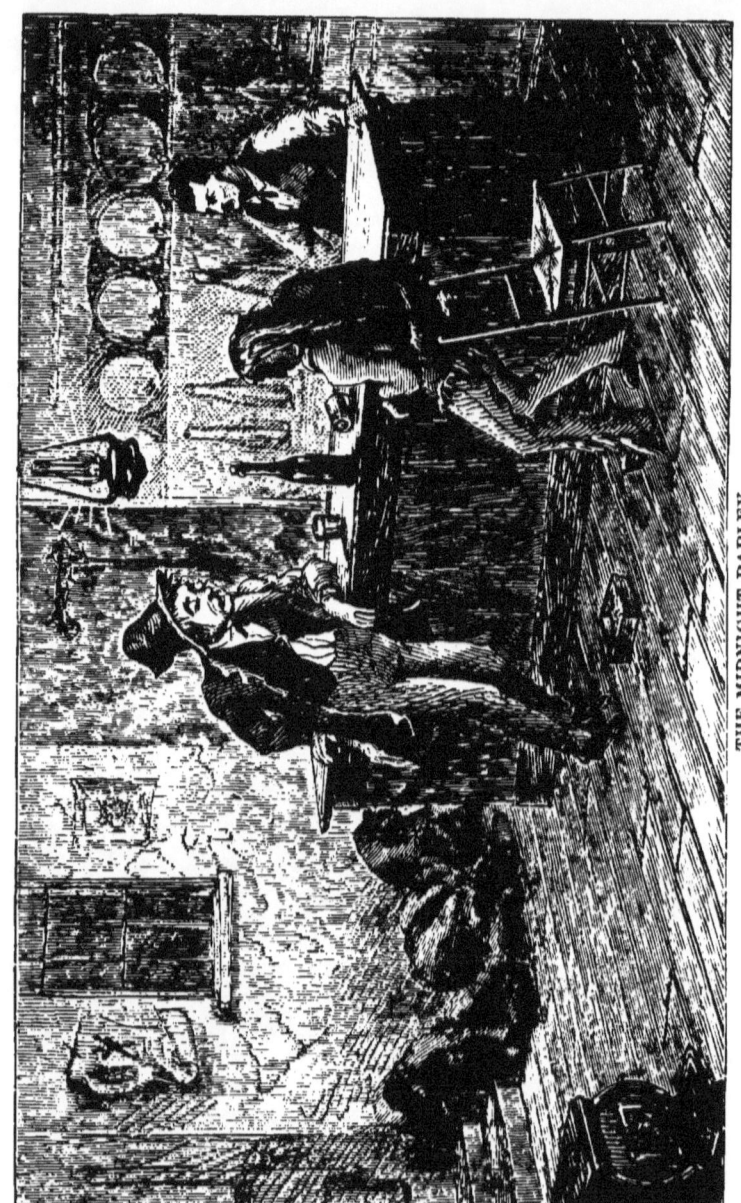

THE MIDNIGHT PARLEY.

people were now a mere handful. The noble chieftains who inspired the pen of Cooper are, alas! no more; deprived of their lands; degraded by firewater; their spirits broken, they, silent and sad, follow the trail of the setting sun.

One of our number gave out before ten o'clock; he staggered and fell heavily to the floor while trying to reach the bar. In about half an hour after that another of the party fell over the stove, burning him severely. We dragged him up into the corner, where the one who had first succumbed to King Alcohol was snoring away like a Mississippi steamboat, and laid him alongside.

At midnight the Indian and myself were the only ones of the party who could keep their pins; and the old warrior stood leaning on a chair complacently surveying the recumbent forms, and seemed as proud of his victory as some of his forefathers would have been on entering their village from a successful war-path. We held a council, and concluded to share the victory, although each was positive that he was the more sober party.

I thought that a breath of fresh air would not be bad to take for a change, and started for the door; but I made the discovery that the aforesaid door was playing circus. I stood in the position of a cavalry man at sabre exercise, and waited until it should come around to me; then, making a desperate rush, I reached it, made out to grasp the handle, and to pull it open. I then attempted to step out, but I reeled, and fell headlong in a snow-drift.

How long I lay there I do not know; when I returned to consciousness I found myself lying on a buffalo-robe, and my companions of the previous night were still snoring away on the opposite side of the room. My head was aching; my temples throbbing; my tongue and throat were parched and swollen; my whole body seemed to be on fire. I was suffering great agony in body and mind. Rum I must have to relieve me. I was suffering all the tortures of the damned. The landlord had not as yet made his appearance. I dragged my tottering form to the bar, climbed up, reached over and grasped a decanter of liquor; no one saw me; all in the room were in the arms of Morpheus. My nervous system was in such disorder that I could hardly raise it to my lips; but I succeeded at last, and drank it dry.

Replacing the decanter I got off the bar, and soon could walk around the room. The liquor had put new life into my frame. I cursed myself for being so foolish. I thought of mother, and how she would feel did she but know what a wretched condition I was in. Did those who do not drink know but a thousandth part of the intense misery suffered by one who has indulged his appetite too freely they would use words of kindness instead of censure. Many a poor fellow trying to recover from a spree, has been driven again to drink by the cold looks and words of those who ought to have taken him kindly by the hand, and sympathised with him in his great, almost unbearable sufferings.

After walking about the bar like a sentinel at his

post for an hour or so the landlord made his appearance, and the slumbering forms in the corner began to show signs of life. One after the other sat up, rubbing their bleary eyes, probably thinking that it was about to take their morning dram.

They were a sorry looking crowd take them altogether. I had not taken much notice of them the night before, showing that whisky blinds a man to appearances. I have often noticed that when a young man of respectable associations gets intoxicated he is not very particular about his companions. They say poverty makes strange bedfellows, but whisky will make stranger ones. Many a man has, on sleeping off the effects of a debauch, found himself in the company of those whom he would look upon with disgust in his sober moments; in fact he would consider himself disgraced by being seen with them.

These men who now staggered to their feet were not very prepossessing in their appearance. Their clothing would not have commanded a very high price among second-hand clothing merchants in Baxter St. There was one thing that all seemed to be unanimous on, and that was the propriety of taking a drink. They would all agree to that without wasting words on argument.

Such were the thoughts that occurred to me the last few turns I made in that bar-room; but the brandy I had drank soon drove them from my mind, and I soon mingled in with the rest of the crowd, drinking as often as any, and heedless that I was lowering myself by being in their company.

We were soon feeling rather elevated and the sufferings of the early morning hours were forgotten—all drowned in drink. None thought of the pain and anguish which the liquor they were drinking was sure to produce; all joined in pouring as much down their throats as possible, drowning all those better feelings which mankind possess more or less of. Kind friends, far or near, were forgotten; none thought of the tears that would be shed did some dear one know what was transpiring in that bar-room by the wayside.

It is astonishing how rum will change a person; some will sacrifice their best interests and friends to their appetite for drink; pawn mementoes of dear and dead friends to purchase this great destroyer of health and happiness.

We continued drinking until about four o'clock in the afternoon, when I made up my mind that I must leave the crowd sometime, and that it might as well be then or my money would be exhausted; for I noticed I had most of the bills to pay. I stole away with the excuse of looking at the landlord's horses, and, keeping the barn between myself and the bar-room windows, I made my way as well as I could to the village where I had my headquarters.

CHAPTER XVII.

FOR the next three days I was so ill from the effects of that prolonged spree that I was confined to my bed. My thirst was most unbearable, and I drank bowl after bowl of water, still craving for more. My nerves were in such a state that my trembling hands could hardly raise the water to my parched lips.

The horrible sufferings emanating from thirst are known to the travelers on the African deserts, the Llano Estacado of America, and those who are unfortunate at sea; but the poor drunkard, after a debauch, can sympathize with them. Many of our soldiers in the late war saw more or less of the sufferings caused by a scarcity of water, especially the wounded on the battle field-who first call for water, and some die with the word on their lips. Hunger can be borne a long time with plenty of good fresh water, but without it the victim soon succumbs. How I have suffered for the want of it none but myself can know.

When I was sufficiently recovered I resumed business again, firmly resolved to give King Alcohol a wide berth in the future; and I am happy to say that I adhered to my resolution for some time. My business increased, and I soon furnished the country stores with the articles that I manufactured.

As this business did not call for all my time, and as the oyster trade presented a good opening, I concluded to embark in that business. The first supply I received I concluded to raffle off, as it seemed to be the most expeditious way to sell them.

There was a young man who kept a store in town who consented to have me come and hold the raffle at his place, after his business had closed for the day. During the raffle one of the party proposed beer; a collection was taken up and two gallons of beer were brought in. On its appearance my former good resolutions vanished, and so did the beer.

After that supply was exhausted we sent for more; and when the last can of oysters had been delivered to the winner, we opened several cans and had an oyster supper. We remained, a happy party, until the "*wee sma' hours o' the morning.*" I paid for my night's dissipation by a violent headache, but had mind enough about me not to relieve it by drinking more.

At this time, having some little capital unemployed and pork being very cheap, I invested in hogs, salting the pork, and also smoking the hams. I found myself before long with quite a trade in these articles, and, with my other two branches of business, was doing well.

One day, about this time, a wealthy friend of mine

from the West called on me, and during his stay he offered me a situation to sell improved machines for use in saw-mills.

This seemed to be a good chance; so I formed a co-partnership with two other men, and our advertisements soon appeared in the papers. My friend shipped us a supply of machines, and, as soon as possible, I gave up my former business and devoted my whole time to my last enterprise.

One of my partners traveled with me, and the other remained to ship machines to our order. Procuring a team for the purpose, we took a sample machine with us, and struck off to the Black River country where these machines would be in the most demand.

The snow at that time was quite deep in Northern New York, and our progress was slow. The weather being very cold we were compelled to stop often at roadside taverns, and, believing as many deluded men do that rum would keep out the cold, we seldom left them until we had imbibed several drinks.

At about eight o'clock in the evening of the second day we found ourselves at the Checkered Tavern on the West Fork. Being chilled to the bone, we were scarcely able to drag ourselves into the house. Seating ourselves by the warm fire I said to the bartender—

"Make us each a hot whisky-punch, and don't be afraid of the whisky."

He was proficient in his line of business, and soon had the drink prepared for us. Its effect on me was like magic; it penetrated my whole system in an instant. I forgot the sufferings of the day, and felt myself to be the happiest man in existence. The large fire-place was piled high with good old hickory wood, which crackled and blazed, lighting up the whole room as bright as day.

We ordered supper; and while it was being prepared I took advantage of an opportunity to look about the bar-room. At the opposite side of the fire-place sat an old, grey-haired man, clad in rough, coarse garments, with a rope tied around his waist. He had a crooked staff in his hands, and between his teeth a black clay pipe. His hair was very long reaching down to his shoulders, while his beard made me think of the patriarchs of old. Looking over to me he remarked—

"This a very cold evening."

"Yes sir," I replied, "it is indeed a cold night."

"You are traveling I judge," said he.

I informed him that I was. After a moment's pause he said—

"Young man; did you ever see a railroad car?"

I answered in the affirmative, and he remarked that he was over seventy years of age, but had not ever seen a railroad car or steamboat, and had no desire to see them. I made up my mind he was not much interested in improvements, and concluded to drop the conversation, but continued to observe him, thinking, after due reflection, that he belonged to the family of Rip Van Winkle.

There were several other men there who looked like lumbermen. One of them who seemed to be the principal spokesman, emphasized his words by bringing down a pair of number thirteen cowhides which shook the glasses in the bar, and ended his arguments with—"That's so! by the jumping Jerusalem."

I thought by his appearance that he must have been an actor in an incident I had heard related, which was as follows:—

There was a certain man who was very ugly, and, being different from most men he knew it, and prided himself on it. He lived, I think, in old Kentucky, and had taken an oath to shoot any man he should ever meet, who was less favored by nature than himself.

Being out on a bear hunt alone one day, he saw his man crawling towards the same bear that he had his eye on, and immediately cocked his rifle and aimed at the man instead of the bear. The hunter heard the click of the lock, and, looking up and perceiving the other aiming his rifle at him, yelled out, at the same time bringing his rifle to a poise,—

"Halloa, stranger! what in thunder's up?"

Says Ugly—"Stranger! I made an oath a year gone that if ever I met a man who beat me in ugliness I'd shoot him, and I reckon the time has come for me to make that oath good."

"Look a here, old feller," says Ugly number two, "if that's the case, go ahead; for by the great Continental Congress and General Jackson, if I'm as ugly a looking chap as you are, shoot away, for I'm blamed if I oughter live."

It's needless to say that they both became friends,

and eat bear-rump steaks by their camp-fire together that night.

While I was observing this uncouth looking character, my partner poked me in the ribs and remarked it was about time to patronize the bar again, which we accordingly did. The supper bell rang soon afterwards, and we repaired to a small but neat dining room where we partook of a supper, and enjoyed it as much as any epicure ever did his at Delmonico's or on the Cafe de Paris, even if the adornments were not of a gorgeous description.

The interval between supper and retiring was filled up with smoking, drinking, card-playing and story-telling as is usually the case at a back country tavern.

The next morning after breakfast we started on our journey not forgetting to prime ourselves well with the preventative of chills. It is a good excuse for those who have a thirst for rum to take it to keep out the cold; also to indulge in the same remedy to keep cool of a sultry day:—poor rule that don't work both ways.

Our road led through dense forests of timber, the snow on each side of the road forming walls nearly as high as the horse's back; it having been cut through by the many timber teams that had passed. Occasionally we would pass a clearing, and there the snow was so deep that the fences were entirely buried. Sometimes the roofs were the only portions to be seen of houses and barns, and in some instances there was only a chimney in view to indicate that a dwelling was beneath the snow.

After a hard day's travel we arrived at the village of G——, situated in a deep valley surrounded on all sides by high hills densely timbered. The village consisted of one tavern, blacksmith shop, grocery, and several small dwellings. On an excellent water course for power were also a number of saw-mills. On driving up to the hotel we saw the windows of the bar were filled with faces, their noses flattened against the glass, looking out at us with as much interest as the loungers at the Astor House steps would have shown had a war party of Apaches rode up Broadway as they appear on their return from an excursion into Mexico.

The landlord soon came to the door and took our team to the stable; while we were glad enough to make our way towards the bar, remarking to the knight of the toddy-stick, that if he did not produce in about three shakes of a sheep's tail, a good article of ardent, there would be a row in the vicinity.

He laughingly passed out a well-filled decanter of brandy, and we took two stiff horns of as good an article as any reasonable person could expect to procure in that part of the state. The bar-room frequenters here were of about the same cut as those we met at the Checkered Tavern,—only more so.

As we entered the dining room for our tea, we saw at once that we were in a hotel altogether different from that of the Checkered Tavern. There was but little food on the table, and the article they passed us for bread would have made a New York beggar throw up his trade; the butter was strong enough to go alone. The tea was not the finest Gunpowder or Oolong, and I venture to say no heathen Chinee ever rolled a grain of it in his digits.

We went through the ceremony of eating and the landlord must have thought we were a pair of profitable boarders. Our case was nearly parallel to that of a poor drunkard I once heard of, who, on going home to his family after a long spree and calling for food, on being informed by his wife that there was not a morsel in the house, bade her set the table, and they would go through the ceremony of eating dinner.

We retired early, feeling confident that we should not be troubled with night-mare on account of our supper at any rate, and fully resolved to get our money's worth of sleep. But alas! how vain are all human calculations; we were both soon awakened from our slumbers by other occupants, who appeared to be at home and well acquainted with the character of the tavern they were in, and desperately resolved that when a good square meal awaited them, as in this case, they would take advantage of it. Lodgers, judging by the blood-thirsty demonstration of these miscreants had been but few and far between of late.

We tried to sleep, but it was impossible; and, at last, growing desperate, we arose, relit our lamps, and made a fierce onslaught on our tormentors.

The laughable incidents of our search for these pests brought to my mind a story of a gentleman who once put up at an ancient hotel, and on our retiring found himself in the same fix as ourselves. Being unable to sleep he lighted his lamp after using up in doing so, nearly a box of poor matches which he threw one by one into the wash-basin. He then took a hunt after his torturers, and amused himself by throwing them also into the basin; after which he once more tried to sleep but was prevented by a musical serenade which seemed to originate in his room. Again lighting his lamp he went on a voyage of discovery which brought him to the wash-stand, when he found that the bugs had built a raft of the burned matches, and were sailing about on it, singing, "A life on the ocean wave."

We were not feeling very energetic when we set out for the mills next morning. In fact the fare at the hotel, as I remarked to my partner, was not calculated to promote energy in a man; and I did not think there was any danger of the boarders being afflicted with the gout. We came to the conclusion that we had better hurry up our business and not linger in that locality any great length of time, or our friends would not recognize us on our return.

We found one man who had sense enough to appreciate our improved machine and we left it in full operation at his mill, took his note in payment, and then started for home.

CHAPTER XVIII.

ON our arrival home the next day we found an order waiting, and started off with the machine as soon as possible. Our business continued increasing for some time; finally it was arranged that I should go to Ulster county where I was successful in extending our sales. After some months I retired from the firm, being dissatisfied with some business transactions connected with the mode of making sales. I then began to look out for some lighter business which would suit me.

The stencil-plate enterprise was at that time almost in its infancy; and I accepted an offer to travel, taking orders and furnishing the plates. A few short trips were sufficient to convince me that I never should make a fortune if I continued in this trade.

During my travels I fell in with a gentleman going my way, who invited me to take a seat in his sleigh, which I gladly did.

On our journey he informed me that he was the editor and proprietor of the Herkimer County Advertiser, and was then on a circuit obtaining new subscribers and hoped at some future day to make it one of the leading advertising journals in the country.

I found him to be very much of a gentleman, and he seemed to take a liking to me. We conversed on different subjects, and our ideas and opinions seemed to coincide. After a long conversation he informed me that he was in need of an assistant and would be glad to engage me if I was at liberty. His proposition was a favorable one for me, and before we arrived at our destination I had engaged to work for him.

I soon found out that Mr. P——, the editor, was a strong temperance man, and respected him the more for this reason. He knew nothing of my past life; and I said to myself,—God helping me, I will keep sober while in his employ. I gained his confidence to such an extent that he soon gave me the handling of all the money received and he afterwards left me to do all the canvassing alone, while he went to the west, leaving competent men to conduct the business of the office. While in his employ I conceived the idea of publishing a paper myself.

When my term of service expired I went on a visit to a friend a short distance away, and as it happened, he had in his office a demijohn of gin for medicinal purposes. On an unlucky day for me he went out and left me in charge of his room, when a strong desire possessed me to try the quality of that particular medicine. Twice I found myself grasping the demijohn, and both times reluctantly replaced it without removing the cork; but the third time I approached the closet where it was kept my appetite overcame my conscientious scruples. I pulled open the closet door, grasped the perfidious destroyer, and took a long, deep draught, replaced it like a guilty thief, and stole silently back to my chair.

This aroused the demon of thirst which had been chained within me for some length of time. I sat thinking:—There is the jug and my friend will soon return, and then there will be no way of access to what I know I must have after having had a taste. So I improved the opportunity while it lasted.

When my friend did return, at last, I was not in the same condition he had left me in. It did not take a second glance for him to observe that I was far from being sober. He walked deliberately to the closet, and shaking the demijohn, said—

"George, what do you think of the quality of that gin?"

I replied that if I was considered a judge I should call it a prime article. I inquired if he had a large supply on hand, and said, that if he had I should probably prolong my visit.

He replied that he generally had a stock on hand for persons who were sick, and that if I stopped long, and continued as thirsty as I was in his absence, he would have to send for a new invoice.

I remained at the house of my friend over night, and in the morning went to a rum-shop where I could allay the raging thirst that was torturing me. When I had drank several times I did not feel like meeting my friend again; so I purchased a bottle of whisky, and started off on the road to an adjoining village, where I remained a week, drinking deeply all the time. I took a bottle of liquor to my room with me every night, being obliged to take a drink at intervals to drown the trouble I was in—all caused from what I was using as an antidote.

I knew no one in the village; had no friend to speak a kind word of warning. The venders of alcohol wore a smile of welcome as I entered their dens, and were ready to deal out the poison to me as long as I could stand—knowing that I had the money to pay them.

When I mustered sufficient courage to stop drinking I thought—What a fool I have been, wasting time, money, health, and reputation, all for the sake of rum. It was several days before I became strong enough to travel. On balancing my accounts I found I had squandered over fifty dollars but still had quite a little sum of money left.

I deliberated as to what I should do next, and I recollected my resolution in reference to publishing a newspaper. I resolved to carry it into effect, for I could not remain long inactive. I must have something to occupy my mind or I should again go to drinking. How to commence, I did not know, nor in what place to locate.

Finally, I decided to establish myself in the city of Syracuse. I soon had several canvassers out soliciting subscriptions to my paper, called the New York Central Advertiser, and by the time I was ready to issue my first number, I had quite a large number of subscribers. It was my intention to make it a first class advertising paper. The plan of publication was new at the time. The business card of every subscriber was to be inserted free of charge.

My success was quite flattering at first, and I might have done well had it not been for my old enemy, rum, who still followed my footsteps.

I resisted temptation for a while; but one day my appetite overcame me, and I thought a glass of beer would not do me any harm. But it proved the means of plunging me once more into the stream of dissipation; and the next thing I recollect I found myself lying on a hard bench, chilled to the bone, and unable to form any opinion as to where I was.

I was in terrible agony; my tongue was swollen, throat parched, and it seemed as though ten thousand pins were penetrating my flesh. I was in total darkness; but I could hear the rats scampering in every direction.

I cried out loudly to ascertain if any human being was near, but received no answer. I crawled off the bench and groped my way about, feeling before me with my hands until I came to a damp wall, which sent a cold, horrible thrill through my body. Thinks I to myself, I am either in a prison cell or a tomb; and my imagination pictured to me the forms of the departed, in their winding sheets, hovering around me, and waiting for me to join them in the unknown world.

The rats seemed to become aware of my helpless position, and began to be so bold as to jump on and off my form as I lay reclining against the wall. The awful thought entered my mind—am I to be devoured by these loathsome creatures? Then I thought that if I could only strike a light I could disperse the rats, and at the same time ascertain the character of the quarters I was in.

I felt in my pockets, and as luck would have it I found two matches and a half-crushed cigar. Without thinking, I scratched one on the damp wall and it failed to ignite; but with the other—my last hope—I was more careful, and rubbed it back and forth on my clothing until, to my great joy, it burst into a bright blaze.

The rats beat a hasty retreat, and I discovered that I was in a small basement. Old whisky barrels were piled in one corner; but the most welcome sight to me was a window in one end of the cellar. Throwing down the match, which had burned to my fingers, I groped my way to the window; not being able to open it I raised my foot, and soon the glass and frame went crashing out. I soon followed them, and in a careful manner let myself down to the firm ground, and once more breathed the free air of heaven.

It was quite dark and cloudy; the darkness had been so intense in the cellar that I could, by steady looking, make out that I was in the rear of some building. I made the best of my way around until I found myself in a narrow street, but in what portion of the city I was I had not the remotest idea. Following up the street for some distance, and down a cross alley, I found I was in one of the principal thoroughfares, and felt safe.

From that day to this I do not know in what portion of the city is located the place where I awoke from my drunken sleep. On investigation I found my watch and money were gone, and came to the conclusion that I had been drugged, robbed, and left locked into some old deserted building. I wandered around for three or four days more, drinking all the time, and borrowing money from my friends to do so.

One night I entered a low grog shop in the outskirts of the city, and during my stay there I witnessed a fearful fight among the drunken occupants, and received a severe blow on my own head. Chairs, bottles, etc., were used as weapons, and one unfortunate man was stabbed. This gave me a fearful fright, and I resolved to stop drinking and return to business. But my system was in such a condition that I was unable to accomplish anything for some days.

I felt my degradation deeply, and thought that every one I saw must know of all I had passed through; therefore I avoided the gaze of all—even my friends. When I saw one of them approaching me I would cross the street so not to meet him.

Why is it that man will so degrade himself, knowing the results that rum must eventually bring upon him? Dear reader; have you ever tasted of the intoxicating cup? if so, look not upon the wine when it is red in the glass, for it will surely bring sorrow and woe in the end. If you have not taken your first glass, I entreat of you, in God's name, never do it; you will then be safe from the misery, and degradation that it has been my unhappy lot to experience.

DISGRACED AND DISCOURAGED.

I recovered from the bad effects of my spree sufficiently to conduct my paper for a short time, when I again fell. I drank for about two weeks deeply, and at the end of that time found my paper behind-hand, and myself heavily involved in debt. I felt myself a ruined man. I became desperate, purchased a jug of whisky and hid it away,—going after it in the dark, and smuggling it into my room, resolved to drink it up and then die.

I meditated suicide in different ways, and took a fierce delight in thinking that my sufferings were about to end. I did not think with Shakespere that—" Tis better to bear the ills we have than rush to others we know not of," but rather exclaimed with the poet—

> "Oh let me die! since earth hath lost
>   Its every charm for me,
> My bark of life is rudely tos'd
>   Upon an angry sea;
> It madly leaps from wave to wave
>   Amid the deepening gloom,
> A shattered wreck; I would not hide,
>   From this impending doom.
>
> Oh let me die! Why should I live?
>   Since all is lost to me
> That could one happy moment give,
>   Or ease my misery.
> My life is darker than despair,
>   On earth, why should I stay?
> Friends pass me by without one word—
>   Cold as a winter's day.
>
> Oh let me die! though all is gloom
>   Beyond this life to me,

> The untried darkness of the tomb
>   Cannot more fearful be
> Than is this burning, withering breast
>   Where youth's bright visions lie:
> Oh take me from this heartless world,
>   I'm weary—let me die."

I did not make any attempt on my life; no doubt I was restrained by an overruling Providence which had watched over me up to that time, and has through all my subsequent life. But feeling discouraged, disgraced, and unsatisfied, I abandoned the thought of publishing my paper any longer. It passed into the hands of others, and I found myself once more adrift on the rough sea of life.

What next to turn my attention to I did not know; some kind of employment I *must* have. After becoming in a degree temperate for the time, I took an agency for the sale of fruit and ornamental trees. I continued in this business about three months, meeting with some success. During that time I only drank to excess once. I stopped at a tavern in a small village, and the devil led me into drinking with another young man until we both became intoxicated.

That night he undertook to walk on the railroad, was run over, and instantly killed. What an impression that event made on me as I saw him dead and mangled in the depot! If the ground had opened and swallowed me up it would have been a relief.

He was an entire stranger to me, and unknown in the neighborhood where he came to work at his trade; but rum caused his death, and his body was buried by strangers in a strange land. Far away in Canada were dear relatives and friends, to be soon shocked by the terrible news of his melancholy fate. He now lies in the pauper's corner of that village church-yard, with naught to mark his last resting place but a simple plank, which is fast wasting away.

Many such graves are scattered over our land; let us try to make their number less in the future; let us all join hands in this great conflict, and fight the monster intemperance as long as life and strength are left us.

Such an end to what might have been a useful life, is a sad warning to all who tamper with this fell destroyer of man's happiness—rum. He is dead, while I live to tell the history of my shame. It makes me shudder to think of the many times I have exposed myself to death in the same manner and under similar circumstances. How thankful I am that I have been preserved from many dangers while under the influence of rum, and that I may do all in my power to prevent mankind from following the same road.

I could now weep bitter tears of sorrow at the lonely grave of my companion of an hour; and though I had the golden millions of the El Dorado added to the wealth of Golconda, I would gladly surrender it all to raise him up to life again.

CHAPTER XIX.

SOON after giving up the business of selling trees I determined to go to Philadelphia to sell sewing-machines, and started for that city.

When the cars arrived at Rome, a young man who was accompanied by his mother on their way, I think, to Boston, stepped out on the platform of the car in which they were riding. Just as he reached the railing the engineer reversed his engine, which threw the young man between the cars and under the wheels. I stood near when he fell, having alighted from the same car for the purpose of procuring a drink of whisky.

I took hold of him, and with the assistance of two gentlemen lifted him up and carried him to the depot. One arm was crushed from the elbow down; his face was scarred and bleeding, and I noticed the thick soles of his boots had been torn nearly away. He kept crying out, "Oh mother, mother, what shall I do?" but never shall I forget the look of horror that overspread that mother's face when they brought her to her boy.

Language is inadequate to express the intense grief and misery that was stamped upon her features.

A surgeon was summoned, his arm dressed, and his father telegraphed for at Seneca Falls. I remained over until next train, and then proceeded on my journey. Several years passed before I had occasion to visit Seneca Falls, when I learned of his father, Mr. Downs, that his son had lost his hand—amputation being necessary—but otherwise he had fully recovered.

I arrived safely at Philadelphia, and while stopping in the City of Brotherly Love I fell in with a young man, and he volunteered to show me the sights.

The first place we visited was the Continental Hotel, the most extensive public house I had ever seen. The bar was the most attractive portion of the house at that time, and we lingered around it a good while, taking at intervals some very stiff drinks.

We then repaired to the Navy yard and inspected the U. S. Marine to our satisfaction. I conclude that there were not as many vessels in dock as we thought we saw, as the drinks we had taken had the effect to double objects presented to our view. Our inspection was not prolonged to such an extent as to interfere with our thirst, and we left the minor articles, such as field-pieces, fixed ammunition, etc. etc., for some future day. Leaving the yard in search of a saloon we had observed on our entrance near the gate-way, we soon found a whisky-shop, and as we were about entering I noticed a dejected-looking man sitting near the door, and invited him in to drink. He accepted the invitation with a thankful expression on his countenance.

We took our drinks and started on our way; but on my accidentally looking back I noticed that the stranger I had asked to drink with us was following in our footsteps. We slackened our pace, and he soon joined us and commenced a conversation in which we learned that he was from Scotland; that he was a baker by trade, and had been so far unable to procure employment; also, unfortunately, he was out of money and had no friends in this country. He had fallen into the delusion of many others who think there is no necessity for emigrants to have more money than enough to pay their passage over; that when they arrive here they can get along easily.

I felt interested in his story, for by his appearance he was honest and could not be an impostor. So I told him we would assist him to find employment to the best of our ability, and he need not fear present want, for I would see that he had food.

I gave him money to keep him over the night, and made him promise to call at my hotel the next day. The noon following he called for me, and I was the means of his getting a job at his trade. I paid his board for a week, bid him good-bye, and wished him good luck in the future. He left us with tears of thankfulness in his eyes, and I have never seen him since.

My volunteer guide around Philadelphia and myself promenaded the suburbs and town, seeing all that was to be seen worthy of attention, and spending my money freely. I found—as many a man has in similar circumstances—that my cash was nearly gone, and I came to the conclusion that it was about time to suspend operations in the line of amusements, and turn my mind to something that would bring money in, instead of paying it out continually. But I found nothing that I cared to undertake in Philadelphia. So bidding my companion a kind farewell—and I know he was sad to part with me—I took the train for New York City, thinking that in that great metropolis there might be some business to suit me.

How many young men are deluded in this same manner; they leave their pleasant country and village homes, kind friends, and every thing that should make them happy; when they arrive in the city they discover their mistake, especially if they have no influential friends, and are not well supplied with money. I have seen three hundred men waiting to answer an advertisement for a store porter. Many young men from the country linger on from week to week, still hoping against hope; few of them find anything to do, and some of them, when their money is all gone, are ashamed to apply to their country friends for money to take them home again.

You can see plenty such in the public parks any day, with woe-begone countenances, almost desperate from want and exposure. They sleep in lumber-yards and around the docks until they are arrested by the police, and sent to the Island as vagrants. I do not say all turn out so, but I know a large percentage of them do. After an apprenticeship at the Island in company with the most depraved, they become contaminated, and in many instances learn to be thieves themselves.

In July, 1866, a young man of good education who had never before known what it was to want, was found dying between some cotton bales on the levee in New Orleans. He stated before death that he had left a good home in the north to see what fortune had in store for him at the south. He expected to easily procure a clerkship in that city, but had wandered over the town week after week until his funds gave out. He was too honest to steal and ashamed to beg, and having been without food for three days he had crawled in among the bales to die. This instance came under the personal observations of a friend of mine, who also saw young men wait anxiously for the negro hod-carriers, working on the Masonic Hall after the fire, to finish their dinner, when they picked up the bones and crusts thrown away, and gnawed them like starving dogs.

After traveling the streets of New York for some time without any prospects of bettering my fortune, I made up my mind it was no place for me and immediately took my departure for the flourishing town of N——, where I engaged to work for a man who had a contract for manufacturing doors. This was new business to me, but I had some knowledge of tools and I readily worked into the trade. I remained in this shop for about three months, and during that time on several occasions I indulged too freely in strong drink.

I then went into business for myself, taking a job at manufacturing blinds which occupied me several months, but I often absented myself from the bench to drink in the low grog-shops. Sometimes I wandered off into the country, stopping wherever rum was to be obtained, and drinking deep potations which threw my system out of order and rendered me more like a lunatic than a sane man. I was greatly emaciated, and so reduced in funds at times that I had to beg the liquor I could no longer purchase, and which I must have or die.

It is one of the strangest effects of rum that it will cause a naturally proud man, who under other circumstances would scorn to ask a favor from any one, to cringe before some low, coarse vender thereof, whom perhaps he has never seen before, and beg of him a glass of liquor, to buoy his sinking spirits up and give him a moment's forgetfulness.

If so lucky as to obtain it, how dreadful it is to see the poor slave grasp the glass in both hands and, nearly spilling the—to him—precious contents, raise it to his lips, while his eyes brighten for the moment.

Oftentimes when on a spree I became so reduced in circumstances that I would sell any thing I had which was available, to appease my appetite and stimulate my poor shattered frame. Sometimes I was so debilitated that I could scarcely walk; the cords of my limbs seemed to contract and lift my feet with a nervous jerk from the ground while walking.

Under such circumstances I must have rum; all my soul was concentrated on the one thought—How can I get liquor? Nothing in the world that I possessed was too sacred for me to part with—the very coat from my back, the shoes from my feet; I would even have given a limb or bartered my immortal soul and said—"Take all, but give me rum! bring me burning rum! and let me quench my unbearable thirst although I sacrifice all that is dear to man in this world and the world to come."

On one occasion I had nothing to dispose of but two books which I had cherished; for, when I was myself I always loved to read good books when I could spare the time to do so. I must have money to get liquor, and I had nothing else to sell. I took them under my arm, and going along to a book-store asked the proprietor to buy them, which he did, giving me but half their value; but I would have accepted the price of one drink rather than have taken them back. I hurried to the nearest cheap grog-shop and spent it all for rum.

There are a great many, perhaps, who are connected with the drinking man, who never drank themselves, and know not his dreadful longing for drink, and cannot sympathize with him, and who, by their looks and manner toward him show a coldness which drives him to drink again. This ought to be avoided. Show kindness to the poor drunkard, for God knows he needs it if any one. Harshness and unkindness never reformed a drunkard; such treatment will only make him sink lower. Recollect this, my friends, and abide by it. Remember also that a drinking man is doubly sensitive at times, and small trifles have great influence.

Mr. H———, a very wealthy man belonging to one of the first families of the Empire State, was seen in

New York City in a reduced condition. He had been on a protracted spree, and his nervous system was so prostrated he could not raise a glass to his lips. He was observed to call for liquor, and to depend on his little son, about eight years of age, to hold it to his lips, he meanwhile kneeling on the floor to accommodate himself to the reach of his boy. What an incident for that young lad to remember! Mr. H—— was taken in hand by a friend to humanity—an entire stranger—and received from him great care and frequent prescriptions of kind and sympathetic words. He finally recovered after a severe illness which he was not expected to survive. I am happy to say that he is now a faithful and zealous supporter of the temperance cause, and has done good service therein.

My protracted spree had rendered me a pitiable object to behold. I had an emaciated look, for I was unable to eat; my stomach craved only drink, and strong drink at that. I knew if something was not done soon that I must die.

I resolved to reform, and try once more to conquer the appetite which ruled me with a rod of fire. I had no one to go to for advice or help; all seemed to have deserted me; I stood alone on the broad desert of despair, but I could faintly discern the outlines of my guardian angel, hovering above me in the azure expanse of the sky of hope.

I had found by sad experience that I could not depend upon myself. I must look only to God for help in my great hour of need. I went to my room, brought out my long-neglected Bible, and placing the sacred volume on my tool-chest knelt by its side, and poured out my soul in earnest prayer that I might be kept from again falling.

Oh, how happy I felt after this! New hope seemed to fill my heart; the blood in my veins grew warmer; the sun shone brighter; and the flowers gave out a sweeter perfume. All nature seemed changed; and the chains of intemperance hung loose around me;—would that I could shake them off at once and forever!

When I went out into the streets it seemed like a new world to me, and after I had passed a grog-shop I would exclaim to myself—Thank God I had the strength to resist the strong temptation to enter and call for rum! At times the desire to enter one of these gates of hell would so overpower me, that when I was sure I was nearing one I would rush across the street to avoid it. At other times I would clench my hands and grind my teeth, and run with all my might to get past one of these dens. Some who have not become enslaved to drink may perhaps doubt this; take warning that you do not know its truth by bitter experience.

Fortune soon favored me, for I obtained work at carpentering, and was enabled to earn enough to gain a good living and some more. I was before long able to make a respectable appearance on the streets, and experienced great pleasure when my friends, and some others with whom I had not been acquainted, took me by the hand to congratulate me on my improved condition and express the hope that I would continue in the same path. I attended church regularly, and the weekly prayer-meeting where I was brought within a circle of people who strengthened me and encouraged me greatly in my new-formed resolution.

The want of suitable society is a great bar to the reformation of many drinking men. They are in their sober moments so ashamed of their weakness, that they are backward in going among respectable people, and resort to their old haunts to pass their time, where they again fall into old habits. They should be encouraged by their female friends—not avoided like a leper. Women do not know what influence they have; they can do great service in the cause of temperance. I admit that they have done and are now doing much; but the field is wide, and the harvest is ripe for the gathering.

A few years ago, in the city of P———, a young lady was singing a song of this character, when a poor, miserable drunkard came staggering along. The melody charmed him, and he stopped to listen. After she had ceased, he groped his way into the house and asked if that was sung for his benefit. She told him it was for the benefit of all to whom it applied. After some minutes he requested her to repeat the song. She complied, and when it was concluded requested him to sign the pledge; he did so with tears in his eyes, and has kept it to this day. He is now a respectable physician, surrounded by numerous friends, beloved by every one, and a great worker in the cause of God and humanity.

Ladies, remember this your great power, and use it for the benefit of mankind.

CHAPTER XX.

I CONTINUED to work at the carpenter business for some time but did not feel satisfied. One day a gentleman came to me and said that he had been induced to call as parties in the town had recommended me to him. He expressed a desire for me to take some goods which he had on hand and sell them for him. He would set a certain price on them, and would wait until I had disposed of them for the money. After deliberating on his proposal for a while, and seeing that he was anxious for me to enter into his plans, I consented to do so, and embarked in the enterprise on his terms. I shipped some of the goods into the country, and soon followed them.

I found it rather up hill work to dispose of some of my stock, and had to work very hard traveling around the country. I had faithfully kept my resolution not to drink; but my business required me to patronize hotels, and one night I joined in drinking a glass of liquor. I had often refused to drink with parties when invited to do so, and do not know what came over me in that moment of weakness to make me forget myself and do so then. I certainly did not dream that that single glass of whisky would be the means of causing me days and weeks of the bitterest sorrow I had ever known. That one glass paved my way with thorns of affliction, and caused me in the end to suffer more in my mind than I thought I could suffer and still live. That single drink awakened the sleeping demon of thirst within me, and glass after glass I poured down to keep the first company: in fact, I was at the late hour of my retiring feeling very unlike myself.

The next morning the natural consequences of a night's indulgence—a parched throat and intense thirst—were the penalty. I was obliged to drink before I could eat my breakfast. I did not go on and indulge freely as I had on previous occasions, but I took several drams every day, and as I never drank alone it cost me more to pay my bills, at times, than my sales amounted to.

On my return from my first trip, I paid the man for some of the goods and started out with a new supply. I bargained with a customer for quite a large quantity of goods and returned again to procure them.

I arrived in the evening, and the next morning the news came that electrified the nation. Fort Sumter had been fired upon by the rebels, and the whole town was in a state of excitement which I never saw equaled during the entire war which followed. Merchants left their counting-rooms and mechanics their benches; laborers threw down their tools, and men, women, and children stood in groups conversing about this great event in the history of our country. Was it possible that we were to be involved in all the dreadful horrors of war? Had the time come when the father should turn his hand against the son, the son against the father? when brothers with hatred in their eyes should meet in mortal combat?

In a few days intelligence came that Major Anderson had been forced to surrender the fort after a desperate resistance against great odds, having no means of obtaining reinforcements; stipulating however with the victors that his flag should receive a salute ere it was lowered to the ground.

The dear old flag! hitherto respected by all nations, loved by all who owed it allegiance, and feared by all who had ever sought to rend its starry folds. Through the wild, untrodden wilderness the red man's cheek had paled before its waving stripes; its stars had flashed their brilliancy in the halls of the Montezumas; and it had been nailed to the mast in many a bloody conflict on the briny deep, coping successfully with the proud mistress of the seas.

Were men, born under its protecting folds, now to learn to hate it, and meet their countrymen in war's dread carnage? Who could realize that such would be the fact? All true citizens were ready to exclaim—

> "Stand by the flag! all doubt and treason scorning,
> Believe, with courage firm and faith sublime,
> That it will float until the eternal morning
> Pales, in its glories, all the lights of Time."

The President asked for seventy-five thousand volunteers, and the country responded to the call:—

> "Lay down the ax, fling by the spade:
> Leave in its track the toiling plow;
> The rifle and the bayonet-blade
> For arms like yours were fitter now;
> And let the hands that ply the pen
> Quit the light task, and learn to wield
> The horseman's crooked brand, and rein
> The charger on the battle-field."

A company was formed in the village and was soon on its way to the front. I was very anxious to enlist, but only those went who were in the militia and knew the drill somewhat; consequently I was not able to get my name enrolled. I saw them the night they left, marching through the streets. Their flashing torchlights were quite a display, and the quick tap of the drum and strains of martial music by the band made many a heart beat with true patriotism. Under such excitement I could not refrain from drinking with others. Some who were not in the habit of drinking liquor at all, now drank quite freely under the excitement.

I heard that Major Anderson was coming to New York, and I went down the river to see for myself what the feeling was there in reference to the coming struggle. He was to have a reception at Union Square, and thither I turned my steps on my arrival in the city. Such a crowd of human beings I had never witnessed before; the excitement was intense. Men and women seemed to be almost frantic. The housetops in the vicinity of the park were covered with people waving their hats and handkerchiefs and singing "The Star Spangled Banner." I truly believe that if a man had said one word against the Union he would have been torn in pieces. The flag which had waved on the ramparts of Fort Sumter, was hanging on the horse supporting the Equestrian Statue of Washington in the square. When Major Anderson stepped on the platform which had been erected for the occasion, cheer after cheer rent the air. He explained to the people his position, and what occurred at the fort during the bombardment, to which the crowd listened with great attention.

On my return home I made up my mind to go out and arouse the people by holding meetings and speaking as best I could on the state of affairs. I consulted some of my friends, who said, "Go by all means and do what you can." So I procured a large number of posters, and started out on my mission.

The first meeting that I held was a success as to numbers, and passed off very satisfactory. I continued to speak evenings, and during the day made sales of my merchandise. I also indulged in liquor while on this tour, and was sometimes considerably under its influence. Many of the men who enlisted were not satisfied unless they could have a good time before they left home for the seat of war, and whisky was an indispensable article on such occasions. I was brought into close companionship with these recruits, and must drink and have a pleasant time with them; and I soon found myself drinking almost as much as ever. I did not however get really intoxicated, but, to use a term

I ENLIST A COMPANY.

much in vogue at that time, I kept *chuck* full. The excitement kept me up, for I was continually holding war meetings, making speeches, and disposing of my goods as fast as possible, although my sales were sometimes too small to pay the extra expenses I incurred.

I soon made up my mind to raise a company myself, and offer my services to Uncle Sam. I succeeded in getting the necessary number of recruits, but the strain on my mind and body had been so great, going without sufficient sleep, drinking large quantities of vile whisky, and exerting myself beyond reason, that I found myself on a bed of sickness. Tired nature could hold out no longer. It was some time before I could leave my room, and in the meantime the regiment I was attached to was ordered into service at the South, and not being able to be mustered in with them I was left behind, my men having another captain appointed over them.

After I had recovered sufficiently to walk out I concluded to go to the village of ——, on the Hudson, where my parents had recently located, and try to dispose of some of my merchandise. While seated on the steamer's upper deck, meditating on my situation and thinking about my checkered life, oblivious of all around me, a hand was laid on my shoulder and at the same time a voice exclaimed—

"Holloa, George; where you bound for now?"

This brought my reverie to a sudden termination. Casting my eyes up to the intruder I met the gaze of an old familiar friend, whom I had previously known in Albany. After shaking hands and passing friendly congratulations he proposed that we should adjourn to the bar, and take something to refresh the inner man. I felt quite weak after my sickness, and forgetting or not thinking of the principal cause of that illness, I accepted his invitation.

After drinking I thought I would return the compliment by asking him to join me in another glass, and again we indulged. The second drink put new life into my veins, and I felt cheerful and soon forgot my past misfortunes. We talked over old times, and I almost forgot where I was going and cared less.

When the boat arrived at the place where I was intending to stop, we were both in a condition that made it difficult to navigate. My business being a secondary object in the condition I was in, I acceded to his proposition to accompany him to Albany. On our arrival at the capitol we repaired to a rum-shop, and spent the remainder of the day and evening drinking, making sure at the same time that all those in the bar-room should drink at our expense. About ten o'clock I determined to go to a hotel if I could keep on my feet long enough, for I was powerfully under the influence of the poison I had drank during the brief time I had spent with my friend. How many men have been plunged into a long protracted spree by being induced to take one social drink with a friend, ending, perhaps, in delirium tremens and death.

Oh drinker of this vile stuff that has destroyed thousands of our most promising youth, if you will still persist in treading the broad highway of death—

to hell, do not, I entreat you, induce others to join you; do not show a false light on the rock of destruction by asking others to drink who are weak and easily influenced.

How I managed to get to the hotel I have no idea, but the next morning I found myself in a room, in bed, and noticed that there was a glass of liquor on the wash-stand. Probably I had brought it up with me the night before, but I did not remember it. My feelings cannot be described; death seemed to be near; it was different with me than at other times, for I was so debilitated by past sickness that I had hardly strength to move. My whole body seemed to be on fire, and I could not repress my groans. I held my poor, quivering hands up, and looked at them; they did not seem to be mine, and I felt a pity for whoever they did belong to. I could hardly feel one with the other, their sensitiveness had become so dead.

I looked at the glass on the wash-stand and thought—If I drink it, it may be the means of my death; but I will drink it though I die, for I shall surely die if I do not have relief from this agony. Mechanically I reached out my hand, and could not feel the glass when I knew it was tight between my fingers. I raised it to my lips and drained it to the dregs, sinking back again on my pillow. I could feel the liquor burn in my breast, and feel the hot blood leap to my cheeks. My sluggish brain once more began to act, and the tremors of my body gradually abated.

I knew that more must be procured before the effect of this glass passed off, and that I must make an effort to rise from my bed. I succeeded in getting out, but was obliged to sit on the edge of my couch for some time, I felt so weak and ill. After several attempts I finally made my toilet, and went down stairs and directly to the bar. The first one I saw was my friend, who was in the act of drinking a glass of rum. When he saw me he dropped his glass, saying—

"What in Heaven's name is the matter with you? You look like the ghost of Hamlet."

I replied that I felt rather ghostly, and that my looks did not belie me.

"Come! come!" said he, "you are better than half-a-dozen dead men yet. Cheer up and take a drink."

He filled a glass to the brim and passed it to me. I soon set it down on the bar, empty, and took a chair beside my friend. I found that he did not know what had become of me the night before, I disappeared so suddenly, and he had been to several public houses making inquiries for me. Finding my name on the books of this one, he had waited for my appearance, not liking to disturb me.

We soon took more rum, and then started out around the city, traveling all day, and frequently refreshing ourselves at the low grog-shops in our way. Just before night I stepped into a wholesale liquor store and purchased a five gallon keg of gin. I then conveyed it to a boarding place where they sold bad whisky and had lodging rooms to let. I asked the proprietor if he would give me a room, and at the same time allow me to drink my own liquor and treat whoever I felt disposed to.

He intimated that he had liquor for sale at his bar; but I informed him that my gin was a superior article, and I wanted to get rid of it, and knew no better way than to drink it. He complied with my request in regard to the room provided I would pay him his price, and we soon came to terms.

It was several days before my drinking friend and myself emptied the keg; and during the time I did not draw a sober breath. We had sense enough to eat while we were drinking, and by the time we finished the keg we were somewhat bloated. Liquor effects persons differently according to their temperament. Some men who drink hard wear a flushed face, and those who are not conversant with their habits would suppose it a sign of health. Others look pale and emaciated; their eyes wear a wild wandering look: they are never at rest; their limbs are in constant motion; a nervousness is noticed about their every movement; one glass of rum will awaken their appetite, and they cannot stop until they become so debilitated that their stomach rejects food, and in the latter stage, liquor itself. These last, if they do not break off the habit, must soon succumb to the destroyer. But no matter how constituted, all who pour down this liquid fire must eventually come to a miserable end, **and be the cause of misery to all connected with them.**

CHAPTER XXI.

HAVING remained as long as I could without using all my money up, I determined to try once more to go home and see my parents, and again took passage for C——, bidding my friend farewell. Five years afterwards I met him once more; he was then clothed in rags, and entirely destitute—all the effects of drinking rum.

I continued to drink on the boat as she glided down the placid waters of the Hudson on her way to the great metropolis. When we stopped at the nearest landing to my destination I went on shore, but concluded to put up at the hotel that night rather than go home, as my appearance was not very presentable.

I was somewhat of a stranger, but soon made plenty of friends by my liberality in treating everybody that came up, and before ten o'clock there were but few sober men in that bar-room. One fellow who had drank rather freely began to impose on me. This the bar-keeper would not allow, and, jumping over the bar, he dealt him a powerful blow which caused him to change his base, and he retired from the field rather crest-fallen; we saw no more of him until next morning. After he was gone the bar-keeper took my hand and said—

"I'll see no one misuse you, or he does it over my dead body."

From that hour we became firm friends. He was a young man of ability, and with his manliness and enterprise would have made his mark in most any situation. The last I knew of him he was the proprietor of the largest hotel in the town, and I hope that he is keeping a temperance house now. He often said to me in after days—

"George, I sell rum I know; but I cannot let you have it for I know it would be doing you a great wrong; one glass, and you are no longer a sane man."

I remained at this village nearly a week, drinking incessantly. At the end of that time my father heard that I was there and sent my Uncle James down to try and induce me to go home. He said my mother was nearly frantic about me, and if I did not come directly she would come after me herself.

Thinking it best to comply with her request, I started off with Uncle James. On our arrival I found my folks filled with anxiety, and at the same time overjoyed to see me, for I had been absent about two years.

I remained at home some three or four months, going nearly every day to the village where plenty of rum could be had, and being well supplied with cash I lavished it freely on my drinking associates. At night I would purchase a quart bottle of whisky, and take it along home to quench my thirst until I should again visit the village. In this way I managed to keep pretty well stimulated.

My health at this time began to fail me again, and my finances became reduced. I had disposed of my goods from time to time, until but half of my original stock remained. I well knew that the people in the vicinity were informed as to my bad habits, and I had not the courage to offer anything for sale during the last month of my stay. My dear, good mother was almost broken-hearted no doubt; she wept and prayed for me each night, but never with one unkind word or look did she greet me, though she often plead with me to stop in my wild career of dissipation.

My father would frequently expostulate with me. Often would he repeat these words—

"George, I know I drink, but I never drank like you. Your life will be short if you continue to do as you are doing."

One afternoon, after taking on board a large cargo of assorted liquors I made sail for home. By repeatedly standing off and on I made some headway, but the nearer I came towards home the harder it was to navigate; in fact I became liquor-logged. I would look up and mark an object to take my course from, but soon lose it and have to tack ship and come around again, my sails all aback. As my ballast consisted principally of whisky, it was no wonder I rolled about so.

There was a stiff northerly breeze, but wing and wing was out of the question, and at off and on I lost ground, and was in a quandary how my voyage was to terminate. Having lost all control of my steering apparatus I drifted into the trough of the sea, and soon found myself on a lee-shore—in fact bearing up fast against the orchard wall.

My mother was watching me from the door of our house, and seeing that I would founder unless I received aid, she sent my brother-in-law out to pilot me in. When we came within a few rods of the house I concluded I could make the remainder of the voyage alone, and giving up his arm I started off, but soon brought up and capsized on the green-sward, just missing being precipitated into a deep well which was without a curb.

My mother screamed aloud, and my father came out and picked me up and led me into the house. I must have cut a very comical figure while navigating across that ten acre lot, for, as mournful as the sight must have been to look at it in one point of view, my mother could not refrain from laughing, although her eyes were filled with tears of sorrow at seeing me in that condition.

Reader, have you ever stood on a pier and seen a noble ship start out on her first voyage across the ocean? How grand she looks! almost like a thing of life, as she moves majestically through the waters. You almost wish you stood upon her deck, with her to traverse the pathless ocean. Her voyage may be prosperous for a time, but soon the signs of a storm appear gathering over her head; the winds begin to moan through the rigging; low muttering thunder is heard, and the vivid flash of lightning glances across the blackening sky. At first faint ripples agitate the waters; then comes rolling in all its majesty a raging wall of waves. The helm is brought about; the ship is headed to the wind; the heavy sails come rattling down to the yards, and busy hands make fast the reef ropes. She rears her head to meet the boiling flood, and plunges like a frenzied horse; the monster wave sweeps her deck and buries her beneath the waters. She recovers herself for a moment, her timbers creak, seams open, and the briny liquid finds its way to her center. The pumps are rigged and worked by desperate men until it is a hopeless task. She gives one frantic leap, and plunges with all on board into the lower depths; not a plank remains to show where she went down.

It is precisely so with some young men. They start on the voyage of life with staunch hearts, determined to breast the tide. Bright are their prospects; to reach a haven of happiness to them seems easy. But in a moment of unguarded danger the storms of temptation overwhelm them, and they perish in the great sea of Intemperance.

One day the thought occurred to me to take a trip to the town of L——, about eight miles distant, and I soon started on foot.

On arriving there I took up my quarters in a rum-shop where I remained some two days, drunk all the time. I then turned my steps towards home, and after walking about four miles I became so weary that I thought I would lie down under a tree by the road-side, and rest. I soon fell asleep and the sun was just disappearing in the west when I awoke.

I had slept off the effects of the rum that had sustained me, and when I regained my feet I could hardly stand. About two miles beyond was a rum-shop, and I dragged my weary limbs toward it. My whole frame was in a tremor; every slight noise startled me; fear took possession of my mind. I crept along as though escaping from some deadly enemy. Strange noises seemed to issue from rocks and trees; fiends peopled the dense shades and mocked me in my terror; the faster I went the nearer came the prowling monsters, and I feared they would out-flank me and cut me off from the grog-shop, which now seemed to be my only salvation—my haven of relief and safety. I was on the borders of delirium tremens.

It was a wild, rocky section of country, and as I made the best of my way through a rocky glen, a copperhead snake sprang from a hole near me, and buried his fangs in my pantaloons. I sprang wildly into the air, and the woods echoed with my yells. My frantic struggles shook the serpent free, but my courage was not strong enough to kill it. Oh, I thought, what a narrow escape from death! If its deadly fangs had entered my flesh what a horrible end would have been mine there alone in the woods, and what a termination to a useless life!

This occurrence stamped itself deeply on my mind. I shall never forget it.

I reached the groggery, and drank glass after glass of liquor in succession. I was soon free from the horrible images which had haunted my imagination, and purchased a bottle of liquor to keep them off on my way home. I arrived at my father's at about ten o'clock and went to bed.

The next morning I went to the village and remained nearly all day. At night I imagined that my room was filled with fiends, and I could hear them talk and whisper to themselves, and beckon me to come and join them in their horrible orgies. They then became more bold and sat in conclave on my bed, some pressing the breath out of my body, and I could hear a grating sound like the grinding of teeth. Cold perspiration stood in great drops upon my frame, for I was filled with horror. Slimy creatures crept over my body and made the very hairs of my head twist with agony. Monster serpents hissed their hot breath into my face, and glared at me with unearthly eyes.

During this dreadful suffering I remembered that I had a bottle of liquor under my pillow, but my hands were powerless—nerveless; hours of most intense agony seemed to elapse before I regained the use of them, and then I thought there were serpents under the pillow coiled around the bottle. I felt their cold forms, and my hand flew through the air to escape the touch, striking, as it happened, against the back of a chair standing near the bed, which brought me in some degree to my senses. I then grasped the bottle as a drowning man would a plank, and poured down its contents until I nearly strangled. I drank enough to keep off the demons who had haunted me, but the morning found me in great suffering.

I did not leave my bed that day. Every object looked strange to me. The features of my own mother seemed to be distorted, and she seemed to glide across the floor like a spirit. I called frequently for some buttermilk, and poured it down to relieve my burning thirst. I could hold no conversation with any one; I could dwell on no particular subject; my thoughts would flit from one thing to another without control, and I did not even know my own name.

I drank no liquor for several days, and could eat but little. My appetite gradually returned to me and my mind began to regain its balance, but I was far from recovered.

CHAPTER XXII.

ONE day while seated in the house two men entered and one of them, unknown to me, approached, and laying his hand on my shoulder said—

"I am sorry to inform you that I am on a very disagreeable duty. I am a sheriff and must ask you to accompany me; consider yourself under arrest."

If a cannon had been discharged in my ear I should not have been more surprised. My heart beat quick and I felt as though I should sink into the floor.

When I had sufficiently recovered my wandering senses I asked why they made the arrest. The sheriff pointed out his companion and said—

"That man is the one to answer you."

Then for the first time, as I had been so frightened, I looked at the other man. It did not take a second glance to enable me to recognize the man of whom I had purchased the goods several months before in N——. There was no help for me; the sheriff took my watch and other valuables, and we started off, after having had a very sad parting scene with my parents.

We took the train for N——. It was evening when we arrived. As I was arrested for debt and had no one to go my bail, of course I must go to jail. I had taken the precaution to put on my best suit of clothes, and many remarks were passed between the other prisoners as to what could be the cause of my being in such a place, as my appearance did not indicate that I was much used to such quarters.

While standing in the corridor, one of the prisoners passed a cigar through the grating of his door and expressed a desire to have me in the cell with him, at the same time trying to cheer me up. During the conversation which passed between us I found that a too strong propensity for appropriating horse-flesh had brought him to grief. He introduced himself as "Jocky Jim from all around."

The jailor soon reappeared with a huge bunch of keys, and to the joy of my new acquaintance, Jocky Jim, assigned us the same cell. For three weeks I occupied that cell with Jocky Jim, and during that time we enjoyed ourselves as well as could be expected under the circumstances, and related our adventures to each other. I learned that he was the son of one of the most wealthy men in that section of the country.

While in jail I was visited by some of the most influential men of the town, who were desirous of acting as friends and bailing me out, but I would not consent to it. I wished to see the thing through.

There were sad moments while I was in prison when I would wander back to my home, in my imagination, and think of how my parents would feel did they know where I was. My half-brother, hearing of my difficulty, sent me money and engaged the best of counsel for my approaching trial.

One day while Jocky Jim slept peacefully on his prison bunk, I passed my time in composing a *poem* which I here give.

"Kind, loving friends, the die is cast;
In lonely jail I am at last;
Come plead my case—come pay my bill,
Or I a convict's cell may fill.

The charge against me is untrue,
No unjust deed I wished to do;
By cursed rum I was o'erthrown,
Causing my dearest friends to moan.

My mother dear, I'm sad to know
My conduct caused your tears to flow;
Forgive me now, forget the past—
I hope to be redeemed at last.

My prison life is lone and drear,
I have no friends or comforts here;
And if again I am set free,
I'll thank God for my liberty."

I submitted my production to the criticism of Jocky Jim on his awakening from his siesta, and he pronounced it good—which is more than I can expect from my readers. He said he had but one objection to it, which was that it was too solemn, and as he felt in the right mood he would try his talents in the same line. Seating himself in a corner of the cell he soon produced the following—

> "I'm trapped at last, and without bail
> I find myself in this old jail,
> For being caught while riding 'round
> With Billy Wilkin's bob-tail brown.
>
> To Staten Island Jones was sent,
> On catching Jocky Jim intent;
> Then on the Powell we set sail
> And landed at the county jail.
>
> Wilkins and Jones both came to me
> To learn about their property;
> Said I, 'My friends, if you prove kind
> The horse and buggy you shall find."

On the lower part of the manuscript he added a postscript—

> "If you admire the author,
> Please choose him for your daughter."

He carefully folded his production and sent it to the gentleman that he had stolen the horse from. Towards night Mr. Wilkins came to the cell-door, to show his appreciation of the verses by presenting Jocky Jim with a box of cigars, at the same time telling him to let him know when they were gone, as he intended to keep him supplied while he was awaiting trial.

On the day of my trial I had my witnesses ready, and my lawyer was on hand. The man who had me arrested was placed on the stand, and his own testimony would have been sufficient to have proved my entire innocence of any attempt to defraud him of a cent. But we thought best to let all the witnesses in my favor give their testimony. The presiding judge said there was no evidence against me, and that I was free from all charges and released from further durance.

It was a great pleasure to be once more a free man and receive the congratulations of my many friends. One of the most influential men of the town invited me to a sumptuous dinner which contrasted very much with my late prison fare.

My next move was to get employment; and looking over the advertisements in a newspaper my eye fell upon one of a business which I thought would suit me. It was for agents to sell prize packages for a New York firm. I borrowed some money from a friend and embarked in this business, and soon had a brisk trade. After a few weeks I took a partner, and we traveled together meeting with good success. We visited nearly all the towns in the vicinity, and were always sure of doing a good business at hotels where anything unusual was going on to attract people. I still had a desire to drink, and frequently accepted invitations to imbibe with young men.

One night as we were going to a hotel where there was to be a party, we saw an object lying in the snow. It was in the winter season and somewhat dark. We approached, and found to our surprise that it was a man very drunk and nearly frozen. Having no conveyance we could not take him along; so we hurried to the tavern, about a mile distant, and informed them of the facts, and they started after him with a team directly.

When they returned with him he was more dead than alive, and they set about trying to revive him, rubbing him, and pouring hot liquor down his throat, which soon brought him around all right, and in an

FIGHTING THE TIGERS.

hour's time he was dancing and drinking with the best of them. I am positive he would have perished had we not happened along the road and discovered him.

I soon fell into my old habit of drinking to excess and spending all my money, and I became discouraged and concluded to remove to some new field of operations. Gathering up my effects I went to New York city. I engaged a room at the Girard House, where I fell in with a gentleman who was desirous of seeing the sights in and around the city; as I was somewhat posted I agreed to act as his guide. We promenaded the streets all day, drinking freely, and in the evening entered a gambling establishment near Broadway.

Here we were induced to fight the tiger, for we were somewhat intoxicated and easily influenced. I saw that they were cheating us, and expostulated. High words ensued, when one of the gamblers drew a pistol from his pocket and presented it to my head, threatening to blow my brains out.

Knocking his pistol out of his hand I dealt him a blow between the eyes which laid him low, and then, securing his pistol, I sprang back and presented it to the crowd and told them to stand off if they valued life. My new-made friend had flown and left me to fight it out with the cut-throats alone. I kept them at bay until I reached the door, when I opened it, threw the pistol into the crowd, and leaped down the stairway.

On reaching the side-walk I found my friend trembling with fear. He grasped my arm and exclaimed—

"For God's sake let us get away from this dreadful place or we shall be murdered."

I remained in New York until I had not a dollar left, and pawned all my things that I could raise any money on with which to buy liquor, as I craved more than ever before. I walked the streets night after night without a place to lay my weary frame and aching head, suffering not only for rum but for food, repeating to myself—My God! what will become of me?

I eventually enlisted as a volunteer, to go to the seat of war, but was discharged for disability. I returned to New York, regardless of the former misery rum had caused me there, and commenced a course of dissipation which lasted nearly a month.

One day I went to a hotel bar and called for liquor, and after drinking the same I informed the bar-tender I had no money to pay him. He came around the bar, and advancing to my side dealt me a powerful blow on the head which felled me to the marble floor, driving the breath from my body.

I was badly hurt; several gentlemen standing by remarked that it was a shame to strike me, and the rum-vender ought to be served the same way. He seemed to regret that he had struck me after his anger had somewhat cooled; but that did not help me, for the fall on the marble floor had injured me internally, and to this day I feel the effects of it.

As soon as I was able I staggered out of the ungodly place. Having no money I went to the conductor of one of the trains to Albany and stated my case. He gave me a pass to that city and two dollars in money.

CHAPTER XXIII.

WHEN the train reached Peekskill I left the cars in search of a drink, and the train went without me. I entered the village and took several drinks of whisky, and afterwards went into a lager-beer saloon and indulged freely in beer. This made me very much intoxicated, and I went out into a shed and lay down in an old sleigh.

How long I slept I know not; but when I awoke my cap was gone, and I was nearly stiff with cold. There seemed to be no person up in town and no place open where I could procure rum. I pulled off my coat, and putting it over my head and around me I started for the depot, which I soon reached, but I could not get in.

Seeing an old well-curb near, I got behind it to shield me from the wind, and went to sleep again. About daylight I was aroused, and looking up I found three or four men near me, who told me to get up or I would freeze to death. I made several attempts to rise before I succeeded in gaining my feet. I was chilled to the bone, and my teeth chattered like castinets. They got me to the depot and tried to ascertain who I was, but I would not tell them, for I was ashamed and had but little life left in me and did not feel like answering questions.

After a while a freight train came along with caboose attached, and I got on board and rode to Poughkeepsie. Just before the train arrived one of the brakemen spoke to me, and seeing I had no hat on asked me what had become of it. I told him it was lost. He took me to his house, gave me something to eat and an old white hat to wear. It was Sunday, and he invited me to remain with him until Monday. His good wife felt very sorry for me, and expressed a desire that I would reform. She said she knew what it was to have an intemperate father, and felt for any one who was a slave to drink.

At that time they had in Poughkeepsie a society of drinking men, who were organized for the purpose of aiding intemperate persons who needed help. They heard of me, and since my reformation I have understood that they searched the place to find me and give me aid. Many of the men who were members of this society are now reformed, and in the front ranks of the brave army of Temperance.

The next day I made my way home and arrived there nearly dead. After recruiting my strength I determined to make another dash out into the world, and accordingly went to Schoharie County where I had friends living. I engaged to work for a relative at preparing the wood-work for ploughs. The blacksmith in his employ was a hard-drinking man; he kept a bottle of liquor continually in the shop, and shared it with me. Sometimes I drank to such an extent that I was not able to work.

One day Mr. G——, the proprietor, left me to finish some ploughs, and went off on business. As soon as he was out of sight the blacksmith and myself procured a fresh supply of liquor, and for three or four days we drank to excess, and when he returned the work was unfinished. He was one of the best-hearted men in the world, and had once drank himself to such an extent that he knew by sad experience what rum would do. Instead of being angry he spoke kindly to us, remarking that he guessed we boys had enjoyed ourselves pretty well in his absence.

After I had finished work for Mr. G—— I went to a neighboring town and worked in the hop-fields, pulling hop-poles. When the season was over I went to work carpentering, a hundred miles away from this place. I continued to drink, often to excess—especially on Sundays when there was no work to be done as I kept a bottle of liquor in my room. Often, of a Monday morning, instead of being refreshed by a Sunday's rest, I was so weak that I could hardly raise sufficient courage to go to work. I was frequently in danger of falling from the scaffolding of buildings, as my head would swim, obliging me to grasp a brace to keep my footing. Oh, what long days they were to me! It seemed as if six o'clock would never come; but when it did I would hurry home and drink large quantities of liquor.

I remained until winter set in, and then went to a

large town some distance off, and on the Massachusetts line. I engaged to board in a place where two bars were kept—one in the basement and one on the first floor. They did a large business at rum-selling, and many a poor drunkard spent his last ten cents at the counter.

There was one poor fellow who had once lived respected and been well off in worldly goods, who was such a slave to rum that he washed out the bars and acted as a general drudge around the premises, just for what liquor they gave him. One Saturday night I drank with him, and he appeared as well as usual. The following Sunday I gave him a drink, and noticed him drinking several times through the day. That night, at nine o'clock, word came that he was dying. I went to see him accompanied by the basement bar-tender.

He lived in an upper room with quite a large family, and it needed but one glance to show that it was a drunkard's home. Two policemen had hold of him and were walking him across the room; his eyes were rolling wildly in his head, the pupils had rolled up under his brows and disappeared, and he was unable to see. His tongue protruded from his mouth, and blood slowly trickled down his chin, showing that his teeth were penetrating his tongue. He was suffering all the horrors of delirium tremens. His daughter was wringing her hands in anguish, and blistering tears and looks of terror covered the faces of his family.

I never saw such misery before, and hope I never shall again. Yet here, in W———, where I write, but a few days ago there was discovered by the police a family consisting of husband, wife, and several children—one at the breast—who were in a most miserable plight. The husband and wife had been on a spree for nine days and both were suffering from *mania apotu*, while the children were actually in a starving condition, and would probably have died if the neighbors had not given them food. The parents were taken to the police station, the mother being so frantic as to tear her clothing off in shreds, imagining her children dying before her. Her condition is considered critical at this time.

But to return to the poor slave of drink whom we left in such suffering. He died that night. It was a most fearful death, and his sufferings were dreadful to behold. It would take a more powerful pen than mine to describe a fraction of that heart-rending scene. But few followed the poor inebriate to his last resting-place excepting his wife and children. Rum had claimed his victim, and another, who might have been —God knows what, had gone—God knows where. Be that as it may. Judge not that ye be not judged. As no marble slab marks his last resting-place, let this be his epitaph—

> "Stop, stranger, stop, and drop a tear;
> A drunkard's bones lie mouldering here;
> To appetite he was a slave,
> Rum brought him to an early grave.
>
> His wife and children plead in vain,
> That he from drinking would abstain:
> Weak his resolves—temptations great—
> Be warned by his unhappy fate."

The closing scenes of this man's career haunted me for a long time and I was unable to shake them off. I thought that it might have been me in place of him, and I could not help fancying that I might be Rum's next victim. The landlady was in terror for days, and remarked that it was a mean business to sell liquor and they would give it up if they were not so badly in debt. I discontinued drinking for some weeks, but was soon at it again as bad as ever.

Not liking the work that I was doing in the shop here I left, not caring much where I went; but I finally brought up at the town of A——, where I met with a man whom I had become acquainted with in my last stopping-place, and we were soon drinking deeply and kept at it for several days. I then found that I had but thirty-five cents left in the world.

It was midwinter, and my clothing was not sufficient to keep me comfortable. What to do, or where to go to keep from freezing and starving I did not know, and my wants were pressing. I purchased a few fried cakes, put them in my pocket, and started off down the road, not knowing what would become of me.

The day was bitter cold and the wind penetrated my garments, while the blinding snow and sleet dashed into my face. After walking an hour or two I came to a barn, and, thinks I to myself, I can get under the hay and keep warm until morning. Finding the door unlocked I entered and crawled up the hay-mow where I dug a hole large enough to get into, and then drew the hay over me. I felt very cold, but after some time I fell asleep.

How long I slept I do not know; when I awoke I was nearly frozen to death, and it was a good while before I could get my blood circulating freely. I succeeded in reaching the barn floor, where I stamped my feet and rushed back and forth in the darkness trying to get warm. I then opened the door, and was soon on the road again.

As good luck would have it I saw a light in the distance, and found on approaching that it was in a factory. I made the best of my way to the engine room, and took a seat near the boiler where I could get warm. I remained there until morning, seeing no person. Then I eat some of my cakes, and again started on my travels.

About noon I came to the town of P——, on the edge of Vermont, where I soon obtained work. I remained until towards spring, when I attended a party at Bennington, and became very much intoxicated. During the next day I returned home, and continued drinking at the hotel until late at night. Not wishing to be seen by Mr. W—— (for whom I worked) and his family, I went to the barn and slept in the hay with a buffalo-robe over me. When I awoke I was very much chilled and had taken a severe cold.

I felt so ashamed of myself that when Mr. W—— asked me to go home with him I told him I could not stay with him; that I must go away. I thought that every one in town must know how disgracefully I had acted, and that I could not look them in the face. Mr. W—— settled up with me, and I took the cars for Troy where I remained several days.

One day I had taken an unusual amount of liquor which must have been drugged. I lost all sensibility, and when I came to myself I was in the custody of a policeman in the suburbs of the city. I could not tell him how I came there or where I intended to go; in fact I was so bewildered I did not know much of anything. My hat was gone, and my hands were cut and bruised. He took me to a hotel instead of the station-house, and told the landlord to give me a room.

In the morning after I had slept off the worst effects of the rum I made investigations to ascertain my losses, and was fortunate enough to have left a few dollars which I had put into my watch-pocket. I settled with the landlord for my room and went out to get me a hat. I brushed up a little at a barber-shop and took several drinks; then left Troy and went to Albany, not caring to stop longer where I had been so unfortunate.

I soon tired of Albany, and making up my mind to change the scene to some distance, I traveled to the town of N—— A—— in the Old Bay State. When I had got rested from my journey I found that my my funds were rather low, and in a few days I was reduced to my last dollar. I thought I would have the good of that, and went into a rum-shop where I took several drinks in succession, filling the glasses to the brim. The liquor made me wild, and that day I enlisted again, but to this time I have no recollection as to how it came about.

The next morning I felt some one roughly pulling me and calling me to get up, saying that it was most eight o'clock. I inquired who he might be and what place I was in. He told me he was a recruiting officer; that I had enlisted, and was in a room which he had taken for me at a hotel. He also requested me to be ready to start in about an hour.

How I felt no pen can describe—no tongue can tell. I had no money, and could not procure the liquor necessary to keep me from being delirious. I told the officer I should die if I could not get some whisky, and at all events they would have to leave me behind, as I was unable to travel in the state I was in. He kindly gave me two dollars, and told me to go and get what I wanted.

That was a happy moment for me. I could have kissed his hand. I would have become the slave of the man who would give me the means of procuring rum. I went down to the bar and drank several glasses; the death-like feelings soon left me, and I once more seemed like myself. I went into the dining-room and partook of a hearty breakfast; then made my preparations for leaving for Camp Wool.

I purchased a bottle of whisky, which kept up my spirits until I came to the camp; then I was taken ill from the effects of bad liquor, and for several days was on the sick-list.

CHAPTER XXIV.

I WAS so much reduced from long exposure and intemperate habits that I could not stand the ups and downs of a soldier's life, and after being examined by two surgeons I was pronounced unfit for service, and in due time received my discharge with transportation to the place of enlistment.

When I arrived at Worcester Junction, and while waiting for a train, I began to think over my past life, and concluded that it would be well for me not to return to old associations, but to form new ones and try to do better in the future. I finally determined to stop in Worcester, and see if I could not get work there and accomplish something.

With this resolution firmly impressed on my mind, I walked down the railroad towards the city. After traveling a short distance I came to a flag station kept by an old gentleman from Ireland. I addressed him—

"Mister, can you tell me the way to that portion of the city where the most business is done?"

"Sure, an' I can that, me man: you must keep

straight on, and turning to the left you'll soon see the Common, and from there you'll soon be on the Main street."

I thanked him for his kindness and proceeded on my way. I felt sad indeed; my money was all gone except ten cents, and I knew no one in the place. I was a stranger in a strange land.

While crossing over the Common I saw a man sitting on a bench. From his appearance I took him for a wanderer like myself, and sat down and entered into conversation with him. I soon found that he was from the Empire State and we were immediately on the best of terms. He informed me he had been in the army also, and inquired as to the state of my finances.

I told him that ten cents was the size of my pile; he laughed, and said that he could beat me by five cents—having fifteen. He said he was a carriage-maker by trade, and I told him I was a carpenter. As we were both strangers in the city we pledged fidelity to each other, with the understanding that the one who first obtained work should support the other until he was equally fortunate.

We walked down Main Street, and turning off into the poorer portion of the city came to a saloon kept by an Irishman, where we thought we could get a small lunch for what little money we had; but when he found out that we were from the army he ordered his wife to get us up a good square meal, and would not take a cent of us in payment. We thanked him for his kind hospitality, and told him we must go and look for work.

The kind-hearted son of Erin shook hands with us,

and told us if we did not get work to come back when we were hungry, and we should not want for a meal of such as he had to offer. He made no pretensions to gentility, but was nevertheless a true-hearted gentleman, God bless him.

Opposite his saloon was a carriage shop at that time, and we sauntered in to see what the prospects of getting work for my new friend were. The proprietor was wanting a man on fire-work, but my friend, not having been employed on such, was rather dubious about his ability to give satisfaction.

After looking around without seeing anything to encourage us, we thought, as it was Saturday and we had no place to stay over Sunday, we had better make some attempts to ensure against starvation. My friend proposed that I should go to some hotel and put up, and he would continue to look for a job, and meet me in the course of an hour at the Irishman's saloon on Exchange Street.

The reader must recollect that we had no money, and if something did not favor us we should not have any to pay our bill at the hotel on Monday morning. But having been in many a tight place before, I felt willing to risk it, hoping that something would occur to extricate us from our unpleasant situation. I accordingly went to the City Hotel, and engaged a room and board until Monday morning.

At the appointed time I went to the saloon where I had promised to meet my friend, but he was not there. I waited for him some time but he did not come. I then returned to the hotel and tried to sleep, but my thoughts about my desperate situation kept me awake, and my friend's failure to meet me as he promised made me feel very badly indeed.

Next day I visited the saloon several times to learn what had become of my acquaintance, but never saw him afterwards; nor did the proprietor of the saloon ever hear of him, and his disappearance remained a mystery to us.

While sitting in the hotel Sabbath evening, I entered into conversation with a young man who said he was from Canada, and a carpenter in the employ of a builder by the name of Sibley. I informed him that our trades were the same; that I was in search of a job; and, also, that I was in a quandary as to how I should settle my hotel bill in the morning. He set my mind at rest by handing me money enough to pay it, and said he would introduce me to the gentleman he was at work for, who, he thought, would give me work also. I thanked him for his disinterested kindness, and he said he would wait until I had worked a while, before receiving back the money he had loaned me.

The next morning I accompanied my new friend (who had certainly proved himself more deserving of the name than the man I had met on the Common) down to the shop, where he introduced me to his employer and informed him of my wishes. Mr. Sibley hired me at once; he then went out and engaged me a boarding-place, and I went to work with new hopes for the future. Mr. Sibley was a very kind man, and during the time I worked as a mechanic in Worcester I was in his employ.

On Saturday night I informed Mr. Sibley that I was very much in want of a pair of shoes, and he gave me nearly all that was due me. I went up towards Main Street, and as I was passing a well-known hotel I heard some loud conversation inside, and thought I would just step in and see what was going on. I found myself in the bar-room, and being rather weary from unusual labor during the week I took a glass of liquor, forgetting all my former resolutions and the awful sufferings I had endured from indulging in one glass.

I did not once think I should become intoxicated and spend my money for rum instead of purchasing the shoes I so much needed, but so it proved. I began conversing with the bar-tender, and he said that he had seen me in New York and was glad to meet me in Worcester.

This remark—although I did not remember him—caused me to linger around the bar until I had taken several drinks. I then went out into the street, drinking often at saloons on my way.

I continued drinking for several days; at night, after the rum-shops were closed, I would generally walk the streets till they opened in the morning. It was in the month of March and very cold. One night I wandered down through Union Street; coming to a carriage shop and seeing some old cart wheels leaning against the building I crept behind them; though chilled to the bone tired nature could hold out no longer, and I fell asleep.

When I awoke I was most dead; but by trying several times I finally succeeded in creeping out from behind the wheels and staggered down a cross street. Seeing a light through the window of a house I knocked at the door, and a man came and let me in. He seemed to be very much surprised to see me shivering so, for I trembled to such an extent that I could neither sit nor stand. It was a place where liquor was sold and he mixed me up some hot rum and I poured it down, the glass rattling against my chattering teeth. This warmed me up, and on repeating the dose several times I almost forgot my narrow escape from freezing to death.

On the fourth day, in the afternoon, I stumbled on to one of my fellow workmen, and he began to reason with me and persuade me to go back to work.

"No sir," said I, "he will not take me back; after my deceiving him in such a manner I could not look him in the face. I am going to leave this city if I have to beg my way to some other place."

I felt so badly I could not refrain from crying. My money all gone; my poor body weak and trembling from my four days of dissipation and exposure; a stranger to all but a few whom I could not meet for shame —when I say that I felt sad and wretched they are but faint words to express my misery at that time.

After much reasoning and persuasion from my fellow-workman, Mr. Charles Green, I consented to accompany him to the shop. If I had been a culprit sentenced to be hung and on the way to the place of execution I could not have felt much worse. Several times I almost made up my mind to run away from Mr. Green, but I knew he would follow me and soon catch me. When we reached the stairway that led up to my employer's shop I halted; but Green said-

"Come along; I know he wants to see you."

On entering the shop Mr. Sibley accosted me with—

"Holloa George; got back, have you?"

I answered faintly—

"Yes sir; but I suppose you do not want me any longer."

"Why not?" he replied.

"Because sir, I am a poor victim of intemperance, and have deceived you greatly."

"You are not the only one in this city that drinks," said he, "and I do not mean to discharge you; I will keep you because you are unfortunate."

These words of kindness so affected me that I have never forgotten them; and while writing about it my heart seems to swell as it did then, and I am forced to lay down my pen to wipe away the tears that are stealing silently down my cheeks.

Oh, what a vast power there is in kindness! Sometimes a word of sympathy may be the saving of a soul. Kind words are cheap; be not so sparing of them; they do more good than you can imagine; none know their value more than the poor drunkard. A single word of kindness will do more good than all the logic and metaphysics that were ever uttered by mankind.

In one of our New England towns, there was a man who had been for thirty years a confirmed inebriate. No one seemed to care for him; every one called him Old H——, and the boys made fun of him as he staggered along. One day he stood on the street, sad and gloomy, when a lady passing by accosted him with—

"Good evening, Mr. H——."

He was so thunderstruck that he could make no answer, but turning to a gentleman who stood near he said—

"Did that lady call me Mr. H——, or am I crazy?"

The man informed him that she did certainly greet him in those words. From that hour he made a resolution to reform; there must be a mistake; he could not be past all hope, or that lady would not have addressed him as she did. He joined the Sons of Temperance, and at this time holds a high position in that order and is known and respected as a great worker in the cause. Saved from a drunkard's grave by a few kind words. Remember this, my readers, and see if you cannot spare a few such words to some poor, suffering wretch.

But to return to my interview with Mr. Sibley; he was kind enough to go with me to the boarding-house again; the lady who kept it was one of those good souls who delight in seeing any one try to do well, and she took me back as a boarder. It was some days before I felt strong enough to resume work; but when I did again take the bench I resolved to do the best I could, and for three months I did not even take a glass of beer. I purchased clothing suitable for moving in decent society, and attended church on the Sabbath; and I can say that they were three very happy months to me. They were to me what an oasis in the desert is to the weary traveler.

One day, on taking up a daily paper I noticed an

advertisement of a temperance meeting and lecture which was to be held in Washburn Hall, and having attended but one temperance meeting in my life I concluded to go and hear what the lecturer had to say. He related some very amusing anecdotes and incidents relating to those who had been in the habit of drinking, and I was so much pleased that I gave nearly all that I had with me in the way of money. He had never been a slave to drink, and his remarks did not reach me as they would if he had related his own experience.

On receiving my pay at the last of the third month I started out to make some necessary purchases, and while passing a hotel I thought I would stop in and look over the papers in the reading-room. On my way out I passed through the bar-room. The smell of the liquors so excited me that after I had reached the sidewalk I stopped bewildered. My appetite was fast overcoming me, and a terrible battle was going on within me. To go back or not to go back—that was the question; my evil spirit solved it for me, and sent me to the bar where I ordered something to drink. I drank in that saloon until I had squandered thirty dollars or more.

Some people who read this will say—"Why did you not resist the temptation?" All I have to say is that I tried hard to do so, but could not; and many a man will say that he has had the same experience.

It is related of a drunkard, that when asked by his friends why he did not say, "Get behind me, Satan," when tempted to drink, he answered that Satan was always behind to push him forward into the rum-shop.

The reader, unless he has passed through the same ordeal, can have no idea what I experienced for the next few days. It is unexpressible in words. The first I can recollect is that I met Mr. Sibley, and that he told me to go to my boarding-house and take a rest, and when I felt sufficiently recovered to come to work. I did as he advised, and the landlady—a good, motherly Yankee woman—made for me a decoction of "yarbs," which brought me around to myself, and I was soon able to resume work. But the old habit was so strong that I could not stand it, and I was soon under the influence of my old enemy.

On becoming sober again I commenced work, but felt so ill that before night I was compelled to leave the building on which I was engaged, and it was finished by other hands than mine. It stands on Burnside Court, and whenever I pass that way the old days, now gone forever, are brought vividly to my mind.

Although seven years have elapsed, I sometimes look at the last nails I drove there, and think of the condition of my mind at the time, and thank God that I am disinthralled, and have been the humble instrument of saving others from that dark road of suffering and death.

CHAPTER XXV.

HAVING given up work, I visited New York city, where I had some business to transact. After calling on the parties I wished to see, I took the first train for Springfield. Rumshops were numerous there at that time, and I am sorry to say there are a great number at present. I fell into my old habit and went from one to another drinking deeply; this lasted for several days until my money was expended.

I was again among strangers, with no money to purchase food or lodging. I had nothing to pawn, as luckily for me I had left my trunk in Worcester. But necessity is the mother of invention. I inspected my wardrobe, and came to the decision that I could get along with less clothing than I was wearing.

Without hesitation I pulled off my vest, and, hanging it on my arm, started down Main street to try and find a purchaser. Stepping into a liquor store I offered it for sale. The man I addressed proved to be the proprietor of the store.

"Why sir," said he, "what under the heavens do you want to sell it for?"

"For a very good reason," I replied, "for I have no money, and no friends in this place."

"What is your business, sir?" said he.

I informed him that I was a carpenter and joiner. This seemed to strike him favorably, for he immediately remarked—

"I am going to build me a house; in fact the timber is ready for framing, and if you wish I will give you employment—that is if you are a competent workman—and I will give you the best wages your work commands."

I joyfully accepted his kind offer, stating that if my work did not suit him he had his remedy, and that was to discharge me. He then asked me to take a drink, and I was glad enough to accept his invitation. The next day I commenced work, and for several weeks I abstained from liquor although I often visited my employer's establishment where it was kept for sale.

One day, a young man whom I had become acquainted with invited me to accompany him in a ride to Suffield in the state of Connecticut, and as it was Sunday I accepted his proposal. When we arrived there we went to the village hotel, and drank several times; and before we were ready to return home were considerably intoxicated.

Having commenced drinking in this way I could not stop, but went on a long spree, and eventually found myself in New York city. I remained there drinking hard for two weeks, and during the last half of this time I do not think I took any thing excepting liquor into my stomach.

When my money was all spent and I could obtain no more rum, I started to walk to Springfield. After traveling some distance from the city, I felt so weak that I thought I could go no further without food and stepped into a saloon kept by a woman; during my walk I had found a small scrip in my pocket which I lay down on the counter, asking her to give me the worth of it in gin. She filled a glass about two-thirds full and passed it to me. My hands trembled so that I had hard work to raise it to my parched lips.

After pouring down the burning fluid I told her of my situation, and asked her to be kind enough to give me a crust of bread or any thing she chose to keep me from starving. To my dying day I never shall forget the look she gave me. She put all the savage dignity she could muster into her repulsive countenance, and said in a shrill voice—

"We don't keep nor feed beggars here, sir."

I left her saloon without further delay and have never seen her since. I have been before the public in that town and spoken three times, and have always mentioned the circumstance and have told them that I thanked God I was no beggar now, and that I fully realized how merciful the Lord had been to me in saving me from suffering and want—from the dismal road of intemperance and beggary. How often I hear people saying, "I wish I was situated like so and so;" or, "If I had this or that how happy I should feel," when, at the same time, they are surrounded by all the comforts of a happy home—all that should make life desirable—food to eat—clothes to wear—a bed to lie upon, and plenty of kind friends to cheer them and make the sunlight brighter as they journey along. Could they be placed in circumstances such as I and many a poor fellow have been in, methinks they would value the pleasant home they have and thank the Lord that it is as well with them as it is.

It was with a heavy, sinking heart that I left the abode of the pitiless woman who had refused to give me even a crust of bread, and trudged along through the deep mud, not knowing what I should do, or what was to befall me. I continued walking until I could scarcely see the road; soon it began to rain, and the darkness to increase, and while groping my way along I fell from off a bridge into a ditch, and landed in the mud and water some feet down from the level of the road. I managed to gain the bank and got into the road again, but my clothing was completely saturated. I must have been a pitiable object to behold but I was thankful that no bones were broken.

Joy nearly overcome me when I observed in the distance ahead a light, and I hastened towards it praying that there I might find some kind soul who would take pity on my forlorn condition. When I reached what I fondly hoped would be a haven of rest to me, for a short time at least, I found it was a wayside oyster saloon, kept by an old lady. The appearance I presented was not calculated to impress her very favorably in my behalf. I went up to her however, for my case was desperate, and stated my wants as well as I could in my excited state. She seemed to take pity on me, and offered me a glass of whisky as she saw I needed it badly, and I drank it eagerly. The kind old lady then made me seat myself and gave me a generous bowl of warm oysters and said—

"Eat them my poor boy, they will do you good; you look hungry and sick."

She then sat down by my side, and said she—

"I have a poor boy roaming about this wide world, God knows where, or whether he be dead or alive. He looks like you, too, dear soul, and loves drink too much. He often comes home to me hungry and in rags. God help him and strengthen him to do better, that he may return to me sober and a changed man, to close my eyes when I die. I cannot sleep of nights at times thinking he may be wanting a place to lay his head. Don't your good old mother worry about you, think you?"

Her kindness and the mention of my mother brought the tears to my eyes and made me realize how wretched I was, and how wrong it was to do as I had been doing. I had a good cry with that dear old charitable lady. When I told her I had no place to rest that night, she said she had but one bed in her house, and I rose to depart, not wishing to trouble her too much. She followed me to the door and, slipping a few shillings into my hand, told me that there was a boarding-house across the street where she thought I could be accommodated; but she first made me return, and brushed the mud from my clothing.

With a warm grasp of the hand and many thanks tor the kindness she had shown me I launched out into the darkness and made my way towards the boarding-house, thinking of the great contrast between the woman I had just left and the one who had refused me a crust of bread. I felt encouraged from knowing that there was some charity left in the world. With much difficulty I found the boarding-house, but they had no vacant room in the place and could not keep me. I had nothing to do but journey on my way.

I soon came to a large iron-works and entered the office. Although it was late, in fact near to midnight, the clerks were still writing. On my entrance they cast a look of surprise at me, for the lady had not succeeded in removing all the stains of the ditch from my clothing; indeed my personal appearance was not calculated to introduce me favorably. However, I stated to them how unfortunately I was situated and offered to sell my undercoat to them for five dollars. It was one I had purchased in Worcester and was worth about twenty dollars. The head book-keeper after examining it said he would take it, and handed me the money.

I procured something to eat and then started on the railroad track, intending to walk back to New York. While traveling on the track I came to a bridge and was obliged to grope my way along slowly. The rain had subsided, but it was still quite dark. Just as I had reached the center of the bridge I heard to my horror a train coming in my rear, and on looking around saw—oh God! that it was on the same track that I was. Heavens! thought I, this is the last of Dutcher. I saw almost certain death approaching, yet prayed for escape, although I had often meditated self-murder. All the dreadful past rushed with lightning speed through my brain—what I might have been and what I was—what a death, to be mangled into an unrecognizable mass of humanity, perhaps never to be seen again but thrown into the boiling torrent below. Ten thousand thoughts came to my mind; dear friends passed in review before my eyes in a few fleeting seconds.

But the time for action had arrived; the bright flash of the reflector revealed my form to the engineer who whistled "down brakes." To drop between the timbers was perhaps death by drowning; but there was a chance for life, and none where I stood. I stooped to make the awful plunge, and there—a Godsend to deliver me—I saw an iron rod beneath the timbers. Quick as thought I lowered myself by the supports, grasped the rod, and swung off over the dark waters just as the flashing, roaring engine with its long train swept above me. The noise was deafening, and I thought I should have to let go my hold before it passed; but the merciful Providence that had watched over me for so many years gave me the strength to hold on and to clamber up again on the timbers, where I lay for a long time panting for breath.

That was a very narrow escape from death, and as I pen these lines a shudder runs through me, and in my imagination I am again hanging for life to that bar of iron, and cringing from the fiery monster which thunders over my head. Often since my redemption I have dreamed over that awful situation, and started from my sleep with the cold perspiration standing in big drops upon my forehead.

After a long and dreary walk I reached the city, and after taking several drinks to straighten me up, started on the train for Springfield. The money I obtained for my coat enabled me to pay my fare.

CHAPTER XXVI.

ON reaching Springfield I obtained some more money and started out drinking again. At nine o'clock in the evening I entered a saloon kept by some colored men, where they played billiards and cards. I have a faint recollection of seating myself to play a game of cards with some one; the next time I came to know myself or where I was, I found that I was in bed and that several men and women were standing around the room. There was also a doctor who was seated at the bedside. They told me I had been a raving maniac for three days and nights. I had suffered all the horrors of delirium tremens.

The terrible objects and frightful scenes which passed before my shattered vision will never be effaced from my memory. God grant that I may never have to pass through such a fearful ordeal again. There is probably no pen that can portray anything approaching the agonies of a person who has delirium tremens. This side of the grave, man can suffer nothing to compare with it. The soul seems to leave the body and wander alternately in Heaven and hell—principally in the latter place; but at times it has glimpses of the former, making the agony more excruciating.

At one time I would imagine myself to be in a beautiful palace, the walls hung with the most splendid tapestry; fragrant perfumes filled the air, while soft sweet music lulled my senses into a half repose. I was in no pain, and would gladly have remained in that state of ecstasy forever. Petite, fairy forms with gossamer wings, dressed in white, came dancing, flitting through the air. They were beautiful to behold, and seemed bent on my service, trying to amuse me and drive ill thoughts away. But almost in an instant the scene would change; the beautiful colors would turn to blackness, the sweet music to horrible wails and groans, and the fairy forms enlarge and transform into the most hideous monsters, with blood-red, glaring eyes, and gnashing teeth. Some would approach me, and I would flee, only to rush into the horrible embrace of others, who with fiendish howls and laughter would bury their dreadful claws in my quivering flesh, tearing me to the vitals. Oh, what anguish was concentrated in that terrible conflict. I fought desperately to drive them away, and shrieked wildly for help in my great suffering.

Then in an instant they would disappear, and I was walking through verdant fields where cool shades invited me to repose, and sparkling rivulets glided and dashed alternately over smooth white sand and rocky falls. I threw myself beneath a tiny stream falling from a moss-grown rock, thinking to quench my great thirst and cool my fevered body; but before I could drink, a peal of ten thousand thunders rent the air, and the stream of water became a hissing serpent, whose fetid breath came hot into my face. I sprang backwards, and discovered that I was surrounded by the most horrible shapes, serpents and lizards, dragons, and animals of the most hideous appearance, driven on by fiends in human shape, who lashed them towards me with scourges of fire. Turn which ever way I would, the same fiendish crew would greet me with taunting laughter. Cold, slimy serpents came dragging themselves from the rocks, and twined themselves about me; my brain seemed turned to molten lead, my heart to be bursting; when it seemed that I could endure these tortues no longer, everything which had so tormented me disappeared as quickly as it had come.

Then I seemed to lay panting and exhausted in a cool grotto at the entrance of which were festoons of rich purple grapes in great profusion, nestling among the green leaves. I longed to eat some of the delicious clusters, but tried in vain to raise myself to do so; my muscles refused their office, and I lay as if carved from granite with my soul imprisoned in the solid rock. How long I suffered while in this state I know not, but it seemed as years of anguish. I finally realized that I was able to move again; my jaws relaxed their lividness, and I seemed to crawl along towards the mouth of the grotto, to endeavor to pluck some of the cooling grapes, for I was suffering greatly from thirst. I found that I could not stand, and that the clusters were beyond my reach. I grasped the flinty, ragged rocks, and strove to clamber up to the vine; but just as I thought I had them in my grasp my hold on the rock gave way, and I fell torn and bleeding to the stones below. Time after time I endeavored to reach them and at last succeeded in grasping the vine, when it turned into a writhing serpent and coiled itself about me, and we rolled down the rocks together, as my bones crushed beneath its tightening folds.

Then, methought, a huge-winged demon swooped down from the black heavens and grasped us both, and flying through the air, escorted by others laughing and howling, suddenly dropped us into a deep chasm. Down, down we went, the serpent changing into a laughing, mocking satyr, who seemed to be taking me to untried tortures. Far up, at the mouth of the pit, I saw an angelic form, weeping, and beckoning me to come to her; but I was in strong fetters, and dared not struggle for fear I should drop. We seemed to descend with great velocity, and I soon beheld the bottom of the pit, which was covered with dark water full of snakes and reptiles, while around the sides stood devils and fiends pointing their bony fingers at me and filling the air with howls of exultation.

Suddenly I was plunged into the slimy water, but in place of cooling me it seemed like molten iron, scorching the flesh from my bones. As I rose to the surface I seemed to float around it, thereby obtaining a view of all the horrors of the place. All at once the rock opened at one side of the infernal lake, and a woman emerged from the dark cavern. She had a most fiendish face, and her hair was composed of long, slender serpents which writhed about her shoulders; her eyes seemed like balls of fire, and as if ready to burst from their sockets. She stole softly towards me. I tried to shrink away, but the attendant demons held me fast, and she soon stood bending over me, so near that I could feel her hot breath in my face. Then she laughed in a horrible manner, while the fiends set up an awful howl, and commenced a dreadful conflict among themselves, during which the woman was torn to pieces and partly devoured before my eyes. Then all was darkness, and I saw them no more.

These are a few of the many horrible imaginary scenes that I passed through while suffering from delirium tremens as well as I can describe them in words. After I became rational I was so weak and feeble that at times I would think I was dying; my breath would seem to leave me, and a sinking feeling, indescribable, would come over me, and I would be unconscious for a time. But through kind treatment I improved, and in two weeks time I was able to walk about. I must here acknowledge my gratitude to Mr. Ezra S. Stiles, at whose house I was stopping, for his great kindness during that period of my life, and also his good wife who could not have treated me better had I been her own son. Their names will ever be endeared to me by the strongest ties of friendship, and I hope some day to be able to pay, in a degree, the deep debt of gratitude that I owe them. Mr. Stiles is now a resident of Bridgeport, Conn.

After such a drain on my physical and mental powers I could not think of doing heavy work, and I took an agency for selling books. I succeeded beyond my expectations, and had it not been for rum should have made a large amount of money.

In the midst of my prosperity, while traveling in Massachusetts I met a young man of my own age. After a somewhat lengthy conversation in which our views on various subjects coincided—both of us having had some sad experiences in the army—we seemed to glide swiftly into friendship. Though both of us had been addicted to drinking and suffered greatly thereby, we forgot all our bitter experiences of the past, and took a drink to cement our newly-formed friendship. This was enough to kindle the flame in both our breasts, for he had also been struggling against his worst enemy.

We could not remain in the place, as his people lived there, and rum had not succeeded in killing his respect for his family. We started on a spree and visited several towns in Worcester county—Fitchburg among the number—and finally went to Boston. There we became separated in some unaccountable manner, and the next thing I remember I was in Albany, at a hotel, in bed with my boots on. I dressed myself and went to the bar to drink, for my desire for liquor was terrible. I drank all day, and at night started for Worcester where I arrived, and having some money left, continued drinking.

Leaving Worcester I went to the village of Fitchburg, where I again had an attack of the tremens which lasted me about two days. I suffered all that mortal man could and live. When I was able to walk about

I tried hard to control my appetite, but the temptation to drink was strong; my mind was so shattered that I had but little strength to resist, and I again fell.

During my wanderings I reached New York city, and before a week was penniless. What to do I did not know, but made up my mind to start out afoot, either to die on the way or reach some place where I could obtain employment. When night came I lay down by the side of a fence, but no sleep could I get. My thoughts were as follows—What a poor wretch I am; no one to care for me; every man's hand raised against me; goaded by this desire for drink what will be the end? I am sure I shall never be any better, I have tried so often to no purpose. My good resolutions are as writing in the sand, and what is the use in my living any longer such a miserable life, being of no benefit to any one and an evil to myself. I had much better be dead; then I shall trouble no one.

With reflections like these I made my way over the fence and across a field, and came to a swamp. Picking my way through the bushes I discovered a large tree with projecting roots, and I once more lay down, finding a comfortable place between the roots; but I did not sleep. I could hear the frogs and lizards making their peculiar noises, while near by a whip-poor-will chanted his midnight serenade. Out in the adjacent swamp I could hear the shrill cry of the loons. I wished myself a loon, frog, or anything but what I was.

Getting up from where I lay I followed in the direction of some water which I heard dashing over the falls. The thought occurred to me that I would drown myself. On reaching the falls I fully determined to shuffle off this mortal coil. I thought to myself—No one will ever know who I am even if I am found. Mother will never know what has become of me, and I shall be free from all my sorrows—at least those that pertain to this world.

I never was more intent on carrying out any project than at that time. I went to the edge of the precipice and it looked as though it would be a favorable spot for my purpose, for I could hear the water roar below me as it struck on the rocks, and in the faint starlight I could see a black pool at the foot of the falls. The king of all evil was behind me urging me on, suggesting—This is just the place to end all your troubles; jump; don't stop to think, for if you do you will not. But my good angel whispered in my ear—Do not do it; for if you do you will awake in the regions of the damned.

A shudder passed through me at the thought of the great Hereafter and what would be my condition in the unknown world that I was about to rush into, unprepared to meet the Great Judge, and unable to say that I had ever done any good in the world I had left.

I began to step slowly back from the tempting spot —tempting, but still horrible to look down into as I imagined my own white, dead face floating on its dark crest. The thought became dreadful to contemplate; I turned and rushed wildly from the spot, not daring to turn my head. Tearing through the bushes as though the arch-fiend was in pursuit, I did not stop until I was panting with exertion at the distance of half-a-mile from the scene of my strong temptation. I then fell down on my knees in the grass, and poured forth my soul in thanks to God for my deliverance from such a death. I was all alone; no one to sympathize with; no one to help me; in a dismal swamp at the midnight hour. I wrestled in prayer with Him who truly is a friend to the friendless.

That night I shall never forget. The surrounding swamp, the tree beneath which I tried to sleep, and, above all, the dark pool and water-fall, are photographed on my brain. I sometimes dream it all over again, and when about to take the fatal leap, awaken in deep terror. Finding myself safe in my comfortable bed I am lead to realize the goodness of God, and to thank him for the many blessings that he has showered upon my unworthy head.

All the next day I traveled without food, but when night came I ventured to ask an Irishman who stood at his gate for something to eat.

"Sumthin' to ate, is it, me mon?" said he. "Sure an' ye shall, 'pon my soul; it never was said of Teddy O'Neil that a hungry mon passed his cabin whin he knew it. Hould on a bit till I spake to Biddy, an' sate yeself; sure, yer're looking weary."

I sat down on a bench by his humble cot, thinking how many of my own wealthy countrymen would have turned me from their doors, while this poor son of Erin was glad to divide his limited store with the needy. I heard his cheery voice in converse with Biddy, and was soon called into the cabin to partake of their humble but welcome fare.

"Now me mon," said Teddy, "yees can just ate as much as ye like of what is an Irishman's food—mate and pertatees—and welcum to yees."

I made a hearty meal and began my thanks. He stopped me with—

"None o' that; yees welcum and that's enuf; but is it drink that brought ye to this?"

"Yes, it is," said I.

"Well, I'm sorry for yees; you mustn't take too much; but take a glass wid me before yees travel."

That night I slept in a barn, and after traveling all the next day I came to a small village tavern. I had no money, yet I made up my mind to go in and trust to luck to get something to eat and drink. On entering I saw several men drinking at the bar; they seemed to be rather a jovial crowd, and considerably under the influence of liquor.

Weak, hungry, and faint, I made my way to the bench that ran across one side of the bar-room, seated myself, and was soon in a deep reverie, thinkingth at I was indeed a poor wreck of humanity doomed to a life of misery and wretchedness.

While pondering on my condition, one of the men came up and took a seat by my side; slapping me on the shoulder with his brawny hand, which made me cringe, he said—

"Well, stranger, which way are you traveling?"

"No particular place, sir," replied I.

"You don't look very well," said he, at the same

time giving me another slap on the knee, so forcibly that it brought me to my feet. "You are a tender chicken."

I informed him that I was tender, weak and hungry, dry, tired and wretched, without one cent in the world, or any one I could call my friend.

"Why, stranger! is it true that you are so situated?" said he, "I'll be your friend, and you shan't suffer as long as I have got a cent;" and he brushed a tear from his eye as he made the remark.

He had a noble heart, and was ready to open it to me although a stranger to him. Many times since my reformation have I thought of that man, and if I knew he was in want I would divide my last crust with him. He gave me a good meal of victuals at the hotel, and when he went away he told the landlord to keep me over night and not to take a cent from me. He also gave me five dollars, and said—

"Now I do not want you ever to pay this back; but when you are over your present difficulties and meet a man situated as you now are yourself, why, give him a helping hand, and by so doing I shall be amply repaid."

This man lived a few miles from the hotel and was a blacksmith, and if he is a sample of the men who follow that trade, God never made a better class.

For several days after this occurrence I traveled on foot, and faint and weary I reached a small village in Western Massachusetts, where I found work. I remained there several weeks, and then went to Valatie, New York, and worked at my trade for a time.

After giving up work at Valatie, I started to visit my parents who lived in the town of Catskill, near the village of Leeds. As usual, I stopped at several places and drank until I was unable to go farther, and lying down by the roadside I fell asleep. While there sleeping, a gentleman by the name of Henry Plank came along, took me into his carriage, and carried me home. By the time we arrived there the effects of the liquor had subsided and I was nearly sober.

On entering the house I first saw my mother, who sprang to meet me, but sank to the floor overcome. My father and sister also entered the room, and there was a new rendering of the Prodigal Son, although my case was not parallel with his; I had not spent my portion for a very good reason—I had not any to spend. But as to living on husks and sleeping on straw my experience somewhat resembled his.

The next day my mother told me how much she had suffered through rum, and how many sorrowful nights and days she had passed on my account. She pointed me to the grave of my dead brother, and told me how happy she was when we were all small children, although my father drank at the time. Then looking me in the face, a silent tear stealing down her withered cheek, she asked me if I wouldn't promise her to drink no more; that promise would smooth her way to the grave. Then I said to her—"*God helping me, not another glass of rum shall ever again pass my lips.*" Over six years have passed away, and I leave the public to judge whether I have faithfully kept that promise.

After some days of rest, my brother-in-law proposed to employ me to build him a house, which kept me busy for some time. When the house was finished he paid me, and I purchased a few necessary articles of clothing. One of my half-brothers, who had returned from California a few weeks previously, gave me some good advice, which strengthened me in my newly-formed resolutions.

It was my firm determination to lead a temperate life in whatever condition I might be placed; and not only to lead a temperate life, but to go out into the world and try and lead other suffering ones into the paths of sobriety. I had at that time no idea of ever becoming a Temperance Lecturer; but having had such bitter experiences, I felt a longing in my heart to tell the glad news that I had been enabled to keep my promise to my mother for such a length of time.

With about three dollars in my pocket I started out not knowing where I was going, and determined not to inform any one of my object. I went to Catskill, and found I could pass a rum-shop without going in to get a drink, although I had to fight hard against my appetite.

CHAPTER XXVII.

WHEN the steamboat came along I took passage for Albany, and from there I made my way to a small village less than a dozen miles from Troy. The name of the place I think was Pittstown. It was Saturday night, and not a person in the place had I ever seen before as far as I knew. Oh, how lonely I felt. I did not know any temperance men anywhere, and had no one to give me a helping hand. But I thought that the Lord would perhaps open the way for me.

I found out the residence of the minister, having made up my mind that it would be well for me to call on him. All the way to his house I prayed earnestly to God for help and strength to lead a sober life and do some good in the world.

I found the clergyman at home and he invited me into his house. After some time I mustered up courage enough to tell him my object in coming to the place. After hearing my story he asked me if I had ever spoken on Temperance. I told him I never had, but I thought I could tell some of my sad experiences and it might be the means of doing good. He did not seem willing to give me an opportunity, but said I had better go into something else, for it would be hard for me to get along and keep soul and body together in the Temperance cause.

"Well sir," I replied, "that may be good advice, but my mind is fully made up, and if I starve it will be fighting rum; I must combat King Alcohol, or else I may yet die a drunkard."

He said my cause was good, but he could not allow me to speak in his church. He invited me to stop over night with him, but no sleep came to my eyes. I lay thinking—What shall I do and where shall I go? Will the Lord put it in the heart of man or woman to help me in my good resolution?

Sunday was a stormy day, and on Monday I started on my travels. About two miles below I came to a small village, and on inquiring learned that a Methodist minister lived there. I called on him, and on conversing with him found that he was a noble-hearted man; the name of Rev. Mr. Creag will never fade from my memory. He was lame at the time and could not walk about, but when I told him how much I had suffered through rum, his great heart was opened, and he gave me to understand that he would help me to the extent of his ability. He informed me that there was to be a temperance meeting that evening about two miles from there, and he would arrange it so that I could speak after the regular address, which was to be given by a minister who was very much interested in the cause.

That evening I went to the meeting. After the clergyman had spoken about an hour he informed the audience that there was a stranger present who would like to say a few words, and then introduced me to the people. How I got to my feet I cannot tell, but I managed somehow to stand up; my knees trembled, and the perspiration stood in beads on my forehead. A weakness came over me and my brain reeled, for it was my first attempt to speak on Temperance. In a very embarrassed manner I told them what a life I had led and what my determination was. I never have had the pleasure of knowing what impression I made on the audience, but on taking a collection it footed up to about two dollars. After the meeting several came up, and, grasping me by the hand, bid me God speed in my good resolution.

The next morning I walked to the city of Troy and took the cars for Stockport, where I had an uncle then living. There I obtained the privilege of speaking in a school-house, and the people seemed very much interested in my remarks. I obtained twenty-seven names to the pledge and a collection of seventy-five cents. From there I went to Stuyvesant Falls and spoke, obtaining some forty names to the pledge and a dollar in money.

Returning to Stockport I spoke again, and obtained more signers. I continued holding meetings in the different villages with good success as far as obtaining signatures to the pledge went, but my compensation was so small that I was obliged to walk from place to place —often walking ten to sixteen miles during the day to speak the same evening in some dingy school house. Sometimes the boys would gather before the time and fill the room with tobacco smoke, and raise Ned generally. I spoke nearly all winter in and around Columbia county. Among the places that I visited were Chatham, East Chatham, Chatham Centre, Niver Village, Spencertown, Ghent and many others.

At one place a man who had been a hard drinker for many years came up and signed the pledge. It had a good effect on the audience, and I obtained seventy-five names that night and also a collection of five dollars which was the largest I had ever received up to that time. I was very much encouraged, and determined to persevere.

On one occasion an old man arose and said—

"Now Ladies and Gentlemen, this ere young man is doin' a good job, and he can't live on nothin'. S'pose we give him a donation. Now friends, go down deep in yer pockets."

He was a rich man, and I began to think I should get a good contribution. When the boxes were passed the old gentleman fumbled in his pockets and after a long search fished out three cents which he threw into the box, exclaiming—

"The laborer is worthy of his hire."

The whole amount given by this audience was about two dollars and a half. It was then about the middle of winter and I could get just enough to keep from actual starvation, but I did not feel discouraged in the least. I fought my appetite daily, and worked on.

One of the coldest days we had that winter—known

by many as "Cold Monday"—I had an appointment to speak at a place about seven miles from Valatie, where I was then stopping. No one ventured out on that day excepting on urgent business; but I made up my mind to go. About five o'clock I started on foot. When about half-way I became so chilled that I could go no further without warming. Rushing into a house I told them I was freezing, and they gave me a chair by the fire. When I had warmed I again started on, after thanking the family for their kindness. When I reached the building where I was going to lecture I found no fire. On going to the minister's house he seemed surprised to see me, and informed me that no one would venture out such a cold night, and said I had better stay by the fire with him and not think any more of speaking that night. He inquired how much money I had, and on learning that I had but ten cents in the world he put his hand in his pocket and handed me a dollar saying—

"Take that; it is all I have; if I had more you should have it."

I refused to take it, but he insisted and I accepted. This man was the Rev. Mr. Mead—one of the noblest men I ever met.

After I had got warmed I told him I must return to Valatie. He urged me to stay, but I thanked him for his hospitality and kindness, and walked through the piercing cold seven miles to my father's house.

CHAPTER XXVIII.

WHEN spring arrived I returned to Worcester, and made a visit to Mr. John B. Gough. Not finding him at home I was most hospitably entertained by his wife, and in the morning she sent her carriage with me into the city. Just before I started she handed me an envelope, at the same time saying—

"There is something to help you along: Mr. Gough is not at home, but I will do as he would if he was here."

On arriving at Worcester, I stepped into a store and opened the envelope, and found therein twenty dollars. It was a Godsend, for I was completely out of money.

I was acquainted with quite a number of people in Worcester, but knew no temperance men. On making inquiry, I found that Rev. Samuel Kelly, a good old Methodist Minister, was at work in the cause, and to his house I directed my steps. I found him to be a good man, and he introduced me to Mr. William Mccorney, a noble, self-sacrificing man, who had fought

King Alcohol all his days, and was then doing his best to defeat him. Mr. M. greeted me cordially, and promised that he would do all he could to aid me; up to this time he has done so faithfully, and in many ways. He proposed me as a member of the Sons of Temperance, and I joined the order. Never shall I forget the night I was initiated in old Rainbow Division. What a thrill went through me as they gathered around me, and called me brother. Well, thought I, if this is not a heaven on earth it comes near to it. It was new to me, and everything pertaining to the order shone in my eye with more than regal splendor.

I spoke that evening for a few moments, and they were so well-pleased that they wanted me soon afterwards to go to Boston with them on a visit to the Old Bay State Division. About sixty of us went down, and I was one of the speakers. I thought it was a great contrast to my first visit to Boston, for I was then on a regular spree, and, as before stated, awoke at an Albany hotel, in bed with my boots on, not knowing how I came there.

Soon afterwards, some of the temperance men of Worcester proposed to get me up a meeting in Mechanic's Hall, and give me a chance to speak to a large audience. The lecture was advertised for Sunday evening, and before the hour of meeting the hall was filled—seats, standing-room, and every available place; and hundreds went away unable to obtain admission. I never had stood before so large an audience, and when I saw such a sea of faces turned towards me as we sat on the platform, my heart beat quick and loud, while my courage nearly forsook me. I kept praying to myself that I might have Divine assistance to carry me through. Rev. Mr. Tyler presided, and after prayer introduced me. On rising to speak I felt a chill run through me, but after saying a few words I felt more at home, and spoke one hour and a half. No one left the hall during my address, and the clapping of hands gave me to understand that the people were pleased.

The next day the Spy, and the Gazette, gave reports of the lecture, complimenting it, probably, more than it deserved. I would here insert the notices, but it would border too much on egotism were I to do so. Vanity and pride I hope will never find a lodgment in my heart. I have nothing in the world to boast of. All I am and all I ever expect to be, I owe to the cause I advocate. They endeavored to take a collection for me, but the hall was so crowded that it was found impossible to get through it, and it was abandoned after securing about thirty-five dollars.

Soon after this meeting I began to receive calls to go and speak in different places in the vicinity of Worcester. Among the towns to which I was invited were West Boylston, Shrewsbury, Northboro', Sutton, Millbury, Cherry Valley, Oxford, Webster, Charlton, Southbridge, Brookfield, Hubbardston, Clinton, Lancaster, Ashland, Hopkinton, Marlboro', Hudson, etc. I remained in Massachusetts and Rhode Island during the summer, speaking in some places two or three times. At Woonsocket and Providence I found friends. Peter B. Holmes of Woonsocket and Henry Woodworth of

Providence took me by the hand, and proved themselves friends both by words and deeds, and while I live they will be cherished in my memory as dear and valued friends.

When winter came I determined to go to Maine and offer my services. On my way from Worcester to Boston I fell in with Hon. L. M. Pond, who was then a member of the Legislature from Worcester. He treated me very cordially, and I saw that he was a noble man. On reaching Boston he took my hand, wished me Godspeed in my work, and expressed the hope that I might be enabled to keep my pledge and do much good in the world. As he was about to leave me he slipped something into my hand, and told me to call on him when I returned from Maine, and he would help me more. After he had departed I looked at the little roll, and found to my surprise that he had given me twenty-five dollars. On my return he gave me a check for one hundred dollars more, taking my note on demand which he has never yet asked me to pay. I can truly say that Hon. L. W. Pond of Worcester has helped me more than any other living man.

On my arrival at Portland I found Mr. Rich ready to make my appointments through the State, and I spent some time there. A better, nobler-hearted class of people than the tall sons of Maine I have yet to find. During my tour I visited Lewiston, Bangor, Belfast, Rockland, Augusta, and a large number of other towns.

At Augusta I addressed the members of the Legislature and their wives at the State House. Rev. D.

B. Randall had made the arrangements for my address to the Assembly, and, having never seen me, he was somewhat taken by surprise at finding me so young and such a small-sized man.

"Why," said he, "brother Dutcher, I am afraid you will make a failure; such a little fellow as you are, to go before such big men."

He was a very tall man, and had to look down while speaking to me.

"Well," I replied, "what there is of me is hardy, and you must recollect that it is not always the largest horse that draws the heaviest load."

"Now," said he, "let us get down on our knees, and I will pray for you."

He did so, and on rising he laid his hand gently on my shoulder and said—

"Now, my little fellow, I hope the Lord is with you. Do your best to-night."

The State House was full to over-flowing, and I spoke just two hours. When I got through Mr. Randall laid his hand on my head and exclaimed—"You'll do!" Many gathered around me, taking me by the hand, and some one proposed three cheers, which was responded to with hearty good will.

At Lewiston the crowd was so immense that hundreds were unable to obtain admission to the hall the second evening that I spoke.

The next day a merchant by the name of Darrow, I think, offered me seventy-five dollars to speak the next night and give the merchants a chance to hear me. I consented to do so, and he immediately threw out the notes, made the announcement, and advertised to sell tickets. This fact coming to the ears of some of the temperance men, they came and asked me to decline speaking, for if any one was to make money out of my lecture it should be the temperance men. I informed them that if they desired it I would see the gentleman who had engaged me, and if he was willing to give way I would gladly sacrifice the seventy-five dollars and not speak, although I needed the money very much. On seeing Mr. D. about it he was not willing to let me off, but finally said if my temperance friends would pay him for all the expense and trouble he had had, he would let me off. Mr. Getchel said he would do so, and immediately paid the money; I did not lecture and, of course, lost the seventy-five dollars. The temperance men then told me that they would arrange for me to come again soon, and give me one hundred and fifty dollars if it could possibly be raised.

After a few weeks I went back to Lewiston and spoke again, but it proved a very stormy evening, and the receipts were small. But Mr. Putnum, one of the best men I ever met, gave me sixteen dollars out of his own pocket, making the sum in all about thirty-five dollars. I had a pleasant time at Mr. Putnum's house, and left with many kind wishes for my future welfare.

At Bangor I spoke two nights in the City Hall; both meetings were presided over by the Mayor. The second evening the hall was crowded, and many went away unable to obtain seats or standing room. The Mayor congratulated me, and I felt much encouraged.

The people were not satisfied, as many had been unable to hear me, and it was arranged that I should speak in Norumbega Hall and charge twenty-five cents for admission, which I accordingly did. I wish to express my thanks to George Vincent for his hospitality, and for all the kindness shown me by him and his wife. Long may he live to do good in the great cause that we both love. Mr. Vincent is now a resident of Somerville, Mass.

At Waterville I met the noble Joshua Nye, who for more than thirty years has been a hard worker in the Temperance cause; giving not only his time but his money; opening his house to Temperance lecturers, and striving to do something to save the poor victims of strong drink. At my lecture Mr. Nye distributed Temperance papers to the audience, having a bundle of them under his arm, one of which he gave to every person who came in during the meeting.

After my address they invited me to return and speak again. I accepted the invitation and met Mr. Nye a second time. He is now a resident of Augusta.

After my engagements in Maine had been filled, I was invited to speak in some towns in New Hampshire. The first address I ever made in this state was in Brookline, near the border line of Massachusetts. Rev. Geo. Eaton, a Methodist clergyman wrote to Dr. Stowell about me; and as they were to have a Temperance anniversary I was invited to deliver the address. It was arranged for me to speak in a grove near the town, but when the hour arrived it began to rain, and we were obliged to give up the idea of holding a meeting in the open air and repaired to the church, and it was filled to overflowing.

I had a glorious time, and as I look over my temperance field for the last six years I cannot think of one place where I enjoyed it better than I did in Brookline. A bountiful collation was furnished by the ladies at the Town Hall, and every one seemed to enjoy the meeting to the fullest extent.

Dr. Stowell placed twenty-five dollars in my hand just before I left, and when I seated myself in the carriage that was to take me to the depot, the band struck up "Hail Columbia," while the driver held the prancing steeds. After the music ceased they gave me three rousing cheers, and with the words, "God bless you," from a hundred lips, I left them, realizing what a blessed work it was to be engaged in the Temperance cause and meet such warm-hearted people. The kindness I received stimulated me to renewed effort in the cause, and left such an impression on my heart that it must ever remain burning—I trust—with renewed zeal. There is nothing in this world that will bring the tear from my eye like kindness from any source, and even now, as I think of that good time in that quiet country village up in the hills of the Old Granite State, I can hardly keep back the tears; and my heart swells with gratitude to those kind friends who cheered me on through the toilsome path which every one who works in this cause must travel.

Rev. Mr. Eaton, who was instrumental in introducing me to these good people, once preached in Brookline, and is now at Winchendon, Mass. Up to this time he has been a kind friend to me, and I cherish him as a brother; and his noble wife has been to me a sister. God bless brother George Eaton and his good wife! May their days be many, and may the choicest blessings of Heaven be showered upon them to lighten up their pathway while traveling through life's journey here below; and may they at last be transplanted into the green fields, by the side of the river that flows by the throne of God. My heart is full; I can say no more.

CHAPTER XXIX.

SOON after this I spoke again in Mechanic's Hall in Worcester and then received an invitation to go to Providence. While lecturing in that vicinity I joined the Olive Branch Temple of Honor, and the brothers greeted me so warmly that I shall ever cherish a kind regard for all of them, and especially for Rev. Henry Woodworth. During my stay in Rhode Island I lectured several times in Providence; also in Pawtucket, Phœnix, Newport, Crompton, Woonsocket, and other places. At Newport I met Rev. Charles H. Malcolm, and spoke in his church. I considered him a noble christian, a polished gentleman and a worker for the elevation of mankind, with a pitying heart for all who are the victims of intemperance, or suffering in any way.

About this time I received an invitation to speak in New York and some of the towns adjoining the metropolis. On the expiration of my engagements in New York, I went on a tour up the Hudson, speaking in Saugerties, Coxsackie, Stuyvesant, New Baltimore and Troy.

On returning to New York I was induced to go to Philadelphia, and on my arrival was engaged to lecture for some thirty evenings through the state. The Methodist Conference was in session at Harrisburg, and my first address was to be delivered there. On reaching Harrisburg I made my way to the State House to see the Governor, Hon. John W. Geary. I found him in his private room, and he took me by the hand and said—

"Mr. Dutcher, I welcome you to the state of Pennsylvania. We need your services, and I hope much good will be done by your lectures in the state. I dine at one o'clock, and I would be happy to have you take dinner with me."

I could do no more than to accept his cordial invitation, for I liked him from the first. I saw that he was a polished gentleman, and an open-hearted man. On leaving the State House for his mansion he took my arm as we walked along. He is a well-built, tall, noble-looking man, and I had to look up to talk with him. I remarked—

"Governor, this is quite an honor to walk arm in arm with you, for I am nothing but a poor, reformed man, born in obscurity and poverty." He cut me short by saying—

"Oh, what difference does that make? You are just as good as I am. I do not feel my position at all, and we are all free and equal. I am nothing but a servant to the people, and my greatest desire is to do good. When I was elected governor of this state I made up my mind to do right, whatever might come. I have set up my standard and on it I have inscribed "Right;" and when a question comes before me I look at both sides and then decide for the right." What a world this would be if all governors would do the same.

On reaching his house he gave me to understand that I must make myself at home. When dinner was announced we walked into the dining-room and the Governor and myself were the only ones at the table. I enjoyed the meal very much. After we had satisfied the inner man we repaired to the parlor, where he entertained me in a very interesting manner by conversing on the temperance cause and giving me his experience while in the army. He was several times wounded, and had many narrow escapes, and said that it was only through the mercy of God that he was spared. He has since united with the Church, and is not only a strong temperance man but a devoted christian.

Bishop Scott was presiding at the Conference, and he gave me a chance to speak before the Assembly of Ministers. In the afternoon, announcement was made that I would speak in the Court-House, and when evening came the building was filled with clergymen and citizens of Harrisburg. Rev. Mr. Tasker of Philadelphia presided. He is a man well-known for his liberality and christian character. After my address he arose and said—

"Gentlemen, I have been highly pleased with the address that I have heard; Mr. Dutcher ought to speak in every town and city in the land. Such an experience as his will reach a heart of stone, and I believe if we should crown him with laurels it would be no more than he deserves, and it would not make him proud; I think he would still be the same humble man."

I give this encomium not to adulate myself, but to show what were the feelings of this good man. A collection was taken up which amounted to thirty-five dollars, after which the audience gave three hearty cheers. Mr. Tasker then announced that I would speak again the next evening; which I did to a full house.

From Harrisburg I went to Reading where I spoke two evenings. From there I went to Wrightsville and other places in the vicinity. I then visited Lancaster where I spoke two evenings. Here I met the Hon. James Black, and spent a pleasant time at his house. Many proved themselves my warm friends by taking me by the hand and bidding me God-speed on my glorious mission. I remember Lancaster with no small degree of pleasure. One evening I spoke before the young men in the College near that city, and then turned my face towards Philadelphia, lecturing along at the different towns on the route.

On my arrival at Philadelphia, I found they had advertised me to speak there in a large hall, at the corner of Eighth and Spring Garden streets, I think. The tickets of admission to the lecture and another entertainment connected, were placed at fifty cents; but the hall was crowded. From the City of Brotherly Love I started on my return to the East. When we had got well under way, a young lady came passing through the car, and when she came to where I was sitting she took a seat by my side. After riding about fifteen minutes, she looked towards me and said—

"I have lost my pocket-book."

This announcement rather startled me, for I thought by the way she spoke that she had a suspicion I had stolen it. On my inquiring about it, she stated that she had lost it going from the Northern Pennsylvania Depot to the Kensington, and that it contained all the money she had. She said she could not have gone to New York had not the superintendent given her a pass.

My sympathy was immediately aroused in her behalf. Very soon she took from her traveling-bag a book, and began to read it. I had a curiosity to see what the title was, and she held it so I could plainly do so. I observed that it was the "Life of Jesus." This gave me a more favorable impression still. I said to her—

"That is a very pretty little book you have there, and it must be interesting."

"Yes," she replied, "it gives me great comfort to read it, for I always trust in Jesus when in affliction."

When we got on board the steamer at Amboy for New York I made up my mind to raise some money for her. There was but one man on board that I was acquainted with, and I asked him first. He gave his contribution, and every one whom I asked to do so gave something. During my round I came to a German and solicited his, also.

"Yes," said he, "I gives von tollar, an if dat be not monish enuf I vill gib von tollar more."

"Coming to a gentleman seated between two ladies I told him the circumstances, and he was about to give, when one of the ladies remarked that she claimed the right herself, and gave me one dollar. I succeeded in raising double what she said she had lost, and taking it down to the ladies' cabin placed it in her hand. She seemed thankful, and when the boat arrived at New York I took her in a hack to Lovejoy's Hotel and paid her bill until the next day at which time she was to take the boat for Albany, where she said she resided. She gave me the street and number where she lived, and the name of her uncle. Bidding her good-evening, I took the train for Boston.

Several months afterwards I was in Albany, and thought I would call on the young lady; but I found out there was no such number as she gave me on the street designated, and on consulting the directory I found no such man as she represented her uncle to be. I concluded that I had been sold, and for once in my life been a victim to the wiles of the fair sex. But I must confess that no actress on the stage ever played their part to better perfection than this unassuming young lady of eighteen summers.

She done her level best.

CHAPTER XXX.

DURING the next four weeks I spoke in the different towns near Boston, including Lynn, Saugus, Medford, Malden, Swampscott, Milton, Lower Falls; also in Worcester.

From Worcester I went to Boston, having received a letter from Wendell Phillips inviting me to come to his house. I found him in his study and he greeted me very cordially, making inquiry about my welfare and seeming to take a deep interest in me. I admired him exceedingly, for he had no ostentatious way with him and conversed with me as freely as though I had been the Governor. He invited me to walk with him, and on reaching the street he took my arm and made me feel perfectly at home in his company. When the time came for me to leave, he gave me two very useful books and handed me ten dollars, saying "The strong must help the weak." With a parting shake of the hand I left his house, feeling that my visit had not been without gain to me in many ways. I had received valuable advice and been greatly encouraged in my work, and have since been greatly benefited from his counsel.

There was a great contrast between Mr. Phillips and some other persons whom it has been my fortune to meet; no egotism or false pride were noticeable in his manner, actions or words. I could not realize that I was in the company of one of the most polished orators America ever produced. Descended from one of the first families of New England and reared in opulence, with all his wealth and high position he realizes that there are people in the world needing sympathy and encouragement. I often meet him, and always receive a kind, affectionate welcome, and leave his presence strengthened and encouraged, and go on my way a happier man.

On returning to Worcester I received a call from Franklin Whipple, and after spending a pleasant hour with him he left with many wishes for my continued prosperity, at the same time slipping a five-dollar bill into my hand. From that time to the present Mr. Whipple has been a true friend to me, and I have never been to him for a favor but what it has been readily granted. In looking over my numerous friends, I can think of none who would do more to aid me than this warm-hearted Christian gentleman. The world would be much better if there were more Franklin Whipples.

On my next visit to Boston I received an invitation from Mr. May, who was then Grand Worthy Patriarch of the Sons of Temperance, to speak in connection with that order under directions, and arranged to do so. I spoke in Swansey, South Braintree, North and East Bridgewater, Weymouth, Abington, Hingham,

Kingston, Plymouth and many other places. At Plymouth I had the pleasure of standing on Plymouth Rock, and of visiting Pilgrim Hall, where many old relics are kept. Numerous articles brought over in the May Flower are here to be seen. I was carried back, in imagination, to the time when our Pilgrim Fathers left their homes and all they held dear, to cross a tempestuous and almost unknown ocean, to find a home in the New World where they could worship God with freedom of thought and action. After my engagement with Mr. May was filled I received a call to lecture in New Jersey, and spoke in Elizabeth, Newark, Monmouth, Keyport, Jersey City and other places. The audiences were large and I found a warm reception, and though many consider New Jersey as out of the United States, I believe that it is not only a part of the United States but that the time is not far distant when it will rank as one of the most enterprising and flourishing states in the Union.

From New Jersey I went to Philadelphia, and spoke in Siloam Church. Geo. W. Hicks of that city also made an address. Mr. Hicks has been engaged in the temperance cause for many years; is a fine speaker and a noble man. We need more of the same sort. I hope he may live long to do good, and in the great day to come receive his reward.

One morning on coming down to breakfast at the hotel where I was stopping, I was seated opposite a fine, gentlemanly-looking person. During the meal we conversed on several different subjects and I was favorably impressed with him. About noon he came in, and I saw at a glance that he was considerably under the influence of liquor. Coming up to me, he slapped me on the shoulder and said—

"Come, let us take a drink."

I informed him that I must decline his invitation, for I was a temperance man.

"You a temperance man!" said he. "Well, I am glad of it. I wish I was, myself, but I am not; so I must have a drink."

After he had imbibed his liquor he came to me and said—

"What is your business?"

I told him it was to do all I could to save such men as himself.

"Do you think you can do anything for me?" said he.

I replied that I hoped so; for as fine a looking man as he ought not to fill a drunkard's grave.

"Now, friend," said he, "I have drunk liquor enough to float a seventy-four gun frigate, and have probably spent fifty thousand dollars for rum; I want to be a sober man, and if you will stick to me for three days I will never drink another drop of the vile stuff; but I want you to do just as I say."

I told him I would do anything that was honorable, and would stay with him three days if at the end of that time he would promise to drink no more. The agreement was made, and the first thing he did was to hire a hack. We took seats in it, and he directed the driver to take us to the Park. On the way there he frequently stopped to take a drink at the bars we passed, and when he remained longer than I thought prudent, I would go in, gently lay my hand on his shoulder, and say—"Come, it is time we were going," when he would walk out without saying a word, and get into the carriage. I found out that he was a prominent business man of New York, and well-known in Philadelphia and throughout the country. I remained with him three days, at the expiration of which time he said—

"You have fulfilled your promise. You have taken good care of me, and now, to pay you, I will never drink another glass of liquor as long as I live."

He immediately took the train for New York, where I promised to meet him at a hotel on Courtlandt street at a stated time. I was there punctually, and when I stepped into the hotel he came across the hall with his hand extended, exclaiming—

"Oh, how glad I am that you have come! I want you to go home with me."

We took the ferry-boat and crossed over to where he resided. I found him living like a prince, and a happier time I never spent in my life. His house has always been just like home to me since, and the last time I saw him he said—

"George, my boy, I have kept my pledge."

While in New York I met Col. J. C. O. Redington, who at that time was Grand Worthy Patriarch of Western New York, and he made an engagement with me for my services in that part of the state. The appointments were made for me, and I lectured in many of the towns and cities, and organized several Divisions of the Sons of Temperance. Some of the places I visited were Geneva, Waterloo, Canandagua, Buffalo, Westfield, Dunkirk, and Fredonia. My audiences were very large, and some of the Divisions organized numbered from eighty to one hundred and twenty-five members.

I formed the acquaintance of the Grand Secretary, J. A. Shaw of Jeddo, Orleans Co., and passed a pleasant time with him. He is one of the best men it has been my lot to meet, and has endeared himself to me by the strongest ties of fraternal friendship.

At Buffalo I stopped at the Tremont House kept by Mr. Thorp, a strong temperance man. One day two men came in and inquired for something to drink.

"Yes, gentlemen," said he, "come right this way."

They followed him up stairs, and, going to the water faucet, he let on the water, and said—

"There, gentlemen, help yourselves; this is the kind of drink we have here."

They informed him that they wanted some whisky.

"Well," said he, "if you want that kind of drink you must go somewhere else for it. We drink cold water here in this hotel."

They left, muttering to themselves about being mistaken in the place.

At one town where I organized a large society, some half-dozen of the signers were considerably intoxicated. But they were in earnest, and I obligated them, and I have since heard that they have faithfully kept their pledge and are good workers in the temperance ranks.

During my tour in Western New York I met with

a warm reception, and formed the acquaintance of a large number of temperance men. At one place a hotel-keeper came to the meeting; after hearing me lecture he came up and took me by the hand, and greeted me in a very feeling manner, expressing the hope that the day would not be far distant when no man would be in the degrading business of liquor selling. Drawing a large silver coin from his pocket, he said—

"There, Mr. Dutcher, that piece of money I have carried for years, but I want you to take it and keep it, and whenever you look at the coin remember that one man sells liquor who can think right, although he may not always follow the dictates of his conscience."

After I had finished lecturing in that part of the state I started for New Jersey to fill an engagement. On the way down I called to see my parents. It was late in the evening when I arrived, and they had retired. After considerable pounding I succeeded in awakening them, and my father came and let me in. I had purchased a present for him, and laid it on the table saying—

"There, father, is something I have bought you."

A tear glistened in his eye, for he had a tender heart. After a long pause he looked up and said—

"George, do you ever mention anything about me in your lectures?"

I informed him that I did, sometimes.

"Do you tell them that I am a drunkard?"

I informed him that I told the people that he still drank. After another long silence he looked up and said—

"That don't sound well, for your poor old father to be a drunkard and you trying to do good in the temperance cause."

The next morning he said to me—

"George, I have not slept all night, thinking of what you told me. If you will draw up a pledge I will sign it, and by God's help I will never break it."

I drew up the pledge, and with a trembling hand he signed his name. Mother requested to have her name there also; and a relative of mine who was with us said—

"I guess, George, I will sign it, also;" and he placed his name to the pledge, exclaiming, "I have drank all the rum I ever shall."

He had been a faithful soldier in the army, and no better or more noble-hearted man can be found anywhere, than Andrew Youngs.

That was a joyful time at that little home in the woods; no doubt my dear mother offered up a secret prayer that God might strengthen us all to prove faithful to the vow we had taken—for I had signed with the rest, though pledged as I already was, for I thought my signing might have a good influence. When the time arrived for me to go my way, father brought out his old horse, hitched him into a rickety wagon, and took me to the Hudson River where I could get on board a steamboat for New York. When I alighted from the wagon I took my father by the hand and said to him—

"Remember what you have done," and with the words—"God bless you," I stepped on board the steamboat and was soon gliding down the noble river. I stood and watched him from the upper deck, as he sat in his wagon, straining his eyes to get a glimpse of me as we were being separated, and soon we could see each other no more. I offered up a fervent prayer that he might have strength to keep that pledge. Some time after this I received a letter from my sister, stating that he had done so, faithfully.

A few days afterward I went to Leeds, near where my father lived, and organized a temperance society, and had the pleasure of placing the regalia upon my father's neck and making him a Son of Temperance. Not one drop of liquor has passed his lips since that time. He is now a member of the "Praying Band" in Valatie, N. Y. *"How wonderful are thy ways, O Lord!"*

There had been a great temperance revival at Poughkeepsie, and it was still progressing at this time. Hundreds had signed the pledge, and many a poor drunkard's wife and children were made happy. The work was pushed on through the untiring efforts of Edward Cummings, Mr. Guernsey, and several other gentlemen, including Dr. Barton. Meetings were held in the neighboring towns and the whole country felt their influence. Mr. Cummings was afterwards made Grand Worthy Patriarch of the Sons of Temperance of Eastern New York. I have spent many a happy hour with him, and hope he may live long to do great good.

Mr. Guernsey has also endeared himself to me by many acts of kindness which I may never be able to repay.

My first address at Poughkeepsie was made in Pine's Hall, and they immediately engaged me to speak again. Finally, I established my headquarters there for a time, and spoke not only to audiences in the city, but through neighboring towns—Fishkill, Dover, Rhinebeck, Plattekill, Matteawan, and many others.

One day I met Count Vanwyck. He had suffered from the use of strong drink, and promised to sign the pledge, and he did so at Mr. Cumming's office. He was a man of intelligence, and had formerly practiced law in Brooklyn. He proved himself a glorious worker, and his influence in his native place was so great that hundreds signed the pledge, and much good was done by his efforts. The last I knew of him he was still true to his obligation, with many bright prospects for the future.

While in Poughkeepsie, I was invited to speak in Steinway Hall, New York; after doing so I went to Brooklyn and Jersey City and spoke in several churches. This was in the winter of 1868, and having spent what time I intended to in New York, I went to Cleveland, Ohio, and from there to Toledo, where I spoke by invitation of Col. De Wolf who at that time was at the head of the temperance movement in the State. He took me to his home, and I had a very pleasant time under his hospitable roof. He was also the Superintendent of the Public Schools in Toledo.

From there I went to Detroit, and for the first time met Rev. John Russell, who is now Most Worthy Chief Templar of the United States and candidate for Vice President. He engaged me to travel through the

State, and I lectured in Detroit, Ridgeway, Mount Clemens, Marion City, St. Clair, Saginaw City, South Saginaw, Bay City, Ann Arbor, Battle Creek, and many other places. The meetings were well attended, and at some places the halls were not large enough to accommodate the people who came to hear me.

At one place a poor drunkard came to me, grasped my hand, and told me his misery and degradation. Said he—

"There is a dollar; the only one I have in the world, and I want you to take it and let me sign the pledge."

I told him I did not want his dollar, but he said if I did not take it he would not sign the pledge. I was obliged to accept his money, and he signed, and I have been informed that he has remained firm and is now restored to his family, a happy man.

On completing my engagement in Michigan, I received the following letter from the Grand Secretary.

BELLEVUE, MICHIGAN, APRIL 15th, 1868.
GEO. M. DUTCHER:

Worthy Brother:—

I have just returned from Detroit, and regret that I did not have the pleasure of meeting you before you left the state. I believe you have made many valuable impressions upon the minds of our people where you have lectured and I hope you have formed no unfavorable opinion of us.   Fraternally,

JOHN EVANS, G. W. S.

CHAPTER XXXI.

ON my way from Detroit to New York I fell in with Hon. George M. Buttrick, of Barre, Mass., and received from him an invitation to lecture in that town.

On my return to Massachusetts I spoke in Barre, and all of the expenses were paid by Mr. Buttrick, who is ever ready to give for any good cause. Subsequently, I spent a Sabbath in Barre by his invitation, speaking at the Methodist church in the morning, at the Congregational church in the afternoon, and at the Town Hall in the evening. Mr. Buttrick paid all the bills and allowed no one to give a dollar. I have ever found him a firm friend.

On returning to New York city, I found letters inviting me to lecture in many places in New York and New Jersey. At Nyack on the Hudson, I spoke in the Republican wigwam to a large gathering of people, on the 27th day of August, 1868. During my address, a man arose in the audience, and twirling his hat in his hand, shouted at the top of his voice—

"Hurrah for Dutcher! That's so; every word is truth."

I could not proceed for a time. I knew nothing but kindness would save him; so I invited him to come and take a seat on the platform.

"Certainly, I will," he replied; and he made his way to the stage, and, reaching out his hand, said—

"I know I am a slave to drink; but, God helping me, I will reform." That night he stood up and told the people how rum had robbed him of a fortune and a good name, and he closed up by saying—

"Ladies and gentlemen; I am determined to spend the remainder of my life a sober man. The next morning I saw him, and he was still of the same mind. I believe he has since been true to his pledge.

While in New York I was introduced to James Hodges Esq., a large builder in the city. His place of business was at No. 9 Vestry Street, and his residence was at Bound Brook, New Jersey. He wanted me to speak in Dr. Roger's Church in that place, which I did on Sunday afternoon. After the address, some of the temperance men, including Mr. Hodges, requested me to return and speak in the Methodist church, and I did so gladly, and to a full house. Mr. Hodges has been like a brother to me, and has often encouraged me in my temperance work by acts of kindness; while I live I shall ever remember his name, with deep feelings of thankfulness that it was ever my good fortune to meet him and his family.

About this time I received a letter from Thadeus Fairbanks, of St. Johnsbury, Vermont, suggesting that if I ever came that way, I should speak in his village, and I determined to pay Vermont a visit. I spoke at Bellows Falls, Brattleboro, Chester, Woodstock, Montpelier, Windsor, St. Johnsbury, Lyndon, Brandon, Vergennes, Middlebury, St. Albans, and other places. I enjoyed the tour very much, and was led to believe that the people of Vermont are the most temperate, moral, and happy people whom it has been my good fortune to become acquainted with.

At St. Albans I met the late Hon. Lawrence Brainard, who greeted me with much kindness. He said, as he handed me some money—

"When you first began to speak I made up my mind to give you two dollars and fifty cents; when you was half through I concluded to give you five dollars; but before you finished speaking I determined to make it ten dollars."

On my return home I received from Mr. T. Fairbanks a check for fifty dollars, as a present. Mr. Stewart, of St. Johnsbury, at whose house I was very hospitably entertained, is proprietor of the boardinghouse connected with the large Scale manufactory of Mr. Fairbanks, and, as a temperance man and a warmhearted gentleman, it is hard to find his equal. Mrs. Stewart is a lady of great piety and warmness of heart. She is ever ready to do all in her power to raise up the fallen and relieve the unfortunate.

After my return from Vermont, I visited Lisbon and Littleton, and some other places in New Hampshire, and then went to New York. A Newton Locke invited me to Glens Falls, where I met with success. Mr. Locke is a gentleman of great ability and integrity, and has proved to be my warm friend. During my tour I spoke in nearly all the towns in Washington county.

I then went to Washington, D. C., and when returning spoke two nights in Baltimore, one evening at Harvre De Grace, two evenings in Wilmington, Delaware, and also in Smyrna, Dover, and other towns in that state. From there I went to Trenton, N. J.

Having determined to visit the Provinces, I took the steamer at Boston, for St. Johns in New Brunswick, where I safely arrived. During my stay at St. Johns I spoke three times in Institute Hall. The large building was completely filled each night. I also spoke in Carleton and Portland, and in Fredrickton, the capitol of New Brunswick. I was most cordially welcomed and hospitably entertained during my stay, and my visit to the British Provinces will long be remembered by me. I could give many interesting incidents that transpired there, but will mention but one as a sample of many.

While walking on Prince William street, a gentleman stopped me, and said—

"I heard you lecture last evening, and I wish you would come to my shop and see a man, working for me, who is a slave to drink. He is just getting over a spree, and is all unstrung. He will surely die unless he can be influenced to sign the pledge."

I went with the gentleman to his shop, and found the man he had reference to, trying to press a coat by the light of a tallow candle. The perspiration was streaming from his face through weakness, and his whole frame trembled. Oh, how I pitied that man! He said he had a good mother in Scotland, and she, no doubt, was praying daily for him. After some conversation I requested him to sign the pledge; he consented to do so, and with a trembling hand placed his name on the paper. I pressed his hand, wished him Godspeed, and left him, feeling more fully convinced than ever before, that rum was the most gigantic evil that has visited the human race.

I cannot pass over this sketch of my lecturing tour in New Brunswick, without mentioning the names of Oscar D. Whetmore and John March of St. Johns, and John Richards of Frederickton. Language is inadequate to express my gratitude to them for all the kindness shown me during my stay. In whatever position I may be placed, I will ever cherish their memory, and associate them with happy days which passed away in their company.

On returning to the States I received an invitation from Judge Barbour and Capt. Ezra S. Williams to lecture in Hartford. I spoke in the afternoon on the State House steps, and in the evening in the hall of the Good Samaritans. I then went to Middletown, and spoke four times on Sunday. In the evening the meeting was at the South Congregational church, and the audience was a very large one. I here met Lieut Gov. Douglass, and he gave me a fine letter of recommendation, and expressed the wish that I might speak in every town in the State.

The way being open for me, I passed the winter of

1870, lecturing in Connecticut, speaking three or four times in some places. I spoke in Hartford, New Haven, Bridgeport, Norwich, Waterbury, Litchfield, Winsted, Stafford Springs, Wolcottville, Ansonia, Naugatuck, Birmingham, Norwalk, Danbury, Bethel, New Britain, Fair Haven, and numerous other towns. It was one of the most agreeable winters I ever spent in the temperance field, and whenever I hear people speaking disparagingly about the Wooden Nutmeg State, I always defend it; for I must confess that Connecticut is, to me, a very dear State. The good people received me with such open-heartedness and liberality that I shall not forget them. Often since, I have been called to lecture in many places which I visited that winter, and I am always greeted with large audiences, and they seem to do all they can to make me comfortable and happy. Among my choicest friends, none do I cherish with feelings of greater admiration than Ezra S. Williams of Hartford. I had a very pleasant time with him on a lecturing tour down the beautiful Connecticut, speaking at Higganum, Haddam, Chester, Deep River, and other towns. At New Haven I have always found a home in the family of J. J. Dutcher, and the debt of gratitude I owe them, it will be hard for me to pay. I hope if they do not receive their reward for all they have done for me in this world they will in the one to come.

In the summer of 1871 I again went to New Brunswick, and spoke in Fredrickton, Woodstock, St. Andrews, St. Stephens, St. George, and other places. Also in Calais, Maine, on a Sunday evening, to a very large audience in the Congregational church. While stopping at the Bradley House in Fredrickton, N. B., which, by the way, is a temperance house and a good one, I fell in with a man who seemed to be just getting over a hard spree. In conversation with him he asked me what business I was engaged in. I informed him that I was a temperance lecturer, and was to speak in the City Hall Sunday evening.

"Well," said he, "I am a good subject for you to lecture to." Then he told me that he was a school teacher, and was teaching about five miles above the city, but had been on a terrible spree for a long time; and, certainly, his appearance did not belie his words.

I took a deep interest in him, for he was one of the most intelligent men I had ever met. The next day I went to his house, and found everything as he had stated. Two bright little children were playing on the door step, and his wife looked sad and gloomy. On my return I pictured to him his little home, and how foolish it was for him to drink. At the Sunday evening meeting he came up and said—

"I will sign the pledge if it kills me." He has never broken it; but has ever trusted in God for strength to keep it, and I have no doubt but he will prove true to the end. He is now a teacher of a large public school in Massachusetts.

In the winter of 1872 I lectured, principally, in New England, many times driving from place to place in a private conveyance. One evening, I borrowed a horse of S. E. Carleton of South Worcester, to go to Oakdale. Mr. Edward Stone accompanied me. On the way out, the old horse stumbled, and down he went, and came near throwing us over a high embankment. We managed to arrive only five minutes late, but on the way home we used up the better part of three hours, although the distance is not much over eight miles. We had a hearty laugh over the affair, and Mr. Carleton concluded that if the horse could not stand up on his way to a temperance meeting, he did not want him any longer, and he disposed of the animal shortly afterward.

During the latter part of March and the early part of April, 1872, I lectured in Hartford, Suffield, Thompsonville, and South Manchester, Connecticut; and in Lee, Pittsfield, and Lenox Furnace, Massachusetts. At the latter place I stopped with a gentleman who had been connected with the glass business many years; during a recent revival under the preaching of the Rev. Mr. Wright, he and his whole family, including the hired man, had been converted. A more happy and more devoted family I never met.

At Lee, I met Mr. W. Smith, and received from him not only words of sympathy, but something more substantial. Mr. W. J. Bartlett invited me to his fine home, where I passed a happy time. I gave two addresses on Sunday, March 31st., in the Rev. Mr. Wright's church, and on Thursday I spoke in Dr. Gale's church. I have a high regard for the people of Lee.

I was invited by Rev. J. Warner, of Easton, Connecticut, to spend Sunday, April 7th., with him, and speak in the M. E. church in the morning, in the

12*

Congregational church in the afternoon, and in his church in the evening. It proved a rainy day, but the congregations united at each service, and the meetings proved successful.

The next day, the noble-hearted Mr. Warren took me in his carriage to Bridgeport, and, with many wishes for my prosperity, left me to pursue my way to New Milford, where I was to speak that evening. Col. Blinn had made all necessary arrangements for the meeting, I had a good house, and they invited me to return and speak again.

The following Sunday I spoke, by invitation of Rev. Mr. Walker, in Mason Village, New Hampshire, where I have always received a warm reception. On my way from Mason to Clinton I passed the ruins of Ayre, and, truly, it was a desolate sight. Many lost their all by the fire-fiend. Mr. Stewart, an old and well-loved friend, grasped my hand, and said with tears in his eyes—

"Brother Dutcher; I have no home now to entertain you in; all is swept away." With a sad heart, I left him in his troubles. I spoke in Clinton, Massachusetts, on Monday, April 15th., and shall speak there again on Sunday the 28th.

Before I lay aside my pen, let me say, that to the Clergymen of America I am indebted for what little success I may have had as a lecturer on the great and important subject of Temperance. Their hearts and their homes have ever been open to me, and by word and deed they have aided me in my endeavors to lift up poor, fallen men, and to be, in God's hands, the humble instrument of saving some from a drunkard's grave. To hundreds of others I am also grateful for numerous favors, and especially so to Warren W. Dutcher, of Hopedale, who came to my aid on one of the darkest days which I have experienced since I began to work for the Temperance Cause. May the choicest blessings of Heaven rest upon all who have thus stood by me, and encouraged me on.

During the last six years, I have delivered, by actual count, over two thousand lectures, and traveled not less than one hundred thousand miles. What good I have accomplished no mortal can tell; but when God makes up his jewels, I hope to have the satisfaction of greeting some redeemed ones, saved through my feeble efforts.

I am still working hard to do what good I can. Sometimes I have been long distances to visit poor victims of rum, and in nearly all cases they have reformed. Others I have taken under my immediate charge, and with only two exceptions, they are reformed. Several such are now members of different Churches.

Many ask me if I still have the appetite to drink. I will answer the question here, by saying that I still have to fight my desire for drink. I shall be obliged to struggle with my appetite all my days. But, trusting in Divine Providence, I hope to live and die a temperance man.

And now, dear reader, as I am about to bring this narrative of my past life to a close, let me say a few words of warning. If you have taken the first glass, let it be the last. *Take not another.* If you have never taken the first glass, *do not do it.* I have circulated the pledge through many a dark and lonely prison, and have often heard the words—"Oh that I had never taken the first glass." Often while visiting a prison have I been led to exclaim—"Oh Lord, Thou alone hast preserved me, and Thy right hand has kept me from sharing the fate of these whom I see before me." But instead of looking through grated windows, which many are now doing by reason of intemperance, I am permitted to breathe the pure air of Heaven, and drink in the beauties of nature, surrounded by kind friends, and with a happy home; and I am led to exclaim—"Great is Thy mercy towards me, and Thou hast delivered my soul from the lowest hell."

I am fully determined, while my life is spared, to continue to labor to the best of my ability in the great cause I have espoused. Wherever my lot may be cast, or Providence may lead my feet, I shall ever give God the praise, knowing that He doeth all things well; and as not even a sparrow falleth to the ground without His notice, I do most humbly trust that He will have some purpose even in the fate of one like me.

PART II.

TRIUMPHS AND TRIALS

ON

TEMPERANCE TRAILS.

BY
SAMUEL S. HALL.

CHAPTER I.

THE story of Mr. Dutcher's life up to April, 1872, is narrated in preceding pages. Six years have since elapsed, during which, faithful to his pledge and the determination expressed on the closing page of his autobiography, he has, to the best of his ability, unceasingly labored to reform the intemperate, raise the fallen, and advance the cause of temperance and humanity. Amid trials, temptations, and some things calculated to discourage him, but, it must be added, more to encourage and cheer him on, he has "soberly and cheerfully" accomplished a vast amount of hard work; and never were his services more in demand than now.

Unable from his engagements to respond to the call of his publishers for a continuation of his narrative, the preparation of an appendix thereto has fallen upon me. Before commencing the very imperfect record which I shall give, as my space is limited, it may be well to say something of the intimate associations with Mr. Dutcher which have to some extent fitted me for the task.

Shortly after my return from the army of our civil war, in which I had suffered innumerable privations, I first met Mr. Dutcher in Leominster, Mass., where my father, Oliver Hall, then resided and now resides. Mr. Dutcher was then a traveling book agent, and our acquaintance commenced at the old "Leominster House"—since burned down. In a short time we became quite familiar through numerous potations, and entered on a protracted spree during which we found ourselves in Boston; afterward in some, to us, unaccountable manner, we became separated, as has been detailed on page 227.

In a week or so after I reached Leominster my lost comrade also arrived there, and we passed a night together in the old graveyard, where, after we had drank all the whisky we had on hand, we sat down under the dark and gloomy pines, amid the moss-covered monuments, and began to argue over the possible good that might originate from making a mutual resolve not to indulge our appetites for strong drink any longer.

After reaching conclusions favorable to the temperance question, we raised our hands amid the darkness, gloom and chill night air, and called on God to help us lead sober lives; then, feeling somewhat better for our new resolutions, we lay down together on the sward and slept until morning.

In the morning we separated again, and, as it proved, for many years. Mr. Dutcher went to Worcester, where his wife, who had been vainly searching for him in Leominster, had gone to live with her mother; and I went back to my adopted state, Texas, where I had before the war, when but a boy, fought the most blood-thirsty Indians of America—the Camaches and Apaches—under Sam Houston; and had also, during the first years of the war, served against Cortina, the bandit scourge of the Rio Grande, in that world-renowned corps, the Texan Rangers.

Subsequently I again returned from Texas to New York, and there, as we afterward found out, I lived but one block from where Mr. and Mrs. Dutcher with their first born son resided. Mrs. Dutcher several times remarked to her husband, that from her window she had seen a young man pass who reminded her of me.

Leaving New York I went west, visited Omaha, and roamed about the Sioux country; then I hunted and trapped one winter in Northern Michigan; and then I returned to my father's in Leominster. Soon after my arrival home I received a letter from Mr. Dutcher, inviting me to visit him at his home in Worcester, but before I had done so he called at a late hour one evening and asked to see me at the door. I did not know who it was until he asked me if I remembered sleeping in the graveyard with him.

Thus we once more met; and subsequently our friendship, without the help of whisky, matured into a deep regard for each other. I was somewhat surprised to learn that my friend, who had formerly been noted as a man of great capacity in the drinking line, was now a temperance lecturer of considerable reputation.

After Mr. Dutcher called on me I went to his residence in Kilby street, Worcester, and was most kindly welcomed in a brotherly and sisterly manner by himself and his wife. I found their family increased to two boys and two girls—very interesting children—and Mrs. Dutcher, although she had been in poor health for much of the time, appeared as young as she did when I last saw her, in Leominster, hunting for her George who was enjoying a drunken spree one hundred miles away.

The kindly greeting I received at the Kilby street cottage, the absence of all reserve, and the unselfish friendship—stronger from my roving disposition—into which we unconsciously drifted, led me to thinking how the situation of my friends could be improved.

Mr. Dutcher was paying high rent, and his family expenses were more than he could easily get along with as a lecturer—for he was constantly meeting poor drunkards who needed help, and it was not in his heart to refuse them; besides, there was no time while he resided in Worcester when he did not have some unfortunate victim of rum in his family who was trying to reform. Many miserable men has he clothed and fed and cared for at his home; and too much praise cannot be accorded to Mrs. Dutcher, who has for years had the trouble of these men being in the family, and the fear of them when they were under the influence of drink. In fact, no woman in the land has suffered more from the effects of this curse upon those she loved, and those she has been forced to associate with through the temperance work of her husband. Truly she is well calculated for a temperance lecturer's wife; and I can say with truth, I never met a woman who had more sympathy for drinking men, or who would bear with more patience their foolish and insane actions.

My father had just erected on his farm some two-story cottages, and I induced Mr. and Mrs. Dutcher to go to Leominster with me and inspect them. A pleasant ride of eighteen miles, a warm welcome from the members of my father's family, a good night's rest—then the cottages were visited and one of them approved. In two weeks from that time the Dutchers with their goods and chattels and children were domiciled in what we christened "Buena Vista Cottage"—a Spanish name signifying beautiful view. Mr. Dutcher wrote the latter portion of his autobiography in this new home.

The Dutcher family were now very comfortably situated. Their cottage stood on a hill surrounded by green fields, and from its piazza and windows could be seen the beautiful town of Leominster only one mile below. To the West and North loomed up the two peaks of Monoosnock mountain. Far away to the southward stretched hill and dale, wood and meadow, presenting in summer a most charming prospect. Just down the old lane, bordered on each side by noble apple trees, was the Hall homestead, embosomed in a forest of pear, peach and cherry trees; while in the spaces between grew strawberries, currants, and grape vines. The most beautiful rose garden in the county stretched up from the large yellow barn to the conservatory; and opposite the farm-house towered three gigantic elms, whose long graceful branches, the home of golden robins, swayed gently in the breeze.

The Dutchers soon came to feel as much at home at Gran'pa Hall's—as the children called my father—as myself. My respected mother was ever happy to render them council and assistance; and Lottie R. Hall, my only sister remaining at home, was always on hand to receive and entertain them.

My father's business at this time frequently called him away from home, and shaking off to some degree my roving propensities, I remained to assist him. I also entered into an agreement with Mr. Dutcher to attend to his correspondence, and as a consequence was in constant communication with him, and received from him hundreds of letters detailing his adventures and experiences. These letters, with what I have learned while accompanying him on several of his lecturing tours, and in conversations with him, are my chief sources of information as to what is related on the following pages.

CHAPTER II.

AFTER moving to Leominster, Mr. Dutcher felt at liberty to be absent from home more than he had previously been, and to extend his lecturing tours, knowing that his family were with friends who would care for them in case of sickness.

In the months of May and June, 1872, he lectured in Fitchburg, Clinton, Newton, Natick, and other towns near Boston, and in Nashua, N. H., and vicinity; he then went to Oneonta, Delhi, and other towns in that section of New York State, and spoke to large audiences eleven times in seven days.

In August he was again invited to the Susquehanna valley, and lectured in Worcester, East Worcester, Otsego, Unadilla, and other places. At Cobleskill he was entertained by Hon. Charles Courter, who took him to his beautiful home. He then went to Schoharie County, and at Middleburg found relations —John Cornwell and family, who were overjoyed to see him. Dr. Henry Wells also gave him a hearty welcome, and did all in his power to make the meetings a success. At this town he saw a well-educated man, once highly respectable and wealthy, but then only a miserable beggar. "Give me ten cents," he exclaimed in beseeching tones and with his trembling hand outstretched; "it will not make you any poorer." Mr. Dutcher's pleadings and arguments were all in vain; rum, rum, rum, the man must and would have to keep his soul and body together. A few weeks later he died in the New Haven poor house.

October found Mr. Dutcher in numerous towns in Eastern Massachusetts. At Dedham he visited his esteemed uncle, Hon. Eliphalet Stone, who renewed his interest in the cause and rendered much assistance. At Boston, Rev. J. D. Fulton invited him to speak in Tremont Temple, and raised a good collection for him; he also invited him to his home and treated him as a brother.

At Chelsea, Mr. Dutcher addressed a large audience, and went to the home of his much beloved friend O. E. Downing, where he has always met a hearty welcome. In East Boston he spoke in the Baptist, Presbyterian, and other churches, and received many favors from Charles H. Jenkins, the postmaster.

In November, Mr. Dutcher received a call from Rev. Mr. Griffin of Carbondale, Penn. On arriving there he was greeted by a very large audience assembled in the court house, and his words found a home in the hearts of the miners. Tears flowed down their cheeks as he told them of his experiences as a drunkard and pleaded with them to give up strong drink. Many signed the pledge, and to their dying day will thank the Lord that they were induced to attend the meeting.

At Mr. Griffin's advice, Mr. Dutcher resolved to extend his labors through the Lackawanna valley, and proceeded to Scranton, where he was met by Dr. A. L. Clark, who took him in charge, arranged his meetings, and proved one of the best and kindest of friends. Several meetings were held in Scranton, and their success was wonderful. At one of them, Miss Jennie Pettie, a lady who had suffered from girlhood through rum, spoke with such power that the audience was moved to tears.

Mr. Dutcher made such a favorable impression in this section that invitations came from all quarters, and he spoke in Hyde Park, Providence, Dalton, Wilkesbarre, and many other towns in the Lackawanna and Wyoming valleys. At this time Local Option was being brought before the people, and Mr. Dutcher, being in favor of law as well as gospel, gave this measure his hearty support. Although a strong prohibitionist, he argued, if there was no compromise with wrong, better take half a loaf—if a whole one was not to be had—looking forward to the time when prohibition would become a law of the state. In every town where he spoke great excitement prevailed, and in all but two or three of them Local Option carried the day. For four months he battled for the right in that part of Pennsylvania, and only eternity will show the good accomplished.

One day, in the midst of the Local Option excitement, Mr. Dutcher found himself at a small town where he had to wait some time for the train. Being cold and hungry, he entered the only hotel in the place and ordered dinner. Soon afterward two other men came in and took drinks of brandy at the bar. At the dinner table Mr. Dutcher found himself opposite the two strangers, whose conversation immediately turned to the Local Option topic. Among other things one of them said :—

"Them temperance fellers are hard at work and that Dutcher is drawing big houses. I wonder what he thinks he can do; he better go back among the pinched-up Yankees and fanatics. What can he do if he does make the people cry and vote Local Option? We have got the money, and can buy the legislature. Pshaw! What does Dutcher and his crew amount to by the side of greenbacks?"

They little thought that Dutcher was sitting near them, and that they were contributing hugely to his enjoyment. When they settled their bill one of them asked the bar-tender if he could pray. He replied that he was not very heavy in that line.

"Well," said the other, "My mother learned me a prayer once; all I can remember of it is, 'Now I lay me down to sleep.' Now you can pray that, and add to it the prayer that we may be successful in buying up the politicians and putting Dutcher and those infernal temperance fanatics under our feet."

At this time the Mollie Maguires were very bold and strong in the mining districts, and in some places after a meeting, a hard-looking crowd would congregate about the entrance, with a desire to lay violent hands on the speaker plainly manifest in their rum-bloated features. These rough men had not heard the tender pleading words of Mr. Dutcher, which were calculated to soften their hearts and cause them to respect and love him; consequently they were ready and eager to drive him out of the country.

Under these circumstances, it was the custom for several of the gentleman who were strong both physically and in their love of temperance, to escort Mr. Dutcher after the meeting to the place where he was to pass the night.

This bitter feeling was only made manifest upon the first night of his lecturing in a town; for he made it his business on the next night he lectured to go to the door, and by kind words fitly spoken prevail upon them to enter and hear his address.

The effect of his eloquence upon these rough untutored men was magical; with tears coursing down their coal-begrimmed cheeks, they would rush in scores up to sign the pledge.

At one time some of the hardest cases sent word that if Mr. Dutcher came to the town where they lived, they would use him roughly. Mr. Dutcher went to within a mile of this town and called on a gentleman, who, with his wife and daughter, walked with him to the place of meeting; and out of respect to his escort he was not molested. Every available space was occupied, and some of the roughest men he had ever seen sat before him. The meeting was opened by prayer and singing, after which our friend arose and began to speak, telling them he had come all the way from Massachusetts to do them good; how he had suffered, and his father before him, from cursed rum; of his final redemption and devotion to the cause.

Long before the close of his address it was evident that these rough men were greatly affected, and at the close of his remarks they came in a surging mass to sign the pledge. The acknowledged ringleader of the crowd made his way up to Mr. Dutcher, and grasping his hand, exclaimed:—"Mon, ye ha don weel;" then he assured our friend that he would protect him and that no harm should come to him.

Three wild, hearty cheers for Dutcher rang afar over the hills at the close of the meeting, and as he passed out, rough hands from every side grasped his, and scores expressed their regard, and their wish to hear him again. As he proceeded to his stopping place, many a hearty "God bless you," greeted him from the following crowd of miners.

Mr. Dutcher found many good friends in this section of the country, among whom were several clergymen. Calvin L. Briggs, of Dalton, invited him to make his house his home while there; and he was so kindly treated by him and his noble Christian wife, that their names are still household words in the Dutcher family.

On one occasion, as Mr. Dutcher was hurriedly changing cars at Pittston with a heavy valise in his hand, he missed his footing while attempting to get on a moving train, and was dragged for some distance while holding on to the railing with only one hand.

Had he not been discovered and assisted by others on the train he would have been crushed beneath the wheels; as it was, the train had to be stopped before he was rescued.

On his way home from Pennsylvania, Mr. Dutcher stopped at Port Jervis and lectured for his friend, Rev. Mr. Rogers, one of God's noblemen, and was also entertained there at the beautiful residence of his relative, Judge Dutcher—a worthy gentleman of the old school.

In March, 1873, Mr. Dutcher was invited to Wareham, Mass., and spoke to a large audience in a manner which opened the way for him in Middleboro, Sandwich, Marion, and other towns in their vicinity. He also spoke repeatedly at South Boston, occupying the pulpit of Rev. Mr. Lewis, an Universalist clergyman, who kindly invited him thither. He also spoke on Sunday morning in Rev. Mr. Stratton's church, and in other churches at that place, and much good was done for the temperance cause.

Soon afterwards, Rev. Mr. Stebbins sent for him to speak in his church in South Adams, Mass., where he was cheered by a full attendance, and the people treated him so kindly that he wrote home:—"South Adams people are among the most noble sons and daughters of Adams' race." Hon. Mr. Plunket took him by the hand and said:—

"Go ahead brother Dutcher; the Lord has raised you up for just the work you are engaged in."

Mr. Brown, of North Adams, a noble temperance man and a friend to the unfortunate, invited Mr.

Dutcher to address the people there; he did so before a large audience, and left the place with tokens of their liberality and kindness.

In May and June he lectured in Pittsfield and Irving, Mass., and in Utica, Hamilton, Norwich, Middletown and other towns in the Empire State. At one place a mother came to the meeting, and with tears in her eyes begged him to try and do something for her son, her only child, who was fast going to his grave through intemperance. Mr. Dutcher promised to do all in his power, and told her to pray to God for her son, and that his efforts for the unfortunate one might meet with success.

On the first attempt to see the poor fellow at his home he ran away through the back garden; the same result attended the second visit; but at the third call Mr. Dutcher caught him in the garden, and prevailed upon him to listen to his words. He gained his attention by relating his own sufferings; then told him how his mother was praying for him, how his father suffered from his conduct, and asked him to sign the pledge and pray God to give him strength to keep it. Strong common sense and kind words won the young man over; he signed the pledge, and has kept it.

Mr. Dutcher has revisited this young man and his parents, and been introduced to his wife and child. A happier family could not be found.

How different the scene from what it would have been if the son had persisted in his downward course! The parents, who now gazed fondly on the group beside them, happy in their children and rejoicing in their son's felicity, would then have been sitting childless and inconsolable, lamenting the dreadful fate which had come upon their darling only child and the overthrow of their own bright anticipations.

One day, while walking with a clergyman, Mr. Dutcher met a poor, trembling man evidently suffering the last stages of misery caused by strong drink; and as he passed by he grasped the inebriate's hand and spoke to him a few words of kindness. "That miserable drunkard," said the clergyman, "was for years a professor in a college and possessed one of the finest minds in the country; he has been brought down to this condition by the serpent of the still."

Rum makes no distinction of person; rank and wealth reel side by side with poverty, disgrace, crime and degradation on the road to ruin.

At Ilion, Philo Remington Esq., with many of the other leading men of that place, listened to Mr. Dutcher's address and were pleased to commend his efforts. Mr. R. showed him around the beautiful town, and through the renowned manufactory of arms. On leaving, he presented him with one hundred dollars, saying:—"We make money to do good with, and that will help you a little in your work of love."

Mr. Dutcher next made a tour through Northern New York, and spoke in many churches to the edification of the people, who, aside from the curse of rum, appeared truly prosperous and happy.

CHAPTER III.

AFTER Mr. Dutcher's return home from Northern New York, much exhausted by hard labor, his friend, Rev. A. A. Wright, invited him to speak in his church; and afterward, he occupied the pulpit of Rev. Mr. Russell's church one Sunday morning. He also addressed a large audience assembled in a tent erected for worship by two traveling evangelists. Mr. Wright preached in Leominster for three years, and was the most popular man that ever trod the streets of that town. The secret of it was, he ever had kind words and smiles for all. When he met Mr. Dutcher he would grasp his hand and exclaim :—

"God bless you; how goes the cause of temperance? Go ahead, George; you are right, and the prayers of all good men go with you."

After recovering his strength, Mr. Dutcher, by invitation of Mr. C. B. Travis, lectured at Natick, Mass. Hon. Henry Wilson was present, and gave him many encouraging words as he had often done before. Said he :—"Mr. Dutcher, you gave us a good talk; keep right on as you are going, and the Lord will enable you to accomplish unlimited good." Then taking a bank note from his pocket, he added:— "Take this, Mr. Dutcher; I feel that I did not give enough in my first contribution." Soon afterward Mr. Wilson sent to Mr. Dutcher the following letter, thinking it would be of use to him in some sections of the country :—

"To WHOM IT MAY CONCERN :—I take great pleasure in commending George M. Dutcher, as an advocate of temperance worthy of public confidence. His past experience and present earnestness combine to render his addresses interesting, eloquent, and effective. The friends of the cause will do well to avail themselves of his services whenever they can be obtained.   HENRY WILSON."

Mr. Dutcher first met the lamented Mr. Wilson in Boston, at the funeral of a young man who had for years maintained an almost superhuman struggle against his appetite for strong drink, and whose death is a sad warning to all, and especially to reformed men who think themselves secure; it shows that one who has once tampered with the poison is never safe afterwards, unless he avoid each and every approach to temptation.

Many distinguished men were present at the funeral of the unfortunate Edward H. Uniack. Mr. Wilson stood by his lifeless form and said :—

"Here lies the body of our lamented friend; none knew him but to love him. For years he stood before the public pleading for temperance, but has finally fallen. Never again will his eloquent tongue be heard warning others from the path of destruction upon which he has himself been overwhelmed. His faults we will bury with him in the grave; his virtues we will cherish in our hearts. Let us all learn a lesson from his untimely end, shun the trail of the serpent, and hereafter wage a more determined war against the destroyer of the hearts, homes, and honor of our people."

In the autumn Mr. Dutcher visited Bethel, Danbury, and other towns in Connecticut. He then went to New York State and held enthusiastic meetings in Norwich, Rome, and other places. In Buffalo he addressed the operatives of the extensive rolling mill, and hundreds of them signed the pledge. From Buffalo he went to Ohio, and addressed good audiences in Cleaveland, Akron, Ashtabula, and other towns. At Norwalk he was entertained by Hon. G. T. Stewart, the temperance candidate for governor.

While at a depot waiting for a train, in this tour, Mr. Dutcher noticed a poor drunkard, and began conversation. He learned that the man had a destitute family in a neighboring town, and that he could not go home to them for want of funds to pay his fare, as he had been on a spree and spent his last cent for rum. Mr. Dutcher portrayed to him the dreadful consequences of his acts, and so influenced the poor fellow that he wept and signed the pledge. After giving him some good advice he was presented with a ticket to take him home, and they parted. Subsequently Mr. Dutcher had the satisfaction of knowing that the man kept his pledge, joined a church and was in comfortable circumstances.

During the first nine months of 1874, Mr. Dutcher labored in various towns and cities in New York and Massachusetts, where his services were generously appreciated by the people. In one town a liquor dealer had recently sold rum to a poor fatherless boy and spoken harsh words to his mother when she begged of him never to do it again. He also said to her, pointing to a printed paper hanging behind his bar:—

"There is my license; I am doing a lawful business; and when a customer comes to buy, I am not going to refuse him."

Having heard of the circumstances, Mr. Dutcher at his lecture placed the scene so vividly before his hearers that they resolved to prosecute the dealer and pledged ten thousand dollars for that purpose.

In October, under the direction of Ex Gov. Myron H. Clark and Hon. Stephen B. Ayres, Mr. Dutcher canvassed Western New York for the Prohibition party of that district, whose candidate as representative to the 27th Congress Mr. Ayres was. He spoke night after night to crowded houses with wonderful effect; and his addresses were masterly and convincing. Mr. Ayres was not elected, but failed of success by only a few votes.

After the election was over, Mr. Dutcher continued his labor in New York for several months. His meetings were generally largely attended, and productive of much good. At Fulton he met Mr. Stowell, Grand Worthy Secretary of the Grand Division of the Sons of Temperance, and was by him appointed deputy at large. At Medina, aided by Dr.

Dunns, a noble temperance man, he organized the Sons of Temperance.

From New York Mr. Dutcher went to Detroit, and spoke in three different churches of that city. He also visited Jacksonville, Albion, Hillsdale, Battle Creek, Hudson, Ann Arbor, Kalamazoo, and other places in Michigan. While coming out of a church one dark night, he stepped off from the platform and fell to the sidewalk beneath, receiving a severe injury which lamed him for several weeks. It did not however debar him from his work. Night after night he stood before the people sowing seed which did not fall on barren ground. Many wanderers were gathered into the fold, and a lasting impetus was given to the temperance reform.

After making a short visit to his home, Mr. Dutcher went to Elyria, Ohio, where he was assisted by the Jubilee Singers of Fisk University. Then he went to Chicago, where he spoke in Rev. A. A. Parkhurst's church on Michigan avenue, under the auspices of the Methodist Book Concern. At its close Bishop Harris said to him:—"God bless you; your words did us all good. Have no fears for the future, for the Lord is with you, and many will rise up and call you blessed."

Invited by the Elgin Watch Company he then went to Elgin, where all the churches united in one grand gathering to hear him. Hundreds who listened to his stirring and eloquent address took him by the hand and wished him "God speed." He also visited many other places in Illinois, but limited space will not allow their mention.

His labors now began to wear upon him so much that he was forced to give up his engagements and go home for a rest. His letters during this tour were filled with words of praise of the people of the West. He found them more than generous, and ever ready to do all in their power for the good of the cause.

During the summer Mr. Dutcher made a trip to Portland, Maine; and also to Bangor by invitation of Mrs. Crossman, who, encouraged and assisted by her husband, Col. Crossman, did a great work in alleviating human suffering in prisons and abodes of poverty. He then went to New Hampshire, and then to New York State. At a meeting at Saratoga Springs, Vice President Henry Wilson presided, and introduced Mr. Dutcher in the following words:—

"Ladies and gentlemen—I am highly gratified to witness such a large audience on this occasion. For my part I can say I never indulged in strong drink, but thousands of our fellow citizens are chained down as slaves to the cup which maddens even unto death. Thousands of homes are made desolate annually, and deserving women, brought down to starvation, are forced to see their little children suffer through this great evil. From my earliest childhood I have abhorred and shunned this curse of our race, and to my latest breath I shall do what I can to help fight against it. The gentleman who is about to address us can speak burning words in witness against it from personal experiences. For years I have known him as a man raised up by God to battle against intemperance, and I am happy to introduce my esteemed friend and brother, George M. Dutcher."

After visiting various other towns in New York, Mr. Dutcher made a tour through Connecticut, addressing large audiences with good results.

At one town a man who had been intemperate for years, came to the meeting accompanied by his wife, who, with his aged father, had often begged him to quit drinking. Often had he resolved to do so. Often while recovering from a protracted spree would he shed tears of penitence and remorse as his wife bathed his throbbing temples, and he would exclaim:—"Oh, if I can only live to get over this I will never drink again." But his resolves had proved weak as a bar of sand; the dreadful appetite still ruled him and held full sway over his weakened will.

As this man sat in the church and listened to Mr. Dutcher's tender appeals he was greatly affected; and when the lecturer spoke of redemption from strong drink through God's unbounded mercy, he again resolved to reform, and prayed to God to give him strength to do so. After the lecture was over, the man's faithful wife went up to the platform and requested Mr. Dutcher to call at their house. He did so, and was taken into the husband's store, where after some conversation both the man and his partner signed the pledge on the head of a barrel. This pledge the man had framed and hung up in a conspicuous place in his house, that he might often be reminded of his sacred obligation. At a subsequent visit to the town, Mr. Dutcher found his friend the proprietor of a temperance hotel, and there was no happier family in the state.

Being invited by N. B. Broughton, G. W. G. T. of North Carolina to visit that state, Mr. Dutcher started southward early in December. At Richmond, Virginia, he was induced to halt in his journey, and the churches and temperance societies there gave him a very kind and flattering reception which he gratefully remembers. His audiences were sympathetic and generous. With much reluctance he left the beautiful city to continue his journey.

While walking in Richmond one day, during his stay there, Mr. Dutcher met a poor drinking man, and, as is his custom, took him by the hand. "Dear brother," said he, "I am so sorry for you. My heart aches for you. Will you not come to the temperance meeting and give up drink? Come brother; shake off the slavish chains and ask the Lord to help you." The poor creature replied with quivering lips:—

"Sir; I had as good a father and mother as ever lived; when they died they left me sixteen thousand dollars. I have squandered it all for rum, and am now in poverty and rags. I am obliged to tramp the streets and live sometimes on one meal a day, with no hope of a better condition—no friends to sympathize with me in my terrible sufferings." Mr. Dutcher told him to pray for strength and attend the meeting that night; and he promised to do so.

While speaking that evening, Mr. Dutcher noticed

the man sitting near the door; and when an invitation was given for all to stand up who would sign the pledge, he arose with others. Mr. Dutcher subsequently helped him sufficiently to enable him to appear respectably in public, interested others in his behalf, and with brotherly advice left him hopeful and happy.

At Raleigh, Mr. Dutcher was met by Mr. Broughton, who with the Grand Worthy Secretary arranged his meetings in the state. He spoke several times in the Capitol at Raleigh, to interested audiences. His subsequent trip through the state was a perfect ovation. The people flocked from many miles away to hear him, and in some places remote from railroads, where Northern men were seldom seen, he was considered quite a curiosity. He was everywhere kindly treated by the people he came in contact with. Many members were added to the Good Templars through his labors, and the temperance people were aroused to greater efforts which have since caused much lasting good. It was with many wishes for the prosperity of the people of the "Sunny South," that he left them and returned to his home. While in Raleigh he received two letters of introduction to the Southern people; they were as follows:—

"RICHMOND, VIRGINIA, Dec. 28th, 1875.

The bearer of this letter, George Milo Dutcher, preached for me yesterday (Sunday) at 11 A. M. His discourse was very impressive; I regard it as the most effective temperance sermon I ever heard. Many an eye unused to weeping was wet with tears while he told the story of his own reform, and spoke of the grace of God. Brother Dutcher is making a tour of the Southern States on his mission. I take great pleasure in commending him to our people. He possesses my confidence, my earnest sympathies, and my prayers for the Divine blessing on his noble work.

Very truly,   S. A. STEEL,

Pastor Broad St., Meth. Church, Va. Conf., M. E. Church, South.

RICHMOND, Dec. 21st, 1875.

Brother Dutcher delivered a lecture in my church last Sunday night to a large audience; and I am sure that no lecture was ever more highly appreciated in this city, or made a more lasting impression for good. He speaks with a power, a pathos, and an eloquence which is thrilling; drawing his most telling illustrations from his own previous sad life history. I commend him to the hearts and homes of all God's people, and especially to my brethren in the ministry. By all means secure his services, and let him tell his story to your audiences. No sermon ever preached in this city has done more good than the lecture of Brother Dutcher.   Fraternally,

A. C. BLEDSOE,

Pastor of Trinity M. E. Church, South, Richmond, Va.

CHAPTER IV.

DURING the year 1876, Mr. Dutcher's labors were scattered over New England, New York, New Jersey, Pennsylvania, and Ohio. He was invited to New York City in January by Rev. Dr. Clark, and lectured in his church on 27th street, and in churches in Brooklyn. Thence he went to Eastern Pennsylvania, and to Newton, Dover, and other towns in New Jersey.

At one place in New Jersey while walking to the church where he was to speak, he noticed just in front of him a small boy who was leading an intemperate man. "Come father," pleaded the little fellow, half crying, "throw away that bottle; you know mother don't want to have you bring any rum home; please pa, won't you throw it away?"

Soon afterward as they came opposite the church the boy exclaimed in an excited tone:—

"Pa, please go into the temperance meeting; do go in pa." Then he added, bursting into tears—"What makes you drink rum to make me cry and mother suffer so much?"

The poor man's heart was touched by these tender reproachful words, and he staggered up the steps. As he reached the top step he drew from his pocket a bottle containing rum, and after gazing at it for a moment he dashed it down on the pavement below. He then entered the church, and after listening to the speaker's kind appeals, signed the pledge, and departed with his now happy boy to his desolate home, to turn it into what seemed a Paradise to those who had been so long cursed by a drunken husband and father.

From New Jersey Mr. Dutcher went to several towns in Connecticut, and at Moosup he visited his old friend, Rev. Mr. Ellis. Thence he went to Western New York, and to Clifton and Branford, Ontario, where he was very kindly received. He entertains a high regard for the people in this part of the Queen's Dominion.

At Suspension Bridge he found a valued friend in Rev. Mr. Bennett. As the two were walking out one day, a man under the influence of liquor came out of a bar-room, and in an abrupt manner invited them to take a drink. They declined, saying that they never drank liquor but were temperance men.

By this time several others had emerged from the saloon and clustered around to hear the talk. Mr. Bennett told them that he was a minister of the gospel, and Mr. Dutcher was a reformed man and a temperance lecturer, who was trying to do good to those who drank intoxicating liquors. At this one of the men exclaimed:—

"We dare you both to come inside and sit down."

The rather rough invitation was accepted, and they entered the bar-room, followed by the eager, laughing men who anticipated considerable fun at their expense. Behind the counter stood the proprietor, while several customers were lounging about and drinking. The two strangers shook hands with all in the room, saying:—

"Well brothers, how do you do? We are your friends although we don't drink."

"Pshaw"! said one, "come on and take a drink; 'twill do you good!"

"Sthop yer timperance blather," exclaimed a son of the Emerald Isle, "an take a gude dhrink o' the crayther; yees will be able to judge much better o' the vartues o' the same, wid a small smither in yer stomachs."

"Cume up mine frints," cried a German "and thry vun chuners of bier, und you'll feel much better as goot."

Finding their hospitable invitations all declined they next insisted upon a speech from the temperance man. Mr. Bennett suggested that before hearing Brother Dutcher's remarks it would be well to kneel down and pray. Down went the whole crowd upon their knees, and Mr. Bennett prayed to God so eloquently and earnestly for the poor victims of drink, that tears came into the eyes of some present and others called aloud for mercy. After the prayer Mr. Dutcher spoke for nearly half an hour. When he had finished many were sobbing like children, and one man exclaimed earnestly:—

"Boys, I have drank my last glass—no more rum for me. This is the turning point in my life. To-day my wife and children begged me not to come here, but in vain. I went out on the sidewalk to make sport of these good men, but my laughter was turned to tears. Thank God for this hour!" "Amen," was the general response.

A hymn was then sung, and after receiving an invitation to attend the temperance meeting that night at Mr. Bennett's church, the audience dispersed; most, or all of these men attended the meeting and signed the pledge, as did many others who were influenced by them to do so; among the number who signed was the leading hotel proprietor in the town.

Visiting Lockport, where the temperance cause was at a low ebb, Mr. Dutcher, with the co-operation of the clergymen, succeeded in creating quite an interest, and a society of "Centennial Reformers" was organized with one hundred and thirty-five members; since then this number has been increased to nearly one thousand.

In June he was again in New York City, making his home while there at the house of his friend David Kilmer whom he had known in his boyhood days. He also lectured at Staten Island, Brooklyn, Jersey City, and at the Inebriate Asylum at Fort Hamilton. While speaking one Sunday afternoon in the Erie railroad depot at Jersey City, he was so overcome by the intense heat that he was obliged to return to his own home; he was unable to do any work for several weeks, and feels the effects thereof to this day.

Resuming his work he again went to Ohio, at the call of two clergymen, and spoke to large and interested audiences in churches at Cleveland, Mount Vernon, Mansfield, etc. At East Cleveland he and his son, who accompanied him on this trip, were entertained at the house of his highly esteemed friend, A. E. Bradley. Georgie remained in the family for a considerable time while his father was traveling in Ohio, and both father and son feel under many obligations to the Bradleys.

While in Cleveland, at the close of a meeting, a poor woman came to Mr. Dutcher and begged him to see her husband and try to influence him to reform. "I fear I am asking too much," she said, "but he is a poor drunkard, and although he promised me this morning that he would go to your meeting, he went off and began to drink again. Mr. Dutcher replied that it would be a pleasure as well as his duty to accede to her request.

The next morning he called at her house and found the husband at home and in great distress of mind. "What a wretch I am," he exclaimed; "what shall I do? I wish I was dead." Then springing to his feet he paced the floor impatiently, and with upturned eyes cried out in utter despair, "No hope, no hope for me." His poor wife stood by him sobbing convulsively, but after a while she induced him to sit down and listen to the visitor.

Mr. Dutcher told him that there was hope for him; that God was ready and willing to save the worst sinner that ever lived, if that sinner looked to Him with sincere repentance. He told him that he too had been a slave of the intoxicating cup, and how the Lord had saved him. Then he drew a pledge from his pocket and laid it on the table before him. With his hand upon the shoulder of the inebriate he then called upon the Lord to bless and strengthen the poor sufferer that he might sign the pledge and become a Christian. The wife also joined in the supplications; and her earnest pleadings, seconded by Mr. Dutcher's efforts prevailed; the poor man raised his eyes heavenward as if asking for strength to battle with his craving appetite—then grasped the pen and signed the pledge.

With a hurried "God bless you," Mr. Dutcher softly left the room, and as he turned to close the door saw a sight which amply repaid him the trouble of calling, and brought a sympathetic tear to his eye. The man and wife were clasped in each others arms, while tears of contrition and thankfulness coursed down their cheeks.

Mr. Dutcher saw this couple again the next day, and by mutual arrangement the woman started for her girlhood's home in Ballston Spa, N. Y., leaving her husband with Mr. Dutcher, who kindly cared for him, took him with him to neighboring towns where he lectured, and to Leominster, Mass. when he returned thither. After a sojourn of several weeks at the home of the Dutchers, this reformed man turned out an eloquent temperance lecturer. He rejoined his wife, and many pleasant things could be related of their life since then if space would permit.

CHAPTER V.

IN the spring of 1877 Mr. Dutcher contemplated making a second tour in the Southern States, and after giving several lectures in Massachusetts, he proceeded to our National Capital where he halted for a season.

Here he lectured for the Ladies' Temperance Union, and at a general union meeting of all the temperance organizations in Washington, and met with flattering success in gaining signers for the pledge. He was invited to prolong his stay in the city, but as there was an extensive revival of religion there at the time he thought it not advisable to do so. He also gave up the idea of going any farther south, as the change in the climate seemed already to have affected his health.

It was in rather a desponding state of mind that our friend took his seat in a homeward bound car; but the prospect of soon meeting his loved ones from whom he was forced to be absent so much, soon drove away all feelings of dejection. The train rolled swiftly on, and at length came to a stop at Wilmington, Delaware.

Now Mr. Dutcher had no more interest in Wilmington than in any other town or city through which his route lay; but the bright eyes and cheery voice of a neatly-clad newsboy attracted his notice, and he roused himself and bought a copy of the *Daily Republican*, as much to encourage the gentlemanly lad as for any other reason. Other venders of news with the bold swagger of street Arabs had been through the cars but failed to secure his custom. Upon what trifling things do important events depend, and how are our lives influenced and changed thereby!

On unfolding the newspaper the first item which met Mr. Dutcher's eye was an announcement of a temperance meeting. By a hasty impulse he seized his baggage, and had just time to get off from the car as the train was moving. In the waiting room of the depot he perused the temperance item, and learned that meetings conducted by Major George W. Wells of Wilmington had been held for several nights.

Mr. Dutcher lost no time in calling on Major Wells at his residence on Delaware avenue; and on introducing himself and presenting his credentials in the shape of letters from many prominent men throughout the country, was cordially received and made a welcome guest by the Major and his estimable and accomplished wife and daughters. He was invited to attend the meeting that evening and to make an address.

Temperance was then at a low ebb in Wilmington, and only about one hundred persons were present at this meeting. Nevertheless, the speaker exerted himself to make the occasion an interesting one, and succeeded. His hearers were electrified, and spread among their acquaintances most favorable reports of the stranger advocate of temperance.

The next night Mr. Dutcher spoke again in the same place and to a much larger audience; he gave out as his platform:—"God my Father; Christ my Redeemer; and man my brother."

From that time the success of the cause in Wilmington seemed assured. The audiences and the interest in the meetings increased nightly, and nearly all classes of citizens seemed anxious to aid in pushing on the work. Not only did poor homeless wanderers and destitute drunkards stagger up to the platform to sign the pledge, but men of intelligence, wealth and high social position signed also, side by side with their more unfortunate brothers. Fathers, husbands, sons and brothers recorded their names, while wives, daughters, sisters and sweethearts cheered them on and smiled approvingly. Noble women— some of them occupying the highest positions in society—came into the meetings leading unfortunates to sign the pledge, amid thunders of applause from the audience. Often when some hard-looking penitent man was writing his name, shouts of "Glory!" "Glory Hallelujah!" and songs of praise and thanksgiving were heard afar off in the streets of the city. Prayers too were offered at intervals; and when the services closed, at 10 P. M., the people seemed unwilling to depart.

At the close of the meetings Mr. Williams, who had been appointed secretary, took the poor and homeless men to the Friendly Inn, where food and lodgings were provided for them by the noble-hearted people of Wilmington. A call for cast-off clothing made by Mr. Dutcher was liberally responded to. Kind, benevolent ladies and others came loaded down with garments, and an extensive wardrobe was established where the ragged and tattered victims of intemperance were transformed into decent-looking personages.

Mr. Dutcher was on the platform alone for several evenings; then he invited one of the reformed men up with him, and induced him to tell the audience his experiences. The next night he had two of the men with him, and he increased the number every night until a hundred or more of them occupied the platform. At first these men could say but a few incoherent words, but eventually many of them became fluent speakers and assisted much in interesting the people and helping on the reform. They related many novel and pathetic incidents connected with their drinking experiences, and frequently, as they spoke, the vast congregation would be moved to tears, and shouts of "God bless you" would ring through the hall. One talented but degraded man said:—

"My two children are with their darling mother;" then raising his eyes and hands heavenward, he continued:—"My dear children, your father will meet you in Heaven. Mary, my dear wife, I will meet you again. This moment I seem to hear these dear ones, who loved me with all my disgraceful faults, saying in glory, 'Papa, dear papa, come home.' Pray for me that I may meet them in that bright world."

During the day it was the custom of Messrs Wells and Dutcher to visit the homes of poor and wretched drunkards and persuade them to attend the meetings and sign the pledge. One day they found down at Christiana river, a poor drunkard who seemed nearly dead. They roused him up, brought him to the city, and got him to sign the pledge. As he was in a deplorable condition, they then took him to the hospital and visited him till he recovered. He proved to be a talented man, and made some very effective speeches; in one of them he said:—

"I broke the heart of my wife—one of the noblest of God's creatures. I know she is now in Heaven, and I hope and pray that my sins may be forgiven, and that I may have the strength to so live in the future that I may go to her when I leave this world of sin and temptation."

Another man, well-educated and a member of a wealthy family, who was brought in by Major Wells, said:—

"I have for years been the victim of strong drink. What can I do to be saved? I hear my little daughter ask at night, 'Has papa come home, and is he drunk?' Then bursting into tears he exclaimed:— "O my little darling! is it possible she has a drunkard for a father?" Shaking like an aspen, and with tears dropping freely upon the paper, he signed the pledge, and the scene was so affecting that neither Mr. Dutcher or Major Wells could refrain from weeping.

On the 16th of April, after a spirited address by Mr. Dutcher, the Moral Suasion Reform League was organized with Nelson J. Lee as president. This association was wholly made up of men who had been slaves to drink, who proposed to stand by each other, guard each other's interest, and make war on the common enemy—rum and rum-sellers. Of this society more will be said further on.

The clergymen of the city took turns in inviting the reformed men to attend divine service on Sundays, and marshalled in military style and with their hymn books in their hands, they would march to church and occupy front seats of the middle aisle.

During both the week-day and evening meetings singing was interspersed with other exercises; Mr. Wm. C. Pickles was the leader thereof, while Miss Eva Crouch, Miss Ella Pickles and other persons contributed their talents.

About this time I received at Leominster many letters and telegrams requesting Mr. Dutcher's services at different places, and notified him of these calls. His replies to me were all about as follows:—
"Great revival here; impossible for me to get away." In fact I could get no decided answer as to the probable date of his return, although there was sickness in his family and his wife was anxious to have him at home. At one time he wrote to me:—

"I cannot leave the reformed men or loose the chance of gathering others into the temperance fold. The harvest is ripe, and I must reap before storms arise and the whirlwinds of intemperance dash the thousands of poor inebriates in this city into the vortex of destruction."

The interest had now increased so much that the City Hall would not hold all the people who went to the meetings, and Institute Hall was hired and packed to overflowing every night. People of all nationalities thronged thither, and even sailors from foreign ports left their vessels to swell the crowd. The news of the great reform began to spread over the country, and drinking men came from long distances to enroll their names on the Wilmington Roll of Honor.

The noonday prayer meetings which were started about this time were largely attended, and at times the emotions and sympathies of the audience were greatly excited. One day, after a man had told of his sufferings from the use of liquor in a way that particularly touched his hearers, Mr. Dutcher arose to speak but was so deeply affected that he could not utter a word for some time. At last he said in a subdued voice :—

"Dear friends, I cannot speak; my emotions choke me. But one thing I can do which is more in accord with my feelings; I can cry." A gentleman then tried to pray, but broke completely down; and the meeting ended without further words, the people grasping each others' hands in deep sympathy as they passed out.

The interest in the temperance meetings still spread, and at last even the capacious Opera House was not large enough to contain the crowds who rushed to them. On one occasion when three thousand people were packed into this building, with crowds outside eager to get in but unable to do so, there occurred a scene of intense and dangerous excitement. Without warning, the crowd of people who were near the doors and on the edge of the audience in the balcony and orchestra, with sudden impulse sprang forward, and in a confused mass surged out of the main entrance to the street. At the same moment a young man rushed into the office of the manager exclaiming:—

"There's a fire in the cellar! Do something for God's sake."

Then amid the noise and tumult of a great mass of people in confusion, was heard the crashing of window glass and the heart-rending scream of a poor woman who had been thrown down. One woman mounted on a chair and cried out—"Prepare to meet thy God." Other women fainted; some leaped from the balcony circle windows to the ground; and, altogether, several were severely injured.

Luckily the panic did not extend to the great body of the audience. Mr. Dutcher, from the stage, exerted himself greatly to quell the fears of the people, and other gentlemen by their calm and self-possessed words and actions aided in restoring order. A great calamity was however narrowly averted.

At the first alarm Mr. Baylies, the manager, rushed to the cellar, and there found a smouldering fire in a small pile of sacking, the smoke from which, issuing from the center register in the audience room, had caused the alarm. On examination the fire was found to have been the work of an incendiary. A man had been seen entering the cellar, and he was subsequently arrested, but no positive proof against him could be obtained.

The alarm of fire spread over the city, and the fire department and immense crowds of people were quickly on hand; but the danger was already over, and the exercises of the meeting were resumed before an audience undiminished in numbers.

As the Fourth-of-July drew near, the temperance people of Wilmington arranged for a grand picnic at Riddle's Grove, on the beautiful banks of the Brandywine; and when it came off, five thousand persons participated in the festivities of the occasion. Music, dancing and speaking were among the recreations indulged in; and the bountiful and elegant repast prepared by the noble temperance ladies of Wilmington could not be outdone. It was a temperance gala day—a day of rejoicings over the greatest and most successful temperance awakening ever known, although still gaining in strength and influence.

Besides the Moral Suasion Reform Association several other organizations also sprung up in Wilmington, some of them branches of the original, among which are the "Alliance and Gospel;" all of them have done great good and must have a share of our commendation.

CHAPTER VI.

WE have seen thus far some of the great results which followed the accidental purchase of a newspaper; another extensive reform, in a foreign country, was destined to spring up in as unexpected a manner.

While some of the incidents related in the last chapter were transpiring, Captain Joseph Burrell of Yarmouth, Nova Scotia, happened to put into Wilmington for the purpose of repairing his vessel, and in one of his walks about the city he came within hearing of Mr. Dutcher's voice as he pleaded for the temperance cause. On entering the hall where the meetings were held he became much interested in the speaker and his subject.

Subsequently, Captain Burrell attended the meetings for ten successive nights. As he sat in the audience his thoughts turned to towns, cities and individuals in his own country that might be lastingly benefited by a visit from the speaker, and he resolved to engage him if possible, at any cost. Afterward he appeared on the platform and made a speech; and before sailing away for home he had, under conditions, obtained Mr. Dutcher's promise to visit Nova Scotia at no far distant day.

For the purpose of fulfilling this promise Mr. Dutcher left Wilmington in July and went to Leominster. Thence by direction of a telegram received from Captain Burrell, he proceeded to Boston, and went on board the steamer "Dominion," Captain Clemmens, which was about starting for Yarmouth. He found the Captain a fine-hearted gentleman, and after as pleasant a voyage as could be made by a man who did not take naturally to water (except as a beverage, and in limited quantities) he arrived in Yarmouth, August 2d.

Upon stepping ashore our friend was met by Captain Burrell, and introduced to William Law who is at the present time president of the Dutcher Temperance Reformers of Yarmouth—the largest temperance club on the American continent.

The first evening that Mr. Dutcher lectured he gained the attention of the people, and the interest they manifested argued well for a revival of the temperance cause in Yarmouth.

The first man who signed the pledge was a sea captain. After writing his name he pinned a red ribbon to his coat, said "Good-bye, I'm off" to the audience, started for his ship and sailed immediately.

On the 6th of August the reform society above mentioned was organized by Mr. Dutcher, and its members voted unanimously to adopt his name. Captain John K. Ryerson was chosen president, and John H. Law, secretary.

The enthusiasm and audiences increased daily, and Ryerson Hall would not contain the people who came to the meetings. Aisles, stairways, ante-rooms and platform—all were densely filled. The pledge was signed by sea-captains, sailors, laborers, merchants, mechanics, ministers, women and children, and nearly the whole colored people of the city. Wealthy shipmasters stood waiting to sign by the side of forecastle men, while a colored cook, perhaps, was recording his name. Without prejudice as to color, nationality or religion, all were eager to swell the temperance ranks.

Greetings were telegraphed from the Reformers of Yarmouth—then numbering sixteen hundred—to the Reformers of Wilmington; and Mr. Wm. Law wrote to Major Wells that the greatest uprising in the cause of temperance ever known in the Dominion had been inaugurated.

There seemed to be an absence of the jealousies usually attending a great reform. Clergymen and laymen, rich and poor, men and women—all seemed to vie with each other in aiding the good work; day by day it was pushed forward until over three thousand Yarmouth people had signed the pledge.

Reverends Messrs Reed, Lewis, Day, and Pike were on the platform every night, and many other ministers also did good service in the cause. On several occasions the churches were thrown open.

On the 15th, a grand picnic was held in Wm. Murphy's grove on the shore of a beautiful lake. Although it was a foggy day over three thousand persons were present, and five hundred of them signed the pledge on the grounds. Such a gathering in the cause of temperance was never before seen in that section of the country.

The banner of the Reformers was beautiful and appropriate. On one side was represented a fountain with the words "God's Gift" floating on the water. Above the fountain was inscribed "Dutcher Temperance Reformers," and beneath it, "We will abstain forever from strong drink." On the other side of the banner was the emblem "clasped hands," and the mottoes, "Our great Temperance Brotherhood," "United we stand," and "God speed our noble cause."

The platform of the grand stand was occupied by several prominent men connected with the reform, the choirs of the churches, and the Milton Brass Band which played choice selections with good effect. Mr. Bailey led the choir, and Miss Eva W. Hutchinson presided over a fine-toned organ.

Mr. Dutcher spoke from the grand stand, and at the close of his remarks he took the British and American flags which had been waving above his head, and entwining them together, said:—

"As these two flags are now united, so may the hearts of the people of the United States and Great Britain be united in true and loving friendship—never to be severed as long as the two nations exist."

The effect of these words was beyond description; hats were waved in the air, and cheer after cheer rang through the woods and over the waters.

The wives and children of the reformed men enjoyed the day with their husbands and fathers to a degree which words cannot portray. Before leaving the grounds some of the ladies met on the banks of the lake and christened it "Lake Milo," and another lake near by they named "Lake George," in honor of our friend, George Milo Dutcher. Many times in the future may the cool crystal waters of these lakes reflect scenes as joyous as were seen at the temperance picnic on that day.

Upon returning to the city Mr. Dutcher addressed the reformed men from the steps of the court-house. He told them to trust in God and keep away from temptation, and all would be well with them. Twenty-five hundred men were present at this out-door meeting.

After this he went to Tusket, accompanied by the temperance choir and citizens of Yarmouth, and a club of Reformers was there organized.

Captain Clemmens was now about ready to start for Boston, and Mr. Dutcher was to return with him. Just before going he was invited by Mrs. Joseph Burrell to take tea at her house, and was kindly received and entertained. As he was leaving, she placed fifty dollars in his hand and tendered with the gift expressions of regard for his future happiness and prosperity.

When the time of departure had arrived the wharf was covered with people who came to see Mr. Dutcher off, and many of them accompanied him on board the steamer. After a prayer had been offered, and the hymn "Shall we gather at the river" had been sung, Rev. Dr. Randall handed to the departing guest an envelope containing pecuniary aid and comfort, and introduced him to the vast assemblage. Mr. Dutcher, as well as the people, was deeply affected, and he spoke but a few farewell words. Then his friends who were to remain behind shook his hand and turned back to the pier, the ropes slipped and dropped into the brine, and the steamer surged out into the waters.

From a prominent position on the steamer, Mr. Dutcher saw his friend Captain Burrell, waving his "Good-bye" from the extreme end of the pier; he saw a thousand handkerchiefs fluttering their owners' farewell, while cries of "Come again, brother Dutcher," reached his ears. With tear-dimmed eyes he watched these people who one month before were strangers until they became indistinct, as the vessel steamed onward through the Bay of Fundy.

Captain Clemmens invited our friend to make an address while on the steamer. He also presented him with a free passage and a five-dollar gold piece. "Whenever you wish to visit Nova Scotia," said the generous captain, "walk on board my boat, and you need not buy any ticket either."

On arriving at Boston Mr. Dutcher was met by an urgent telegram from Wilmington, and proceeded thither without going home to Leominster, although he had been absent a month. He reached Wilmington August 27th, and was greeted by thousands of friends who at that time assembled nightly under the great tent erected on Twelth Street.

The following verses published in the *Sunday School Worker*, are copied as a good specimen of the poetry of the Wilmington Reform. The author, R. C. Fraim, Esq., is at the present time a candidate for the mayoralty of that city.

THE RANTING DUTCHER FEVER.

BY ROBIN HOOD.

"What makes you look so sad to-day?
   Good neighbor, Bridget Hughes,
Have any of your patrons died?
   You seem to have the blues."

"Why Patrick, don't you know," says she,
   "We're driven to despair?
Old Dutcher and his reformed crew
   Are tenting in the air.

"They're ranting ever, night and day,
   For what they call reform;
They're driving all our trade away,
   And leaving us forlorn.

"Our bar-rooms soon will all be closed,
   To ruin we must go;
Unless old Dutcher keeps away
   We'll end our days in woe.

"My lovely daughter, Bridget Jane—
   The best-dressed girl in town—
Will have to act as kitchen maid
   And wear a seedy gown:

"Whilst those who gave us cash to buy
   Our daughter's splendid clothes,
Will dress their own girls up so fine
   They'll soon get all the beaus.

"Why, even now, those ragged men
   That joined old Dutcher's crew,
Are all rigged out in Sunday clothes
   As good as I and you.

"They fill the largest halls in town
   With men—and women, too!
While our saloons have empty chairs,
   And we have nought to do.

"Upon the platform, by the scores
   Our former patrons stand,
And tell their hearers what they've gained
   By joining Dutcher's band.

"At first we thought it all a joke
   To see our patrons there;
We thought their pledge would soon be broke
   With free lunch and bock beer.

"We've placed 'Bock Beer' upon our signs,
   With 'Free Lunch' every day;
But Dutcher's band ne'er come around
   To aid us with their pay.

"On every Sunday evening now
   We see the Dutcher bands,
With firm step marching off to church
   With hymn books in their hands.

"They'll all turn preachers, I believe,
   For every one of them
Can mount the rostrum now, to speak,
   And tell what they have been.

"They tell of misery and woe
   Produced by beer and rum;
And if one-half they tell is true,
   We MUST STOP selling rum.

CHAPTER VII.

WITHOUT entering into long details, I will say that through the summer months the temperance reform in Wilmington still prospered beyond the highest expectations and hopes of all concerned; that crowds congregated nightly beneath the folds of the "old tent;" and that scores marched bravely up to the stand to sign the pledge at each meeting.

Some three months after its organization, the Moral Suasion Reform Association elected as its president Col. John H. Moore, a well known and popular citizen, who by his untiring efforts and devotion to the cause infused new life into the association, so that it soon became a power in the city which even rumsellers had to respect.

The club now numbers some four hundred members, who are provided with a good hall fitted up for private and public meetings, with reading room, a very fair library, and an organ. Business meetings of the club have been held weekly, and public meetings oftener. At some of the latter, held at the rooms of the club or at the opera house, an admission fee has been charged. The income from this source, and the very liberal donations of money received from citizens, have been sufficient to defray expenses, and assist members who were out of work and had families in want. Sober men needing employment were always on hand at the rooms.

One year ago nearly every member of this organization was a drinking man. Some have been unfortunate enough to break their pledge, but these have generally been brought back into the fold by their brothers.

The following letter written by Col. Moore to Major Wells, September 12th, 1877, is copied from the Wilmington *Republican:*

DEAR BROTHER WELLS:—

In the following statement I have not had time to do full justice to the subject under consideration, but this far I do know—that since the present temperance revival, commencing, say, with the beginning of Brother Dutcher's labors in our midst, occupying a period of five months and twelve days of uninterrupted temperance work, much of it done under great disadvantage from warm weather, absence from the city of temperance workers, trivial contentions among some of the workers, and many circumstances which would have had a disheartening effect in other localities, the amount of good done in a pecuniary sense (laying aside the matter of health of body, peace of mind, and the happy men, women and children this movement has made in our midst) has more than paid for all the time, labor and money;—aye, doubly and threefold more than paid what has been expended in the accomplishment of it.

Now, I am speaking as a reformed man—one who has

been led by this movement to give up his cups, and who knows something practically about the amount spent in dram-drinking among social and moderate drinkers; and I say without fear of successful contradiction, that over four thousand drinking men and youths have taken the pledge since the beginning of the movement. Allowing for all who have violated their pledge (and remember none are so good they cannot fall, through the temptations and allurements held out by the votaries of the Rum Power and the fatal appetite which forges a chain around the drinking man) and putting the number at the low estimate of two thousand who have spent on an average two dollars per week for intoxicating drinks—and this average is low, for I know many who never spent less than five or ten dollars a week, and some as high as fifty dollars per week—we have here a saving of four thousand dollars per week, sixteen thousand dollars per month, or over eighty thousand dollars in the five months and over that have elapsed since the temperance movement started in Wilmington.

Think of it, fellow citizens! Eighty thousand dollars taken from the rumsellers' tills, and scattered among our merchants, our property holders, our farmers and other legitimate and honorable professions. "Does it pay?" Calculate a reasonable increase if the good work goes on, or calculate it as it is and stands to-day; and if it does not progress, but holds its own, why, sir, that alone is eighty thousand dollars saved from being squandered in dissipation.

Now as to the manufacturers.—We have seen how this movement has benefited the merchants, tradesmen, property holders, and mechanics; let us look and see how it has benefited you.

Has it benefited you in securing to you the services of the skilled artisan on whom you must rely for the success of your mechanical operations? Take a firm for example like the Harlan & Hollingsworth Co., where skilled mechanics are employed in great numbers; where every moment lost is, to the employers, money sunk, lost, and irretrievably gone.

How many men with nerves unstrung and brows throbbing from the effects of drink, lose minutes—aye, hours—where they must necessarily appear to work though incapable of performing it? Does practical temperance benefit and pay you as well as your employees, when they lose no time from the effects of this damning curse of intemperance? Assuredly it does.

Your men are at their places, sober, steady, reliable, with clear heads and steady nerves, to work in your best interest. Your manufactured articles are better made, and more reliable to the purchaser; and, of course, your reputation is constantly being raised higher in the scale of competition in your line of business.

Wilmington has always been noted for the excellence of her manufactured articles, not being surpassed in any locality. Let us keep up our reputation. Let us fight this monster curse with all the power God has given us, and with our money as well, until there is not a grog shop left in our fair city; and then we will have the answer to our question, and it will be:—" It has paid, and paid well." Yours truly,

JOHN H. MOORE.

Previous to Mr. Dutcher's visit to Nova Scotia, Major Wells, taking into consideration the great good already accomplished and the vast field yet open to reform in the state of Delaware, formed, and immediately brought before the temperance people, the project of building a house in Wilmington and presenting it to Mr. Dutcher as a permanent home. This project was favorably received by the thousands of temperance people, who considered it a good method of showing their appreciation of the great work which Mr. Dutcher had done for the good of the community.

Measures were at once taken for carrying out the plan. Contributions were solicited from the many temperance people who were well-to-do in this world's goods; a lot situated upon a hill overlooking the city was bought of Mr. Howland at a low price in consideration of the object; and the work of erecting a house was begun under the personal superintendence of Major Wells. When Mr. Dutcher returned from Nova Scotia, he found a crowd of reformed men working like heroes in the heat of summer, to build for him and his—what they had never yet been the owners of—a home. Two large cherry trees stood on the rear of the lot, and under their grateful shade the workmen ate their noonday meals from provisions provided and brought thither by the noble temperance women of Wilmington.

The "Dutcher Home" was fast looming up into a mass of brick and mortar, when Mr. Dutcher was obliged to go to Leominister by the illness of his wife. Before returning to Wilmington he was induced by urgent calls to make a second visit to the British Provinces.

CHAPTER VIII.

MR. DUTCHER started on his second visit to Nova Scotia in October, and was cordially welcomed at Yarmouth. He spoke there several times to immense audiences and many names were added to the pledge; the local club had five thousand members when he left the place.

The temperance people of Yarmouth had bought up at a high price all the liquor they could get, including the whole public sale of the custom-house, and poured it into the streets amid a joyous gathering of the temperance element.

Captain Burrell and Mr. Dutcher now started on a tour through Nova Scotia and New Brunswick, and Captain Bowman Corning accompanied them as far as Digby. They visited Plymouth, Plympton, Weymouth, Digby, etc., and then went to Annapolis Royal. Then they went to Brier Island, Freeport, and Westport, and on to St. Johns, N. B. They then went east as far as Amherst, N. S., and north to Chatham, N. B., on the Gulf of St. Lawrence. They also visited Sackville, Monkton and Halifax, and from the latter place they went up the Annapolis valley to Windsor, Wolfville, Kentville, Bridgeville, etc., and finally arrived again at Annapolis Royal.

The labors of our friends in this tour proved wonderfully successful, and much good undoubtedly resulted therefrom. Mr. Dutcher's reputation as an orator and sincere advocate of temperance had been spread over the country through the newspapers, and the people flocked to hear him; No building was large enough to contain them, and great enthusiasm prevailed. Only a few of the incidents attending their trip can be related.

At Plymouth nearly all the people signed the pledge. One old man, a hard drinker, refused to do so for a long time, but when his wife went to him with tearful eyes and said—" Won't you sign for your poor old wife?" he could hold out no longer; as he wrote his name the audience commenced singing—" Praise God from Whom all blessings flow."

Another man—a member of Parliament, who had crossed the Atlantic fifty-four times and suffered dreadfully from drinking rum since childhood—signed the pledge at Plymouth, and at the second meeting handed to Mr. Dutcher a Mexican silver dollar, saying:—

" Take that, Brother Dutcher; it was through your kind words that I have reformed. I want you to keep it always, and when you look at it remember it came from a poor slave of drink who is trying with the help of God to live a sober life."

Digby received our friends with a warm welcome,

and Rev. J. H. Saunders did all he could to smooth their path. This town had been a place where much rum was drank, but they left it a sober happy community. Some of the dealers gave up the liquor business and joined the temperance ranks.

A skillful physician of high standing in society was at this time bound firmly in the coils of intemperance, and an unsuccessful effort was made to obtain his name to the pledge. Finally his little daughter undertook the task.

"Father, won't you sign this for me?" she said pleadingly, presenting the pledge.

"No, no, my child," was his reply.

Amid the prayers of hundreds for her success the little one again and again entreated her father to sign the pledge, and though he gave her many firm denials she was at length made happy by his doing so. Her happiness was increased by one of the results of her father's reform: he and his wife, who had been separated through his intemperance, were again reunited and happy in their beautiful home, where Mr. Dutcher visited them on his return that way.

A reform club with six hundred members was established in Digby, and Ed. Wassell, a man of high standing and education, was chosen president thereof. He had been a hard drinker, but came out boldly for the right. Another man who had buried his wife and several children, been a hard drinker for years, and long since made up his mind that he should eventually fill a drunkard's grave, after listening to Mr. Dutcher's appeals, resolved to make a grand effort to reform. He signed the pledge and prayed to God to give him strength to keep it, and was chosen vice-president of the club.

The fire kindled in Digby on the shore of Annapolis Bay is still burning brightly; may its light be a beacon shining afar for many long years to come!

At Chatham, N. B., the results of the work were wonderful. Drinking men by scores and hundreds signed the pledge, and several of them in gratitude for their deliverance have gone out into the adjoining towns to work in the cause, and the movement has spread far and wide. At the present time Hon. L. J. Tweedie, M. P. is president of the "Dutcher Reformers" in Chatham, and nearly every man, woman and child there belongs to the association.

At Amherst and Sackville there was a general uprising, and nearly the whole population was brought into the temperance army. People would say to each other :—" Is not this the work of God? Who would have thought that Mr. A. or Mr. B. would sign the pledge?"

The first man to sign the pledge at Annapolis Royal was Mr. Shannon, a leading merchant, who had suffered much from strong drink. He is now an officer of the "Dutcher Reformers" of Annapolis Royal who number nearly one thousand members.

The last grand meeting held by our two friends was at Annapolis Royal, and was brought to a close near midnight by a general shaking of hands with Burrell and Dutcher; then, with the wharf crowded with men, women and children, they stepped on board the little steamer "Scud," bound for St. Johns, from which place Mr. Dutcher started for home.

The following account of this last meeting, and of the temperance reform in that vicinity, is copied from the Annapolis *Weekly Journal:*

The present week opened with probably one of the most tremendous popular demonstrations ever witnessed in Annapolis Royal. We have seen in the community the wildest enthusiasm on occasions of political contests; but in political ovations there are two opposing parties, both large and powerful, and while the shouts of ten thousand people rend the air in token of victory, they are offsetted by the muttered execrations of the nine thousand nine hundred and ninety whose party is left in the minority.

There were no two parties of nearly equal strength in the demonstrations of the present week. Very few opponents to the movement could be found. The enthusiasm of the occasion has been general. The social elements of the community have been thrown—not into confusion, but into the wildest commotion. Every organization, society, sect and institution, of all classes, ranks, creeds and denominations, has been, for the time, cast into the shade by the Dutcher Reform Club. For once, at least, it seems as if the people had united in a grand outburst of feeling on behalf of temperance reform.

We feel perfectly safe in asserting that nothing like it has occurred in the ancient capital of Acadia during the two-and-a-half centuries that elapse since De Monts first raised the *fleur-de-lis* on the wood-girt slopes of our river side. This has been no frenzied ebullition of an unreasoning and ignorant multitude. We have seen nothing but what would be expected to follow from a general and wide-spread manifestation of the inevitable sentiments of every intelligent citizen, in view of the blasting and blighting effects upon society of strong drink. Customs receiving the almost universal sanction of civilized society, grow into habits, and these habits develop into positive vices of the most hideous character.

The vice of drunkenness had fastened its burning fangs so deeply into the very vitals of the social system, that there is not an individual who has not felt the venom in his own veins, or at all events, who has not been called to grieve, in heartfelt sympathy, over the prostration of some one of his near kindred. Every grade of society is but too deeply affected with the disease not to be intensely interested in the successful application of the remedy. The unparalleled success of the temperance revival in other parts of the country had been winged by the press into every household, and formed matter for discussion at every fireside.

When it was announced some time ago that the campaign was to be opened in Annapolis, there was naturally a considerable amount of learned disquisition among the wise upon the prospects of such an undertaking. The reform movement was inaugurated in Whitman's Hall some four weeks ago. Since that time the ball has been kept rolling through our streets in quite a lively manner.

On Monday evening we had, as announced last Saturday, a fraternal visit from parties connected with the organization in Yarmouth, Digby, Bridgetown, etc. The intimation that Mr. Dutcher would be present, of course drew a large crowd. Many, no doubt, came to see what it would all amount to, and to have their own fun over such fools as might be induced to sign away their liberty by writing their names in the pledge book; but before leaving they made like fools of themselves by gliding down stream with the current that before the close of the meeting flowed in from nearly every bench in the hall to the secretary's table. A strong choir, with a good instrument ably fingered by Mrs. Randall, interspersed the proceedings throughout the evening with the inspiring influences of soul-stirring melody.

T. W. Chesley Esq. made the first advance in a brief but rousing introductory. His exclamation:—

" May the ancient capital be the center whence shall eminate those grand and glorious principles which we are here met to promote," seemed to us to be one of the most appropriate remarks that could be uttered.

Dr. Smith, of Digby, told of the great work going on in his own county; Mr. Burrell, of Yarmouth, made a few forcible and telling remarks; and Mr. Wassel, president of the Digby club, gave in a dozen words from his own experience, a summary of the history of intemperance from the days of Noah down to the present time; namely:—

"For seventeen years I was master of drink; the eighteenth year it was master of me!"

After a rousing piece from the choir, Dutcher took the field and swung himself round among the enemy most vigorously, doing considerable execution as he proceeded. One of his statements we must reproduce, and commend very strongly to the attention of the worshipers at the shrine of Bacchus —that is if there are any devotees of that creed left among our readers. As the utterance of a man who has been frequently over the road, it ought to have a warning effect. The expression is as follows:—

" There is no suffering on this side of the gates of hell, compared with the sufferings of the man who drinks rum."

After Mr. Dutcher's address was ended, then commenced

the signing of the pledge. The vociferous cheers and tremendous applause that shook the building under the feet of many who went forward to sign the pledge, showed plainly that there was a mighty waking up of the latent moral sentiments of the community.

Monday night was a big occasion, but on Tuesday night there assembled in Fullerton's Hall about two-thirds of the whole population of Annapolis Royal. It was the grandest evening in the history of Moral Reform in this place over which the midnight moon ever cast her soft silvery light.

To give any details of the proceedings would demand better descriptive powers than ever nature or education bestowed upon us, as it is not likely that either our mother or our schoolmasters ever expected that we should have to narrate the exploits of a Reform Club.

The hall was filled with such an audience as might well feather the cap of an orator of much less pretentions than G. M. Dutcher. Seats were extemporized in the aisles until they were packed, and the entrance was crowded shoulder to shoulder. Still they continued to come, and by nine o'clock, after many had gone away without being able to gain admission, a rat could scarcely have found room to run from the door to the platform. It was indeed a magnificent turn-out. The enthusiasm at the time of enrolling recruits was, if possible, greater than ever.

Close attention was paid to Dutcher's arguments; rounds of applause greeted his well-executed representations of various scenes in the life of the rum-drinker; and the unbidden tear would steal into the eye as he detailed one after another some of the fearful wrecks of human happiness, and the forever blasted prospects of many promising youths whose names might otherwise have been conspicuous on the roll of the world's honorable men.

We earnestly hope and trust that the walls of iniquity demolished by this siege may never again be rebuilt. It would, however, be denying the facts of the history of mankind to expect that all the recruits will prove true and trusty soldiers in the battle with established habits. But the overwhelming expression of popular sentiment evolved on Monday and Tuesday nights will be echoed along the years for generations. We predict a permanent effect upon the general tone of society with the greater confidence, as we are well aware of the fact that this is by no means a volcanic outburst of elements generated within a week or a month or a year.

Our temperance organizations have for some time been collecting the winds and blustering tempests in the caves of the mountains of Æolia. Dutcher came like Æolus, and whirling the point of his spear, plunged it into the hollow mountain's side, when the blast of popular opinion rushed forth as in a formed battallion, and scoured the community in giddy whirls, and at once, East and South and stormy North-west, ploughed up the deep emotions of the people and rolled vast billows on the shores of Moral Reform.

It may be added, that up to the present time, thirty thousand persons in the British Provinces have become members of Dutcher Reform Associations since Mr. Dutcher began his labors there.

CHAPTER IX.

WHILE Mr. Dutcher was in Nova Scotia the house which his friends were building for him was completed, and to save time he requested that his family should join him at the Union Depot in Worcester, November 22d, on his arrival from St. Johns, and go on with him to their new home. I was invited to be a member of the party. There were six children under twelve years of age to be looked after, and one of them—christened Wilmington Wells in honor of the great reform and Major Wells—was but a few weeks old.

The programme was carried out; it was a happy moment to me when I delivered over to my friend his jewels, and realized that for the remainder of the journey the responsibility and care of said jewels would not rest wholly upon me. Although I felt competent to range the whole South-west without slipping a trail, I was bewildered when trying to take charge of the "tribe of George."

There was half-an-hour to spare before our train left, and Mr. and Mrs. Dutcher and Georgie resolved to improve it by a hasty visit to friends in the city. Before I realized what was going on, or rather who was going off, I found myself seated in the ladies' sitting-room with a baby in my arms and with four other babies of varying size grouped around me. If any old bachelor like myself reads these lines, let him drop a tear of sympathy at my situation.

Now, a long-haired scout in a big depot, with a little baby in his arms and no mother near by is not a common sight, and I soon became painfully aware that I was the center of attraction. Fellow-travelers stared and smiled, and hackmen, loafers, etc., grinned at me through glass doors and windows on all sides. Luckily for some of them my revolver was not at hand, and I ground my teeth in rage and silence. Wilmie preserved his composure, but showed by his roguish eyes that he rather enjoyed the predicament he had got me in. My troubles were ended at last by the return of his mother, and we went aboard the cars and started on our journey.

Tidings of our approach were in due time telegraphed to Wilmington, and on arriving there we were met at the depot by many of Mr. Dutcher's friends who had come to welcome him and his family. The day was extremely stormy, and through torrents of rain we were conveyed to the Dutcher home, to be met by joyous greetings from a score of happy-faced ladies who had come out into the storm to fix things up for the reception of the strangers and to welcome them. They had prepared for us a substantial supper, and their kind words and cheerful looks soon made Mrs. Dutcher and the children feel as if at home and among friends, notwithstanding the strangeness of the surroundings.

The warmth and cheerfulness which pervaded the house contrasted delightfully with the outside storm and darkness; and amid such evidences of the sincere regard entertained for them by the kind ladies present and the people of Wilmington, no wonder that the evening was a happy one for the members of the Dutcher family, and that it will long be treasured up by them as a bright oasis in the desert of life.

Subsequently, when fairly "settled," the family was cheered by numerous calls from the people of Wilmington who sometimes came in large parties, bringing presents, and filling the house with hilarity and gladness. Speeches on these occasions, and serenades by the choir of the M. S. R. A., were also in order.

The Dutcher house is a handsome three-story brick building containing twelve well-finished rooms, and reflects much credit upon Major Wells who superintended its construction. It fronts on Franklin street just beyond the beautiful residence of Mr. Benjamin F. Miller, and its location and surroundings are unexceptionably good. Northerly the country is dotted with fine suburban residences whose owners vie with each other in beautifying their homes. To the west, only a stone's throw distant, is the new park where the children play; and a five-minutes' walk brings one to Delaware avenue with its handsome houses and line of horse-cars.

The view from the "Home" is fine and extended. Below is the city of Wilmington, stretching along the Delaware river, its north-eastern and south-western suburbs cut through by the waters of the Brandywine and Christiana rivers. On the broad bosom of the Delaware may be seen all kinds of river and ocean craft, and across and beyond it the shores of New Jersey, covered with groves, farm-houses and cultivated fields, form the back-ground of the picture. From the roof of the house can be seen a vast expanse of farming country lying in the States of Delaware, Maryland, Pennsylvania, and New Jersey.

Temperance meetings had of late been held nightly in the "Old Foundry," and after Mr. Dutcher's return he addressed large audiences there and at the rooms of the M. S. R. A. He also visited neighboring towns to speak to the people and organize clubs.

Over fourteen thousand people signed the pledge in Wilmington within one year from the date of his first arrival in that city.

CHAPTER X.

SUBSEQUENTLY Major Wells and Mr. Dutcher visited Washington, and held several meetings; their main object, however, was to bring the subject of intemperance before Congress, and obtain the enaction of prohibitory laws in the District of Columbia. They called on many Congressmen, and found some who, to their shame be it said, were ready to ridicule and oppose any scheme for restricting the sale of liquors. They found others who were anxious to help the plan along. The following memorial, prepared by them, was presented in the House of Representatives, January 17th, by Mr. Matthews, read, and referred.

To the Honorable Senate and House of Representatives of the United States, in Congress assembled:—

We, your petitioners, humbly state, that we are citizens of the United States now temporarily residing in the District of Columbia; and we humbly pray your honorable body to make legal inquiry by what authority the traffic in intoxicating drinks is protected and made legal. The Constitution was ordained to establish justice, insure domestic tranquility, and promote the general welfare.

The traffic in intoxicating drinks infringes upon these provisions of the Constitution to a terrible degree; and we again humbly request your honorable body to make inquiry by what authority the privileges and enjoyments of the great majority of the people of this District are interfered with, and the expressed stipulations of the great law of the land abrogated and annulled. We claim that the fruits of this traffic being evil, and that continually, there can be no constitutional right to protect it; and that upon the removal of the protection of law by which it is now surrounded, it could be driven from the community as a common nuisance. And we shall ever pray.   GEORGE W. WELLS.
GEORGE M. DUTCHER.

They also succeeded, through the instrumentality of Hon. Amasa Norcross, of Fitchburgh, Mass., in getting before the House "a bill to prevent the importation, manufacture, and sale of intoxicating drinks to and in the District of Columbia." This bill was read twice, referred to the committee for the District of Columbia, ordered to be printed, and was subsequently printed. What the result thereof will be remains to be seen.

From Washington, Mr. Dutcher, accompanied by Mr. Wells, went to several towns in Pennsylvania, and met with good success in getting people to sign the pledge. "He made here," said the Newton *Enterprise*, "six consecutive speeches to large audiences in the hall and churches. His manner is that of impassioned eloquence, conveying hard unanswerable facts and arguments."

Subsequently he made a tour through Eastern

Maryland and Southern Delaware, and many reform associations were started. At Salisbury, Md., over seven hundred persons signed the pledge. At Seaford, Del., five hundred signed, and on his second visit there, hundreds wearing temperance badges met him at the depot. In one place the liquor dealers sent word to him that they would give him twice the money the temperance people could afford to, if he would stop lecturing and go home.

At Dover, Mr. Dutcher made a most eloquent address; he had been suffering from overwork, and after reaching the home of Rev. C. Huntington, where he had been invited to sojourn during his stay in Dover, he was prostrated from nervous weakness. For a short time the symptoms were serious, but he soon recovered from them and returned home to recruit his strength.

Soon afterward Mr. Dutcher received a telegraph from his father saying that his mother was at the point of death, and by the next train northward he was hastening to Valatie, N. Y., three hundred miles distant. Bravely did he bear up under his grief and weakness, and he had the satisfaction of being with her in her last hours. She died rejoicing in her Saviour. For years she had been a patient sufferer, and her son was never happier than when visiting her and contributing to her comfort. No man ever loved his mother more, and no mother ever more deserved that love.

Through the long years of his childhood, made desolate by his father's dreadful appetite for rum, he had never heard words of complaint or reproach on account of her own sufferings; and when such words were drawn out at the sight of her children's haggard and wistful faces, they were spoken in mild tones, or expressed in earnest prayers that God would send bread for her little ones and cause their father to see the error of his way.

And when George, her George, himself took the same downward road when but a youth, and came staggering home with the insanity of drink in his usually loving and respectful countenance, although it must have caused her brain to reel with an awful, terrible fear for his future, yet no bitter words fell from her lips and nought but kindness and true motherly love did he find in the humble home.

And though in after years he would leave her, and she would not know at times for months or for years the whereabouts of her darling for whose sake she was suffering as only loving mothers can suffer, yet when he did come, delirious with drink, she would nurse him, and pray over him, and when he was again himself she would say with tearful eyes and bitter sadness which would have melted any heart not steeped in rum:—

"Oh George! why will you drink?"

Her kindness and loving words had their effect at last, and her prayers were answered. George became a temperate man, and her declining years were made gloriously happy.

If any persons who read these lines are so unfortunate as to have intemperate sons or husbands, or wives or daughters, I urge them to refrain from harsh words which only tend, when coming from those who are near and dear to the erring ones, to drive them to deeper drinking that they may drown the bitter feelings produced by ill-treatment and cruel words. There is a great curse resting upon them in their appetites for liquor, and they have enough to suffer in consequence, especially if of nervous temperaments and good powers of mind. I hope these words will be well considered by those who are cultivating surly tempers towards their unfortunate relatives and friends.

Like most other reformed men, Mr. Dutcher is a strong advocate of prohibitory laws and in his talks and arguments he endeavors to make his audiences realize that to save themselves, their friends and their children from the curse of intemperance, the manufacture, importation and sale of intoxicating drinks of all kinds *must* be stopped. He impresses it upon them that the saving of intemperate persons should not be the only aim of temperance people, but that the removal of the *causes* of intemperance are equally necessary; that the safety of the next generation should be provided for; and that while by extra exertions many drunkards may be rescued, yet with laws permitting and legalizing the manufacture and sale of liquors, ten times as many as are saved are in danger of becoming inebriates. "And how," he asks, "can reformed men be expected in all cases to keep from falling, when, especially in city life, they cannot walk the streets without being tempted and allured to resume their old habits and associations."

For the rumseller who *persists* in carrying on the unholy traffic Mr. Dutcher has no aid and comfort to offer, and he does not sympathize with those who have. He considers rumselling in this enlightened age a great crime, and believes in and endorses the sentiments of the Hon. Neal Dow, the father of the Maine Law which is now supported by both parties and by an overwhelming public opinion in that state.

In short, Mr. Dutcher makes no compromise with intoxicating liquors in any way, and he believes the ban of society should be put upon those who rent buildings or sign licenses for the manufacture or sale thereof. He considers it a shame that any government will accept a revenue from a traffic which ruins its citizens, body and soul; "and if," he says, "this blood-bought country cannot live without a revenue wrung from the groans of wives, mothers and children—then let it die."

Mr. Dutcher is a man of the people, laboring for all, and making no distinction on account of nationality, color, or social standing, in his efforts to do good. Open-handed charity, modesty, and a "put yourself in his place" feeling characterizes his intercourse with his fellow-men. He visits prisons and almshouses and addresses their inmates as opportunity offers, and works equally well with all temperance organizations and Christian denominations. Often has he incommoded himself and deprived his family of needed supplies by assisting some poor creature who was trying to reform; and not infrequently has he been disappointed and grieved by the actions of men on whom he had expended much money and time.

Mr. Dutcher can say with truth and self-gratulation, that he has never turned away from the pleadings of a mother, wife, sister, or daughter who asked his services in trying to redeem their dear ones, however much it might cost him of money or trouble. In such cases he has always relied on the promise of God's Word: "Trust in the Lord and do good; so shalt thou dwell in the land, and verily thou shalt be fed."

Just as I am finishing my task Mr. Dutcher has returned home from a month's hard labor in New Jersey. He has lately received an invitation to meet the leading temperance men of Philadelphia with a view to an arrangement for his services in that city; he has also pressing invitations to visit New Foundland, Nova Scotia, Texas, and other sections.

www.ingramcontent.com/pod-product-compliance
Lightning Source LLC
Chambersburg PA
CBHW020323240426
43673CB00039B/905